R Blackwell
Coventry
Nov 1980 .

# Training Matters

**Warwick Studies in Industrial Relations**
General Editors: Paul Edwards, Richard Hyman and Keith Sisson

**Also available in this series**

# Training Matters

## Union Perspectives on Industrial Restructuring and Training

Helen Rainbird

Basil Blackwell

Copyright © Helen Rainbird 1990

First published 1990

Basil Blackwell Ltd
108 Cowley Road, Oxford, OX4 1JF, UK

Basil Blackwell, Inc.
3 Cambridge Center
Cambridge, Massachusetts 02142, USA

*British Library Cataloguing in Publication Data*

A CIP catalogue record for this book is available
from the British Library.

*Library of Congress Cataloging in Publication Data*

Rainbird, Helen.
Training matters: union perspectives on industrial restructuring and
training/Helen Rainbird
p. cm. – (Warwick studies in industrial relations)
Includes bibliographical references.
ISBN 0–631–17363–3 (U.S.)
1. Occupational training – Great Britain.   2. Occupational retraining – Great Britain.
3. Employees – Training of – Great Britain.   4. Corporate reorganizations – Great
Britain.
5. Trade unions – Great Britain.   I. Title.   II. Series.
HD5715.5G7R35 1990        89–38390
331.25'a2'0941–dc20

Typeset in 10 on 11½pt Times
by Hope Services (Abingdon) Ltd.
Printed in Great Britain by T. J. Press Ltd., Padstow, Cornwall

# Contents

# Series Editors' Foreword

The University of Warwick is the major centre in the United Kingdom for the study of industrial relations, its first undergraduates being admitted in 1965. The teaching of industrial relations began a year later in the School of Industrial and Business Studies, and it is now one of the country's largest graduate programmes in the subject. Warwick became a national centre for research in industrial relations when the Social Science Research Council (now the Economic and Social Research Council) located its Industrial Relations Research Unit at the University. Subsequently, in 1984, the Unit was reconstituted as a Designated Research Centre attached to the School of Industrial and Business Studies. It continues to be known as the Industrial Relations Research Unit, however, and now embraces the research activities of all members of the School's industrial relations community.

The series of Warwick Studies in Industrial Relations was launched in 1972 by Hugh Clegg and George Bain as the main vehicle for the publication of the results of the unit's projects, as well as the research carried out by staff teaching industrial relations in the University and the work of graduate students. The first six titles of the series were published by Heinemann Educational books of London and subsequent titles have been published by Basil Blackwell of Oxford.

Since the 1970s the scale and pace of restructuring in the economy and industrial relations have raised new questions for analysis concerning the process of recomposition of the labour force. Training is one of the most important means by which this process of recomposition is facilitated. The public policy debate has focussed on the poor record of British employers in training their work forces compared to their main competitors. However, it is not just the domain of employers' decisions in the firm. The state creates the regulatory framework of employment law and intervenes in the training decisions of firms through its labour market policies. Therefore, the public policy debate is concerned not just with the employment and training decisions of firms, but with how government creates a system of incentives and control over training, and how the interest groups of labour and capital bargain within these institutions and over the ramifications of training in the wages structure. It is precisely this system of incentives and control that the government has sought to modify in recent years.

This book makes an important contribution to debates on training and the process of recomposition of the labour force. By looking at different sectors of industry and dealing with problems from the perspective of trade union representatives, it brings out the complexity of the processes of change and their implications for union policy. It provides a wealth of information about how they have responded to government training policies such as the Youth Training Scheme, and to training developments in firms, linked to the introduction of new technology and moves to increase flexibility between trades if, in fact, they are accompanied by training programmes.

The empirical material is placed in a broader framework which considers the significance of changes in the structure of employment to a trade union movement based on occupation rather than industrial sector or political affiliation. It challenges the notion that only craft unions, through the tradition of apprenticeship, are concerned with training and demonstrates that, despite its problems, the Youth Training Scheme has provided a valuable learning experience in placing training firmly on the bargaining agenda. The book challenges the view that trade unions are interested in restricting the supply of skills and emphasizes the positive contribution that they can make, both in policy and in practice, to an industrial strategy based on increasing the skills of the labour force.

# Acknowledgements

The research on trade union policy towards industrial training reported in this book was funded by a grant from the Economic and Social Research Council. It grew out of an earlier research project on employers' associations and training policy that I worked on with Wyn Grant of the Department of Politics at Warwick University. The field-work was conducted between June 1985 and September 1986 and would not have been possible without the help and cooperation of a large number of officials and research workers in the nine trade unions in the sample. I am extremely grateful to all who generously gave of their time to answer my questions and in particular, to those who referred me to colleagues, arranged access to shop stewards and commented on my findings.

The Institute for Employment Research provided a valuable base from which to conduct the research. I am indebted in particular to Rosalie Edkins and Margaret Birch for secretarial and adminstrative support, respectively. The wider research community at the University of Warwick contributed towards a congenial work environment and I should like to acknowledge the intellectual stimuli provided by colleagues in the Industrial Relations Research Unit, the Warwick Vocational Education and Training Forum, the Construction Industry Studies and the Labour Studies Group. My knowledge of training in the construction industry has also benefited from participating in a number of international meetings in Copenhagen, Dortmund, Paris and Warwick. Nevertheless, the opinions expressed in the book and any errors are entirely my responsibility.

Finally, I should like to record my gratitude to Francisco Salazar, for his support and understanding.

*Helen Rainbird*
*University of Warwick*

# List of Abbreviations

| | |
|---|---|
| AEU | Amalgamated Engineering Union (the AUEW reverted to being AEU following its May 1986 conference). |
| AMB | Area Manpower Board |
| APEX | Association of Professional, Executive, Clerical and Computer Staff. |
| ASTMS | Association of Scientific, Technical and Managerial Staffs. |
| AUEW | Amalgamated Union of Engineering Workers. |
| AUEW/TASS | Amalgamated Union of Engineering Workers/ Technical, Administrative and Supervisory Section. |
| BATJIC | Building and Allied Trades' Joint Industrial Council. |
| BTEC | Business and Technician Education Council. |
| CAD/CAM | Computer-aided Design and Manufacture. |
| CAPITB | Chemical and Allied Products Industry Training Board. |
| CBI | Confederation of British Industry. |
| CGLI | City and Guilds of London Institute. |
| CIA | Chemical Industries Association. |
| CITB | Construction Industry Training Board. |
| CNC | Computer Numerical Control. |
| CP | Community Programme. |
| CPSA | Civil and Public Services Association. |
| CSEU | Confederation of Shipbuilding and Engineering Unions. |
| DLO | Direct Labour Organization. |
| EDC | Economic Development Committee. |
| EEF | Engineering Employers' Federation. |
| EETPU | Electrical, Electronic, Telecommunications and Plumbing Union. |
| EITB | Engineering Industry Training Board. |
| ETUI | European Trade Union Institute. |
| FDTITB | Food, Drink and Tobacco Industry Training Board. |
| FMCIT | Food Manufacturers' Council for Industrial Training. |

| | |
|---|---|
| GCHQ | General Communications Headquarters. |
| GMBATU | General Municipal, Boilermakers' and Allied Trades' Union. |
| HNC | Higher National Certificate. |
| IDS | Incomes Data Services. |
| ITB | Industrial Training Board. |
| JIB | Joint Industry Board. |
| MSC | Manpower Services Commission. |
| NAFE | Non-Advanced Further Education. |
| NALGO | National Association of Local Government Officers. |
| NATFHE | National Association of Teachers in Further and Higher Education. |
| NEDO | National Economic Development Office. |
| NJCBI | National Joint Council for the Building Industry. |
| NSTO | Non-Statutory Training Organization. |
| NTI | New Training Initiative. |
| OND | Ordinary National Diploma. |
| RSA | Royal Society of Arts. |
| TASS | See AUEW/TASS. |
| TGWU | Transport and General Workers' Union. |
| TUC | Trades Union Congress. |
| UCATT | Union of Construction and Allied Trades and Technicians. |
| USDAW | Union of Shop, Distributive and Allied Workers. |
| YOP | Youth Opportunities Programme. |
| YTS | Youth Training Scheme. |

# 1

# Introduction

In the 25 years since the passing of the Industrial Training Act, government policy towards industrial training has turned a full circle. Then, as now, concern was expressed at the failure of British employers to train their workforces adequately. Then, as now, lack of training was perceived as a major threat to the international competitiveness of British industry and the emergence of skill shortages was seen as hampering productive capacity. Whereas in the 1960s, the concern was with the growth in the cohort of school leavers exacerbating underlying problems of skill supply, in the 1980s it is precisely the decline of this cohort which exacerbates the training problem. Issues of training volumes and skills supply apart, the political context in which the debate on training is conducted has undergone a sea change. Whilst Perry (1976) reports the 1960s consensus on the need for state intervention and the involvement of the interest groups of labour and capital on an equal basis in the process of policy formulation and implementation, the present government believes that training policy should be determined solely by employers, with no interference from the state. The fact that this flies in the face of historical experience and stands in sharp contrast to the policies of many of our European neighbours, who have successive incorporated trade union interests into the process of policy formulation on issues relating to training and the labour market, has not deterred the Conservative government. In Britain, trade unions have been progressively excluded and marginalized from this policy-making role. The abolition of 17 of the Industrial Training Boards in 1981 marked the start of this process. It continued in 1988 with the reduction of trade union representation on the Manpower Services Commission, the Area Manpower Boards at local level and the remaining ITBs. By the end of 1988, the government finally abolished the Manpower Services Commission in response to the Trade Union Congress' refusal to co-operate with Employment Training. The last vestiges of statutory intervention were to be removed with the proposal to wind up the ITBs and set up Training and Enterprise Councils run by employers at local level.

It is widely acknowledged that Britain does have a training problem (NEDO/MSC, 1984; Coopers and Lybrand, 1985; Prais and Wagner, 1983). At the same time, it is widely believed that developments in technology in the coming years will require both a more highly qualified workforce and the retraining of existing workers. Yet government policy of devolving training decisions to employers is both short-sighted and in direct contradiction with stated objectives of increasing the skills of the workforce. On the publication of the White Paper on 'Employment in the 1990s' (1988) which provides for the establishment of Training and Enterprise Councils, the Director of the Campaign for Work commented that it was '[a]n utterly irresponsible leap in the dark in view of the seriousness of Britain's skill shortages and employers' abysmal training record relative to our competitors' (*Financial Times*, 9 January 1989). Though there are always exceptions to every rule, the majority of British employers view training as a cost rather than an investment, to the extent that their training departments are often treated as separate cost centres. They, therefore, take a short-term rather than a long-term view of their own requirements. Yet whilst there are good grounds for supposing that the firm is the most appropriate locus for learning about the world of work, all the evidence suggests that if this is not regulated by the state it is sure to fall short of the requirements of the economy as a whole, both in the short term and as new skill demands evolve in line with changes in production processes (Streeck, 1989). There is considerable evidence to suggest that not only do employers have differing requirements from the training and education system and are, therefore, unable to articulate a coherent set of demands upon it, but also they do not actually know what their future skill requirements are (Keep, 1988). Therefore, to place the entire control over the training system in the hands of employers represents not a rational strategy, but an ideologically motivated act, inviting the gross neglect of the development of skill resources.

Given the level of debate on industrial training and the publicity given to schemes such as the Youth Training Scheme and Employment Training, it is an opportune moment to examine what training is actually taking place on the ground. Once we cut through the rhetoric of 'training for jobs' and 'training for high technology', a different picture begins to emerge – one in which training is most notable by its absence. In the present book, I aim to look behind the terms of the policy debate and examine training issues facing trade unionists in the workplace and in negotiations at different levels, and the development of trade union policy towards them.

What, in concrete terms, are the training issues currently confronting the trade union movement and how do they differ from those of the past? A recent negotiators' guide to training published by the Labour Research Department identifies three main training areas of concern to trade unionists: initial training; training for the adult unemployed; and training for existing employees (Labour Research Department, 1988). Whilst initial training has concerned many trade and craft unions for generations, historically it has mainly been an interest of the latter and control of apprenticeship training has constituted an important aspect of the regulation of craft labour markets. Non-craft workers have not always received training on entry into employment so that access to and control of training programmes has not formed such an important element in bargaining power. Though the Industrial Training Boards established in the 1960s had the objective of developing training programmes for *all* employees, non-apprenticeship training was relatively neglected and it has only been with the introduction of the Youth Training Scheme in 1983 that initial training has become more widespread. The majority of trade unions have, therefore, had to develop policies only recently towards youth training, even though these have tended to focus on youth wages and conditions of employment rather than courses and curricula.

Training for the adult unemployed also has a long history stretching back to the labour camps of the 1930s and the Government Training Centres set up in the post-war period to retrain ex-services personnel and those made redundant through industrial restructuring. Again, craft unions have been most affected by the threat of substitution and in defending skills against dilution. In the 1980s, the scale of unemployment and the Conservative government's use of labour market policy as a tool for cheapening labour costs have given rise to widespread fears of substitution. A large number of trade unions are now voicing concern at the terms under which the long-term unemployed are forced to accept places on adult schemes.

The third aspect of training affecting workplace bargaining concerns the retraining of existing employees. Advances in technology and employers' attempts to increase labour flexibility in the workplace mean that workers are now expected to learn new skills in the course of their working lives. However, these changes may be introduced with or without recourse to formal training programmes. If they are to result in increased job satisfaction, improved earnings, career and promotion prospects, it is essential that new skills are learnt through formal training programmes and that recognized qualifications are obtained. Formal training increases individual and collective bargaining power. In contrast, a reliance on informal learning or skills specific to one machine encourages employers to simplify jobs. Skills tend to be specific to the firm rather than transferable and it is more difficult to bargain over changes in skill levels.

Beyond the immediate training issues raised in the workplace, an analysis of the strategic significance of training policy is necessary. The Conservative government has devoted considerable resources to its labour market interventions and has introduced major changes in the decision-making structures relating to training both at sectoral level and at national level. However, for the labour movement training ought to be central to a policy promoting the interests of labour. The terms on which new workers enter the labour force and existing workers adapt to changes in technology and working practices contribute to the balance of power between labour and capital. But, given the fact that British trade unions are based on occupational recruitment rather than industrial sector or political affiliation, can the labour movement be expected to develop unified policy perspectives on training? Even if the TUC had not been attempting to cling to the vestiges of the corporatist decision-making of the post-war boom ambodied in the MSC, would it have been capable of providing leadership on training policy to a hetero-geneous membership? If it is true that trade unions have given low priority to training policy in the past, why should they be more interested in it now? If trade unions are unable to pursue effective training policies, does this reflect organizational failure or an unfavourable balance of forces externally?

The trade union role in training policy is important precisely because of the absence of statutory training and retraining provisions. The pro-gressive exclusion of trade union interests from national and sectoral policy-making reinforces the significance of workplace bargaining as a means of obtaining advances in skills training. In seeking training agree-ments through collective bargaining, Manufacturing, Science, Finance argues, '[a]s long as access to training is not a *statutory* entitlement, employees depend to a large extent on trade unions to secure this right for them as part of their contract of employment' (Manufacturing, Science, Finance, 1988: 20). It is at the point of production that many training decisions are made. In addition, it is here that new workers are integrated into the social relations of production, and where changes in technology and work organization are most directly experienced. Indeed, it is at the point of production that workers are best qualified to contribute to decisions relating to labour force planning and development.

## Consensus and Conflict in Training Policy

Training and labour force policies have been viewed as classic areas for the development of corporatist arrangements, whereby the state devolves responsibility for policy formulation and implementation to the interest groups of labour and capital. On the trade union side it may involve the incorporation of the peak interest group, such as the Trades Union Congress in Britain, or the involvement of individual trade unions at sectoral level or in the workplace. This is because, without state intervention, employers may train only for their short-term needs and this may result in skill shortages which are detrimental to the economy as a whole. Grant argues that the rationale for resorting to trade union and employer incorporation into the policy-making process is not hard to find, for

> left to the market, firms are likely to support training in a form and at a level which does not meet the long-term needs of the economy, yet straightforward intervention may be based on highly imperfect information and comprehension of the problems, and may meet resistance from employers and unions to the extent that policy objectives can not be met (1985: 13).

Corporatist arrangements, therefore, provide a forum for reaching consensus on training issues. They draw on the expertise of the interest groups, whilst legitimating and securing the implementation of agreed policy. In Britain tripartite arrangements have been the dominant institutional form for the development of training policy since the 1960s, though the structures have not been static and trade union influence and representation have been progressively eroded. In other European countries corporatist structures have been stronger in general than in Britain (Grant, 1985), and the structures for representing training interests have taken different forms, providing interest organizations with different levels of control over policy-making and variations in the extent to which decisions reached are binding on their memberships. (For example, Anderson and Fairley, 1983; Mason and Russell, 1987; Erridge and Connolly, 1986; Streeck *et al.*1987).

Nevertheless, it is important not to overstate the extent to which consensus can be reached within corporatist structures. In examining the evolution of training policy in Britain, Stringer and Richardson (1982) point out that policy established in this way generally takes the form of conflict avoidance rather than problem solving and thus takes the form of non-radical change. In contrast, Keep (1986) argues that their analysis tends to overemphasize decisions reached rather than the process by which conflicting interests are discussed and accomodated. He points out that the Manpower Services Commission is particularly noted for its consensual consultative style, whilst his own analysis of the planning of the Youth Training Scheme in the Youth Task Group clearly indicates the conflicts and pressures embedded in tripartite discussions. In addition, decision-making structures and representation may remain constant, whilst the policy environment and the demands made by the state on those structures may change. There was, for example, significant continuity in the balance of trade union representation on the Manpower Services Commission between its establishment in the early 1970s and its replacement by the Training Commission in 1988. However, with the deepening of the recession and massive growth in unemployment, the range and scope of its interventions steadily increased. The MSC has been particularly adept at appropriating and redefining the labour movement's own slogans and policies, for example, the NTI objectives of education for all school leavers, an extension of comprehensive principles, the opening up of training to adults, the break-up of restrictive apprenticeship practices, equal opportunities. (Eversley, 1986: 207) The TUC's role in the establishment of the MSC resulted in its continuing support for policies implemented through it long after major shifts in the nature of interventions had occurred. Eversley (1986: 201) argues,

> TUC commitment to the MSC was strong. Not only was it centrally involved in MSC tripartism, it has also played a part in framing the 1973 Act which set up the MSC. Even if the MSC appeared to be falling under the corrupting influence of monetarism, the TUC would be most unlikely to abandon its progeny. As long as the TUC remained loyal to the institution, so too would the majority of affiliated unions, for most of them did not regard training as important, and were happy to follow wherever the TUC led.

Although there are areas of training policy in which employers and trade unions can reach consensus, it is important to identify what they are. Examining the history of the ITBs, it is possible to see that the areas of consensus generally applied to the development of curricula, courses and certification and less to economic matters; for example on the level of the training levy on firms and numbers in training. More importantly, it is obvious why employers and trade unions should want to reach agreement on what constitutes a determinate level of skill. The contention lies in how much a worker with a particular skill should be paid for it. Whilst the training system, understood as a series of structures and institutions for developing and certifying skills, is an important area for the representation of trade union and employer interests, it is through collective bargaining that the value of these skills is realized. It is the way in which training policy relates to pay and conditions of employment which makes it a focus of conflict between labour and capital.

Training gives rise to three broad categories of bargaining. These are:

bargaining over youth or trainee wages and conditions; bargaining over adult wages and conditions linked to differentials in the real and supposed skill levels of different jobs; and bargaining over changes in job definition and the acquisition of new skills and their relationship to pay. In the context of high unemployment and government schemes aimed at training and reintegrating the unemployed into the labour force, the terms on which the unemployed receive training and access to jobs are also subject to bargaining. The institutional form in which this occurs will vary according to collective bargaining arrangements and the structures through which training is organized and validated. The combination of occupational labour markets and industrial sectors in which different trade unions organize will determine the extent to which collective organization can attempt to control internal and external labour markets.

Skills may be transferable between firms and, therefore, externally certified and/or acquired through experience of a specific labour process. Craft skills acquired through formal apprenticeship training are an example of transferable skills in so far as a fitter or an electrician trained in one company has skills which are recognized and applicable to those of another. The regulation of apprenticeship – both the wages and conditions of apprentices and the passing on and certification of skills – has constituted an important element in craft union control of skilled labour markets. (Jackson, 1984; Price, 1980; Turner, 1962). In contrast, tacit skills acquired through on-the-job experience may not be transferable, but may nevertheless constitute sources of control, work autonomy and collective strength (Spies, 1984). Though there may be no formal structure for bargaining over skills in the workplace, equivalent, for example, to the West German works councils, this does not mean that skills and tacit knowledge do not arise as workplace bargaining issues. Whilst employers seek flexible deployment of labour, claims by groups of workers to particular sets of skills and jobs form an important defensive mechanism. Rubery *et al.* argue:

> Within the constraints of the need to maintain an efficient use of labour, which may necessitate a certain fixity of labour costs, an important concern of employers will be to maintain flexibility of labour costs with respect to both output and product prices. By contrast, the aims of trade unions will include securing and maintaining job security, property rights to skills, the separation of particular types of machines and the use of specific materials, and income security in terms of cost of living collective agreements will necessarily be a compromise between the objectives of employers and those employed (1984: 102).

In Britain, the claiming of skills by particular trade and craft unions for their members and job demarcation have evolved as a means of protecting jobs.

> Established working practices and demarcation lines have been portrayed as 'archaic', 'inefficient' or 'outdated'. But these working practices did not come about by accident. In the absence of proper guarantees from employers, they are an important way in which trade unionists can protect their wages, conditions of work and their jobs.
>
> Detailed job classifications and working practices are essential elements of unions' bargaining power. The definition of particular skills or tasks and the establishment of a 'rate for the job' which was universally recognised was a way to prevent employers substituting individuals or groups of workers for others, in an attempt to force wages down to get rid of union activists. It prevents management from trying to combine two jobs into one and is a protection against speed up and job loss (CAITS, 1986: 30–1).

Although the regulation of apprenticeship and the claiming of jobs has constituted an important defensive strategy in craft union policy and practice, it also provides a mechanism for foreclosing entry into particular labour markets and excluding other workers. Therefore apprenticeship training, whilst providing a minority of workers with access to skilled jobs, has restricted the access of women and black workers to training and to skilled work (Cockburn, 1983 and 1987; Lee and Wrench, 1983). Training is, therefore, a phenomenon which historically has divided worker from worker and has been used to justify the division of labour and wage differentials. Access to, and the regulation of, training forms the basis of workers' sectional interests. The way in which worker organization overcomes the dilemma of defending members' jobs against dilution and other groups of workers is a fundamental political problem for the working class movement.

It is also important to examine the significance of the *manner* in which skills are transmitted and their *consequences* for jobs. Training programmes may be used by management to achieve different objectives with varying consequences for collective negotiation. This is particularly significant in the context of an economic recession in which firms are restructuring:

> Training is . . . a source of potential flexibility in the use of labour in all firms. In combination with agreements (official or unofficial) over promotion, specific training can be used either to limit the

internal mobility of employees, thus dividing the workforce into separate groups, or through job rotation and experience to increase their internal mobility (Poole *et al.*, 1984: 112).

The process to be examined is, therefore, not simply one relating to the initial training and socialization of the workforce, but one which also concerns patterns of mobility within internal labour markets. This mobility may relate to patterns of promotion (i.e. vertical mobility) or, in the context of contemporary management objectives of increasing flexibility, horizontal mobility between different work tasks. Training programmes may be introduced by management to achieve goals other than those of transmitting specific skills. They can be used to increase worker commitment to organization through induction programmes or to strengthen internal labour markets (Purcell and Sisson, 1983). They may be used to introduce organizational change, to solve and circumvent industrial relations problems where existing skills are claimed by particular trades (Scarbrough, 1984).

The objectives of training – whether they concern the initial socialization of the workforce or managerial strategies for creating mobility within the internal labour market – can be achieved by different training methods. These have traditionally been categorized as formal and informal methods of training. Formal training normally implies the existence of a curriculum and a structured environment in which instruction takes place. Informal training implies the acquisition of knowledge relevant to the job through experience rather than through formal instruction. These categories do not relate directly to the distinction between off- and on-the-job training, since on-the-job training may be formally supervised and integral to a formal training programme or may simply involve one worker standing next to another and being told 'pick it up as you go along'. More recently, open learning, in which new skills are learnt in the workers' own time have been introduced by management as a cost-effective method of achieving training objectives.

The significance of the training method lies not so much in the skills transmitted, but in the legitimacy it gives to the skills acquired. Where training is formal and off-the-job it is more likely to result in the recognition of increased competence and status within the workplace and thus have implications for pay. Informal and open learning may make it difficult for workers to claim that they have new skills or that they have upgraded existing skills. This is because this type of training takes place outside the sphere of collective bargaining. It is hard for trade unions to argue that jobs should be up-graded where courses are short, skills job-specific and learnt primarily through experience. In contrast, where skills are transferable and learnt through formal coursework they are more likely to result in up-grading.

It would, however, be a mistake to argue that informal learning and skills acquired through experience can not receive recognition in the wages structure and be the subject of workers' control. Indeed, when the Industrial Training Boards were introduced following the 1964 Industrial Training Act, Taylor and Lewis (1973) argued that in the case of informal learning under the gang system in the steel industry, worker control would be greater if training remained outside the collective bargaining system. In this instance, the gang leaders controlled the instruction of young workers in empirical rather than scientific knowledge specific to that labour process. This serves to underline the significance of empirical study of the specific and organizational contexts in which different training methods are introduced as a prerequisite for developing a body of knowledge about both initial training and the retraining of existing workforces.

## Changes in the Policy Environment

The environment in which training policy has evolved in the post-war period can be divided into five distinct phases: *laissez-faire* and voluntarism in the period up until 1964; 1964/1973 state intervention and tripartism; 1973/1982 increasing centralization of policy and weakening of sectoral level bodies; centralized state intervention and employer unilateralism in the period from 1982 until 1988; the final abolition of tripartite bodies at national and sectoral level and the devolution of decision-making to employer-based Training and Enterprise Councils at local level from 1988. In terms of the representation of trade union interests in policy-making bodies, there are continuities in policy style and access to authoritative decision-making in the second and third periods, despite changes in structures. In contrast, since the Conservative Party came to power in 1979, there have been fundamental changes in trade union influence and representation on training bodies, even in the instances in which there has been continuity in institutions.

In the post-war period the state was progressively drawn into intervention in industrial training as *laissez-faire* policies resulted in the emergence of periodic skill shortages. There was a belief amongst educational and industrial policy-makers that a general process of up-skilling was taking place, requiring higher levels of skill and general education for *all* workers. Arguments were put forward for an extended and reformed period of secondary schooling, on the one hand, and for the state to take a more active part in post-compulsory education, particularly in industrial training, on the other. (Finn, 1987: 36). Though the post-war bulge in school leavers exacerbated concern about low levels of training, there were underlying problems of failure to modernize industrial training and to train at the same level of industrial competitors abroad (Perry, 1976). In this respect there are remarkable parallels in the way in which the 'training problem' was perceived then and is perceived now in the 1980s. The solutions proposed are very different.

After the 1939/45 war, governments became increasingly concerned with the development of active employment and training policies alongside the objective of economic and industrial planning. The 1948 Employment and Training Act represented a first attempt in this direction, resulting in the establishment of a National Youth Employment Council, an advisory body with no real impact on training (Perry, 1976: 51). In practice, *laissez-faire* policies continued to be supported by the major political parties until the early 1960s. Emphasis was placed on the expansion of the general education system whilst the two major initiatives were the encouragement of National Joint Apprenticeship Councils to advise employers on training standards and the establishment of Government Training Centres (Anderson and Fairley, 1983: 194). During this period, apprenticeship constituted the main form of industrial training, with 33 per cent of boy and 8 per cent of girl school leavers entering apprenticeships in 1950 (Finn, 1987). Only a minority of school leavers received any training at all on entry into employment.

The first major training reform was the 1964 Industrial Training Act, introduced by the Conservative government but implemented by Labour. The Act resulted in the setting up of the Industrial Training Boards (ITBs) with sectoral responsibilities for training and which represented not a direct intervention by the Ministry of Labour, but a devolved form of policy formulation and implementation through tripartite arrangements. These involved the representation of trade union, employer and educational interests. The main mechanism for increasing training volumes was to be the levy-grant mechanism, which acted as a redistributive tax on training. The ITBs had powers to raise a training levy on all firms defined as being within scope of their industrial training order and to distribute grants to encourage training. In this way, the costs of training were more equitably distributed and firms which were 'good trainers' were encouraged to train beyond their immediate needs through the allocation of grants. The ITBs provided a forum for developing training programmes and curricula. The EITB module system for engineering craft apprenticeship training is an outstanding example of this work and provides a good illustration of how the ITBs contributed to the modernization of apprenticeship.

In 1973, in response to criticisms of the ITB system, particularly from the small firms lobby, the Employment and Training Act was passed. This had the effect of weakening the powers of the ITBs by replacing the levy-grant with a levy-exemption system. Under this system firms which demonstrated that they were training for their own requirements were to be exempted from levy payments. Levy-exemption is more bureaucratic and rests on the premise that national or sectoral requirements equal the sum of the requirements of individual firms. It is no coincidence that the construction industry, in which many firms are unable or unwilling to train because of their small size and the practice of labour-only sub-contracting has retained the stronger levy-grant system in order to organize training on the basis of the training requirements of the sector as a whole (CITB, n.d. quoted in full in Rainbird and Grant 1985a: 100). Provisions were made for the Manpower Services Commission to be set up, with responsibility for public employment and training services. Like the ITBs, the MSC was constituted on a tripartite basis. The Training Services Division of the MSC took over the administrative costs of the ITBs and provided grants for selected training activities. The passing of responsibility for the ITBs to the MSC resulted in many employers perceiving that they had lost their independence and were increasingly becoming arms of state policy (Stringer and Richardson, 1982: 27–8).

In the 1970s restructuring of the economy resulted in a rise in unemployment and a decline in levels of industrial training. A number of special measures were introduced and between 1975 and 1977 the MSC supported 75,000 training places in industry. These measures 'generalised and made permanent the counter-cyclical involvement of public agencies in industrial training, a process started by a few ITBs in the early 1970s' and by 1981 'financed about one third of Britain's estimated 90,000 apprenticeships' (Anderson and Fairley, 1983: 198). By the late 1970s, MSC expenditure had shifted away from skill training and towards social programmes albeit with a training content. The Youth Opportunities Programme (YOP) was one of these. Thus at a time when employers were decreasing the amount they spent on training, the state assumed increasing importance in financing training though much of it directed towards policies of a primarily social rather than industrial nature. Even the Conservative government which came to power in 1979 determined to reduce state expenditure and committed to non-intervention in the economy, has intervened massively in the youth labour market, culminating in the introduction of the Youth Training Scheme (YTS) in 1983 (Dutton, 1984).

The Conservative government's policy towards the labour market appears, at one level, to be contradictory. On the one hand, it has introduced measures to deregulate and reduce state intervention. On the other hand, high levels of youth unemployment and a professed concern with increasing the nation's skills have resulted in major interventions in youth training. However, as Ryan points out, the major thrust of its training policy, the New Training Initiative, marks a significant departure from the objectives of the previous two decades. Prior to this, state policy had concentrated on increasing training in key occupational skills, which were essentially craft skills, transferable across industry and used by a wide range of firms. The Youth Training Scheme, in contrast, attempts to make training in general skills universally available, but the provision of this training is dubiously linked to employment and to the quality and content of jobs available (Ryan, 1984: 31) The rationale for government thinking on training policy is clearly linked to industrial relations reform and to the view that training reform is crucial to any attempt to weaken trade union restrictive practices. This view is to be found in the Central Policy Review Staff report 'Education, Training and Industrial Performance' (1980) which was influential in Conservative Party thinking. Largely as a result of this, it took the view that apprenticeship was simply time-serving as it had been before 1964, in this way deliberately ignoring the work of the ITBs through the 1960s and 1970s in modernizing it and formalizing training (TASS, 1982: 5).

For a government interested in reducing public expenditure and cutting back on trade union influence in tripartite quangos, the ITBs represented a sitting target. State support for ITB running costs was phased out and, in 1981, the MSC conducted a review of the 1973 Act, consulting all the major interest groups on the operation of training arrangements in each industrial sector. Despite the MSC's failure to recommend closure of any of the ITBs, the government ordered the abolition of 17 of the 24 under the powers of the 1981 Employment and Training Act. The TUC greeted this as 'frankly incredible', TASS called it 'an act of industrial vandalism' (TASS, 1982: 6). In the chemical industry, trade unions claimed that the Chemical Industries' Association had 'wrecked the industrial training board in collaboration with the Employment Secretary' (*Financial Times*, 12 January 1983). Six boards were to be retained, including the influential Engineering and Construction ITBs, whilst the Petroleum ITB became Off-shore Oil. (The Agricultural Training Board was similarly retained but this comes under the responsibility of the Ministry of Agriculture, Fisheries and Food and not the Department of Employment.)

Where the ITBs were abolished, employers' associations in each industry had to demonstrate that viable voluntary training arrangements were in place. Effectively all forms of monitoring of training quantities and quality were removed and with them the incentive and control mechanism of the levy-exemption process. Though it was anticipated that the new Non-Statutory Training Organizations (NSTOs) would 'work with' trade union interests (Rainbird and Grant, 1985b) there was no compulsion for trade union interests to be represented on their governing bodies, nor provision for equal representation with employer interests. Initially, many trade unions refused to participate in those that offered representation, in protest at the abolition of the ITBs.

NSTOs are based on employers' organizations or trade associations and in most instances, their training responsibilities are merely an extension of their existing functions. There is considerable variation in the extent to which they are prepared to take a policy-making role and to encourage adherence to codes of practice in their respective industries. Their main function tends to be information exchange, the disbursement of MSC funds to their members and to act as a lobby on training policy. Though some are active this is not true of all of them. In 1986 Sir Bryan Nicholson, Chairman of the MSC stated that many were 'not up to scratch in various ways' (*Financial Times* 29 July 1986). An unpublished report of a study commissioned by the MSC concludes that though some of the 42 NSTOs examined were highly effective others were 'poorly funded, understaffed and armed with too little information'. It further suggested that five of the bodies studied were 'non-serious training organisations' (*Transition*, November 1987: 5). In many sectors, the main purpose of the NSTO has been to prevent the reimposition of statutory training arrangements, whether in the form of the reintroduction of the ITBs or in the form of a centrally administered training tax, along the lines of the French *taxe d'apprentissage*. To some extent, the NSTOs represent a compromise between the government's commitment to non-intervention and recognition that in training policy, the operation of market forces does not prevent the emergence of skill shortages:

> In a strategic political sense, there is no doubt that the NSTOs were used by the government as a smoke screen to defend itself against charges that it was falling back on a pure market solution. Such a position would be difficult to defend when most training experts agreed that training efforts by firms, even if they meet the immediate needs of that firm, would be unlikely to meet the long run needs of the nation as a whole for a supply of highly trained labour. In a deeper sense, the NSTOs were an attempt by the government to cope with the contradiction between its attachment

to market ideology, but the fact that the application of such a policy in the field of training would undoubtedly lead to shortages of skilled labour, or perhaps even more important, a deterioration in the acquisition of new skills (Grant, 1987; 207).

Therefore, training policy exhibited contradictions at multiple levels; ideological commitment to non-intervention resulted in the abolition of the majority of the ITBs. At the same time concern was being expressed about Britain's lack of investment in training, particularly in new technology skills compared with that of major competitors (Prais and Wagner, 1983; NEDO/MSC, 1984; Coopers and Lybrand Associates, 1985). Despite its commitment to an employer-led and funded training strategy, mass unemployment combined with the threat of youth discontent, manifested in its most overt form in the riots of 1981, encouraged the government to inject major sums into the Youth Training Scheme. Finally, the publication of the White Paper 'A New Training Initiative: A Programme for Action' in 1981 with three objectives of apprenticeship reform, the provision of vocational training for all school leavers (YTS) and the opening up of training opportunities for adults (the Adult Training Strategy, ATS) led commentators to question how these objectives would be achieved. 'What sense, for example, is there in publishing a "programme for action" immediately after abolishing, or at least, severely decimating, the only existing mechanism for implementing the proposals?' asked Johnson and Singer, on its publication (1982: 37).

The expression of these contradictions is well illustrated in the YTS, and has had important ramifications for trade union involvement in its monitoring and regulation (Woodall, 1986). Keep (1986) argues that the vacuum left by the dismantling of the ITBs resulted in shifting the responsibility for implementation to individual firms. From an early stage it was obvious in the discussions at the CBI that large employers would be unable to provide many of the training places since they were reducing their labour forces rather than recruiting. It soon became obvious that the CBI, though wanting to support the programme as a means of supporting the Conservative government, would be unable to deliver the numbers of training placements required unless the majority were to be in small firms and in the service sector. This meant that TUC conditions, for example, insistence on trade union involvement in the monitoring of training quality would make the scheme inoperable. It was originally envisaged that pre-vocational training rather than job-specific training should be carried out under the one-year YTS scheme. As a result, in the first year of operation, the quality of training left much to be desired, with placements concentrated in the service sector

(Dutton, 1985) and in private training agencies (TURC, 1986). However, in the construction industry, the size of the CITB managing agency allowed the interest organizations to argue that YTS funding should be directed towards apprenticeship training although this did not meet the MSC's original criteria for funding (Rainbird and Grant, 1985a: 83). In engineering, the adoption of YTS was more piecemeal (Dutton, 1987) though the Engineering Employers' Federation viewed it as a potential lever in negotiations on apprenticeship reform and as a means of depressing youth wages (Rainbird and Grant, 1985a: 61).

From a trade union perspective, the New Training Initiative is bittersweet and policies towards it vary considerably. A number of trade unions, for example, CPSA, NALGO and AUEW/TASS have campaigned actively against it. Others have supported it as means of extending training opportunities, which their members were previously denied. Craft unions have responded to it according to the ways in which it has affected apprenticeship arrangements. For teaching unions, such as NATFHE in the further education sector, it secures resources in the context of public expenditure cuts. As a result, there has been no coherent response from the trade union movement. Eversley argues that the MSC offered something to everyone.

> Education unions were offered cash, jobs and schemes described as comprehensive. The large general unions were presented with programmes that seemed capable of democratising training and opening up the privileges of skilled status to their members. The smaller craft unions were offered youth programmes that seemed to defend apprenticeship. Trade unionists in their capacity as parents, sisters and brothers were told of schemes based on compassion for the unemployed (1986: 201).

This lack of coherence derives from the intrinsic ambiguity of YTS; is it a training scheme or is it social policy? Does it provide genuine training or socialization into low paid, low skill jobs and low expectations? Does it lead to real job opportunities or is it exploitation? Does it have the potential to open up opportunities for women and members of ethnic minority groups who have traditionally been discriminated against in the job market or is it a means of undermining hard-fought-for terms and conditions of employment? These themes have been discussed extensively in the literature. (See for example, Trade Union Resource Centre, 1984, 1985 and 1986; National Labour Movement Inquiry into the Youth Unemployment and Training, 1987; Centre for a Working World, 1986, 1987, nd. and nd.; TASS, 1982; Society of Civil and Public Servants, 1986; Lee *et al.*, 1986; Schnack and King, 1986; Benn and Fairley, 1986; Finn, 1987; REITS, 1987). The process of implementation of YTS, apprenticeship reform and other schemes such as the Community Programme which have a training element will be considered fully in Chapter 2.

Finally, the emphasis on employer-led training policy is paralleled by the development of the 'new vocationalism' in secondary schools and in further education, with the Technical and Vocational Education Initiative and the passing of control of a quarter of the budget for non-advanced further education (NAFE) to the MSC (Bates *et al.*, 1984 ; Dale, 1985; Finn, 1987; Holt, 1987). These initiatives are of interest for the range of areas they cover; for they concern not just changes in course content, in teaching methods and assessment but also the way in which innovation is introduced (Moon and Richardson, 1984) and the issue of local authority versus central control of the curriculum. Therefore, in contrast to the educational and training policies of the 1960s, which sought to expand provision and open up opportunities, those of the 1980s have been geared towards narrow vocationalism, the achievement of 'realistic' job expectations and the depression of youth wages. Trade unions, rather than being partners in the process of consultation and policy development, have been recast as obstructions to the free operation of market forces.

## The Research

Studies of trade union policy towards training have generally focussed on craft union concerns and, in particular, how craft unions have responded to the threat of dilution (Hall and Miller, 1971; Lee, 1979; Rees, 1973; Ziderman and Walder, 1975). The relationship between craft union organization, regulation of apprenticeship, control of craft labour markets and wage bargaining based on differential pay are well established (Cockburn, 1983; Jackson, 1984; Price, 1980; Turner, 1962). Whilst not focussing specifically on training, the debates on the labour process and on labour market segmentation address issues of skill as an element of worker control and in differentiating labour (Braverman, 1974; Wilkinson, 1983; and Wood, 1982 on the labour process; Wilkinson, 1981 on labour market segmentation). Other writers have attempted to address the real and supposed skill differences in the labour force (Armstrong, 1982; Cockburn, 1983 and 1987; Phillips and Taylor, 1980) and the extent to which they are socially constructed by trade union organization, on the one hand, and management, on the other. This body of literature strongly emphasizes the *collective* and *negotiated* nature of skill. It does not require any major leap in the imagination to understand the role of training in creating and maintaining divisions in the labour force. It, therefore, performs an important function in managerial strategies of socialisation and control. Bowles and Gintis (1975) argue that managers deal with collectivities of workers rather than individuals, and maximize profits through a combination of maximizing productivity and suppressing wages.

> Both objectives are pursued through judicious choice of workers and proper specification of the technical, organisational and political structure of the enterprise. The social organisation of production is in large measure a reflection of the capitalist's need for incentive and control mechanisms which will extract labor from workers at the lowest possible wage and prevent the formation of worker coalitions which could oppose their power (1975: 76).

Therefore, it is important to examine training as a process of creating collectivities of workers and as one which is contested both in the workplace and outside.

In this book I examine training policy in nine major trade unions representing workers in a wide range of occupations. I include craft, general and white-collar unions and draw on fieldwork carried out between June 1985 and May 1986, during which interviews were conducted with national and local officials with members in chemicals, construction, engineering and food processing. The time at which the fieldwork was conducted is significant insofar as major developments have occurred in the intervening period both in policy (the extension of YTS to two years in 1986–1987, the introduction of the Job Training Scheme in 1987, the Employment Training Scheme and the abolition of the MSC in 1988) and in amalgamations between trade unions. Furthermore, whilst comments recorded in interviews in 1985 and 1986 might accurately represent the state of policy and success in implementation at that time, the speed of change in the external policy environment has prompted major developments in internal policy and structures. The research, therefore, throws light on trade union policies towards training in general, whilst focussing on policy responses to developments in patterns of employment, the socio-economic environment and in trade union organization which were specific to that conjuncture.

At national level interviews were normally conducted with officers and/or staff of research departments with responsibility for the industry concerned. In some trade unions training forms just one part of a wider range of an official's responsibilities though others designate officers with specific responsibility for training. National interviews were followed up by interviews with regional officials, in order to gain a perspective on local issues and how training policy was implemented in practice. A small number of interviews were also conducted at plant level with shop stewards. In the text, extracts appear from these interviews and the relevant union named in parenthesis following the extract. An open–ended, semi–structured interview technique was employed so that avenues which presented themselves in the course of discussion could be followed up. This open–endedness proved to be particularly appropriate in instances in which it was apparent that questions relating to training assumed that training was actually taking place. In many instances de-skilling, casualization and redundancy were the main concerns of the membership and training had a low priority simply because it did not arise as a workplace bargaining issue.

The choice of industries, engineering, chemicals, food processing and construction, was determined by earlier work on training as an area of corporatist intervention in which the training policies of employers' associations were examined. This is reported in Rainbird and Grant (1985a). This earlier project had its origins in an international research project on business interest associations organized from the International Institute of Management in West Berlin in which 10 national teams focused on these four industries. They were selected with the aid of a sampling matrix based on two clusters of variables; those concerned with economic structure of the sector, such as economic concentration, exposure to international competition, capital intensity and heterogeneity, and those concerned with the sector's relationship to the state, such as the extent of direct state ownership, the importance of the state as a customer, and the degree and form of regulation. The findings of the IIM project are synthesized in Streeck and Schmitter, (1985). Vocational training was viewed as a policy area in which the failure of the market to provide adequate training might lead to the transfer of responsibilities from the state to business interest organisations with the result that the associations might develop means of exerting influence over the behaviour of their member firms.

This book presents a complementary study of trade union policy–making in the same four sectors. Each industry demonstrates distinctive labour force characteristics, trade union representation and collective bargaining machinery. They also exhibit differences in the processes of industrial restructuring and exposure to international markets which have implications both for jobs and employment conditions, and hence to training patterns and trade union perception of policy priorities.

A sectoral focus also enables the relationships between sector–specific training institutions and national policy and institutions to be examined. The abolition of the ITBs in chemicals and food processing and their retention in construction and engineering have affected trade union representation at industry–level and have been significant in the extent to which a coherent sectoral response has been developed to the three objectives of the New Training Initiative.

The trade unions selected for study were those with large memberships in the industrial sectors concerned. It must be emphasized that trade unions organizing in these sectors which have been omitted have not been excluded from the investigation because they do not have policies on industrial training, but because time and resource constraints limited the numbers of interviews which could be conducted. The trade unions interviewed were the Association of Professional, Executive, Clerical and Computer Staff (APEX), the Association of Scientific, Technical and Managerial Staffs (ASTMS), the Amalgamated Union of Engineering Workers (AUEW), the Amalgamated Union of Engineering Workers/Technical, Administrative and Supervisory Section (AUEW/TASS), the Electrical, Electronic, Telecommunication and Plumbing Union (EETPU), the General, Municipal, Boilermakers' and Allied Trades' Union (GMBATU), the Transport and General Workers' Union (TGWU), the Union of Construction and Allied Trades and Technicians (UCATT) and the Union of Shop, Distributive and Allied Workers (USDAW). See the first chart for the resultant sectoral distribution of trade unions interviewed:

*Chemicals*
TGWU, GMBATU, USDAW, AUEW, EETPU, ASTMS

*Construction*
UCATT, TGWU, EETPU, AUEW/TASS (craft sector)

*Engineering*
TGWU, GMBATU, AUEW, AUEW/TASS, EETPU, APEX

*Food Processing*
TGWU, GMBATU, USDAW, ASTMS, APEX

This compares with the second chart representing sectoral distribution of trade unions interviewed on the training boards (prior to abolition in 1982 in the case of the Chemical and Allied Products and Food, Drink and Tobacco ITBs).

*CAPITB* (as at 1980/81)
TGWU (2), EEPTU (1), GMWU (2), AUEW (1), ASTMS (1), USDAW (1)

*CITB* (as at 1985/86)
UCATT (3), Civil Engineering Construction Conciliation Board (3): UCATT (1), GMBATU (1), TGWU (1), TGWU (3), EETPU (2), AUEW/TASS craft sector (1)

*EITB* (as at 1985/86)
EETPU (1), AUEW/TASS (Patternmakers) (1), Confederation of Shipbuilding and Engineering Unions (1), TGWU (1), AUEW (2), AUEW/TASS (1), GMBATU (1)

*FDTITB*
USDAW (3), ASTMS (1), Tobacco Workers' Union (1), TGWU (3), United Road Transport Union (1), Bakers', Food and Allied Workers' Union (1), National Union of Agricultural and Allied Workers (1), GMWU (2)
(*NB:* The General and Municipal Workers' Union became GMBATU following agreement on amalgamation with the Boilermakers' Union in 1982).

The numbers of interviews conducted in each trade union varied not only by representation in each of the sectors, but also by degree of centralization of policy on training and training–related issues. Policy documents and trade union publications were also consulted.

Since the fieldwork was conducted (June 1985–September 1986) a number of developments have occurred which need to be mentioned. Economic recovery has resulted in the emergence of skill shortages and youth unemployment is likely to disappear from the political agenda as the cohort of school leavers declines in the 1990s and employers compete to recruit them. The implications for training are not yet clear. Already in the more prosperous regions of South-East England there have been reports of large retailers abandoning YTS in favour of employing young people on full wage rates (Incomes Data Services, July 1988). General unions, such as USDAW, report considerable progress in training provision since the introduction of the two-year YTS (not fully reflected in the findings here due to the time at which interviews were conducted) and have expressed concern that some of the training gains made through the scheme might be lost as employers seek to bid up youth wages in order to attract young workers. In effect, demographic factors mean that for young people, jobs rather than training schemes will soon be the order of the day.

In the trade union movement itself, a number of developments have occurred, both in terms of amalgamations and in initiatives in training policy. In 1987, ASTMS and AUEW/TASS merged to form Manufacturing, Science and Finance, initiating a major campaign on training in the autumn of that year. A merger between APEX and GMBATU was agreed for early 1989, whilst merger talks continue between the AUEW (now AEU) and the EETPU. If the latter is successful, this will create a major bloc on the right of the trade union movement and could also

form a route for the EEPTU to return to the TUC, following its
expulsion in September 1988 (*Financial Times*, 11 January 1989).


## Structure of the Book

The aim of the book is to examine how trade unions perceive and
organize around training policy issues. It can be divided into four main
sections: firstly, a consideration of trade union policy towards initial
training. This is the traditional area for trade and craft union concerns,
though with the advent of the Youth Training Scheme, policy on initial
training is no longer restricted to the latter. Because of the impact of the
New Training Initiative in this area, both in relation to apprenticeship
reform and the Youth Training Scheme, it concerns training in the firm,
modifications to existing programmes of training for young people and
training in the wider labour market. Trade unions are concerned with
developments in the wider labour market for a number of reasons;
firstly, youth unemployment and the incorporation of young workers
into employment on conditions determined by the state affect not only
those young people directly concerned but also other workers who may
be displaced by a supply of cheap labour. Secondly, trade unions must
formulate policy towards YTS insofar as officials have been involved in
the approval of YTS schemes through the Area Manpower Boards.
These schemes may not affect their own members directly and may
concern training places in small, non-unionised workplaces or in private
training agencies which are outside direct trade union control and
influence. Finally, trade unionists are also parents and care about the
employment and training opportunities of their own children.

The second section focusses on retraining. Chapter 3 is concerned
with retraining related to new technology and Chapter 4 with that
relating to employer demands for increased flexibility. Despite presentation in two separate chapters, theoretically and empirically it is
difficult to separate the two issues. The evidence indicates that patterns
of change are complex and that changes in jobs and working practices
can take place with or without recourse to formal training programmes.
The chapter on flexibility, whilst focussing primarily on changing job
demarcations and flexibility between trades, also examines the effect of
increasing use of casual forms of labour (some of which are promoted
through 'training schemes') on job content and skills and questions the
broader training implications of casualisation.

The third section focusses more sharply on factors relating to trade
union organization itself. Chapter 5 examines training as a policy issue
for each of the trade unions in turn, examining the priority given to it,

internal structures for formulating it and the means by which decisions are implemented. The representation of trade union interests on different training bodies is considered and its relationship to collective bargaining structures. Chapter 6 examines the implications of occupational change brought about by the changing structure of employment and new technology for trade union identity and organization. It highlights, in particular, the implications of employer initiatives on single-union agreements, no strike agreements and a greater reliance on sub-contracting, part-time and casual labour for trade union organization. Furthermore, potential conflicts between trade unions are opened up by flexible working practices and the capacity for new technology to break down the boundaries between jobs. These same factors also pose the possiblity of amalgamation and for the trade union movement to take the initiative and to recognize that in order to defend its own members' interests it must also concern itself with those of workers who are outside collective bargaining structures in the more casualized sectors of employment.

Finally, in Chapter 7 the wider significance of the findings is explored, in particular, implications for the analysis of training as an item which is bargained over at many different levels and for the ways in which trade union interests can be represented in this field.

# 2

# Initial Training

## Introduction

Until the introduction of the Youth Training Scheme in 1983, craft apprenticeship had been the major form of youth training, though apprenticeships were available only to limited numbers of young people entering the labour force for the first time. The Industrial Training Boards had a brief to develop all forms of training, but tended to concentrate on modernizing, updating and validating apprenticeship. Large numbers of young workers, therefore, had limited access to formal, work-related training and those that did have access to apprenticeship were invariably white and male (Goldstein, 1984; Lee and Wrench, 1983). Most young workers, therefore, acquired the skills they needed for their jobs through on-the-job supervision and instruction or by learning through experience. The Youth Opportunities and the Training Opportunities Programmes, introduced in the 1970s as counter-cyclical measures to combat unemployment provided training for young people as a means of improving their employment chances on completion of the course. The Youth Training Scheme was the first attempt to provide universal training for school leavers, whether in employment or unemployed.

The historical development of industrial training has resulted in craft unions having well-developed policies towards youth training because of the tradition of apprenticeship and its significance in forming skilled workers and in differentiating them from unskilled workers. Trade unions whose members have not benefited from formal training programmes tend to have less well-developed policies towards youth training. YTS, while representing the fulfilment of a long-standing labour movement demand for training for all, is a contradictory phenomenon because of its social policy objective of absorbing youth unemployment, which overrides the objective of skill-training. Therefore, whilst YTS might have some positive benefits insofar as it introduces training for young people who formerly might never have received it, there is opposition to its non-training aspects. These relate to the low level of the training allowance which is seen as exerting downward pressure on youth wages, and the fact that the employer has no contractual obligation to employ the trainee on termination of the scheme. It is thus laid open to the criticism of creating a supply of cheap, temporary labour which unscrupulous employers may use as a substitute for permanent jobs. Furthermore, the existence of government funding for an employer-led training scheme has resulted in the wholesale privatization of training provision which to a large extent has been divorced from employment opportunities (Trade Union Resource Centre, 1984 and 1986; National Labour Movement Inquiry into Youth Unemployment and Training, 1987). Because of the contemporary significance of the government's New Training Initiative and, in particular, the Youth Training Scheme, the main focus of this chapter is the development of policy responses to YTS, on the one hand, and the response of craft unions to the reform of apprenticeship, on the other.

In any analysis of contemporary changes in youth training, one is confronted by the problem of rapid changes in policy as new schemes are introduced and existing schemes are modified. Interviews for this project were conducted in 1985 and 1986. The one-year YTS scheme had become relatively well established since it began in 1983 and was viewed as a feature of the industrial training scene that was likely to continue, at least in the short term. Nevertheless, in the course of the project the extension of the scheme to two years was announced. At the time of interviewing the full implications of the two-year scheme were not clear. The trade unions' policy response was still developing and the outcome of negotiations with employers unresolved.

Considerable variations exist in the extent to which trade union members are directly affected by the Youth Training Scheme and apprenticeship reform. Members of the two white collar unions, TASS and ASTMS, are normally adults when they enter their occupations and partly acquire their qualifications through the general education system as well as in industry. The Youth Training Scheme may, therefore, have no direct effect on new recruits. This does not, of course, prevent these trade unions from having clearly developed policy positions on industrial training and on YTS, but training as a policy issue for trade unions will be dealt with in Chapter 5 and does not fall into the discussion here. Even within the trade unions discussed in this section there are variations in the relative coherence of policy which relate to the sectors in which they organize, the range of occupations in which they recruit, the type of initial training received and their own internal structure as organizations (cf. Rainbird, 1986).

Regardless of whether trade unions organizing in particular occupations had an existing well-developed policy towards training or not, the introduction of YTS and apprenticeship reform has required the development of policy perspectives on training. Whilst craft unions, with long-standing concerns with the defence of apprenticeship have had to respond to the potential for dilution and substitution presented by the combination of YTS and the introduction of skill tests on completion of training, general unions whose members have rarely received training have had to respond to a policy which on the one hand appears to offer benefits; that is to say, it has introduced training where none previously existed, whilst guarding against members' fears of job substitution and abuses of young people as a source of cheap labour. Even within the craft unions, response has varied from resistance to attempts to change existing forms of apprenticeship (the concept of a traditional, unchanging apprenticeship is incorrect, as will be argued below) to the embrace of a scheme which, though not fully supported in all its ramifications, in the short term appears to provide a solution to the massive reduction in the numbers of apprentices in training. Trade union perceptions and policy towards youth training will be considered in three major sections: firstly, by examining craft unions and craft sections in those industrial sectors (mainly engineering, chemicals and indirectly food processing) in which there are no national agreements on the scheme; secondly by examining the craft unions and sections which are governed by national agreements and nationally organized YTS schemes (in practice, this means trade unions organizing in the construction industry); and thirdly, by considering the impact of YTS on training, whether or not it existed formally, for trade unions organizing in non-craft occupations. To some extent it is simplification to categorize responses in this way since they are a function both of occupational category, industry sector and the process of amalgamation between trade unions whereby general unions have incorporated craft and white-collar sections and craft unions have extended membership to non-craft grades.

### Craft Training in Engineering, Chemicals and Food Processing

Major developments in craft apprenticeship training in the past two decades have come about largely as a result of the passing of the 1964 Industrial Training Act which provided for the establishment of the Industry Training Boards operating at sectoral level. As far as craft apprenticeship is concerned, the establishment of the Industry Training Boards and, in particular, the Engineering Industry Training Board marked a move away from apprenticeship based on time-serving to a more condensed period of training with increasing emphasis on formal, off-the-job learning conducted at a technical college or training school provided by a company or group training scheme. The Engineering Industry Training Board's module system, developed through its tripartite committee structure, has been significant in establishing standards of engineering craft training both in companies in the engineering sector which are defined as being in scope to EITB (thus paying the training levy) as well as those out of scope by virtue of their size (fewer than 40 employees on their payroll) and by industrial sector. Prior to the abolition of 16 of the ITBs under the provisions of the 1981 Employment and Training Act arrangements existed for the validation of EITB engineering craft training modules by Industry Training Boards covering other sectors. So, for example, the Food, Drink and Tobacco ITB could validate craft training modules for the food, drink and tobacco industry. Since the abolition of the ITBs in chemicals and food processing, statutory training boards have been replaced by voluntary training organizations at sub-sectoral level and based on employers' and trade associations. In some instances, these Non-Statutory Training Organizations (NSTOs) make provisions for validating and developing engineering craft training modules whilst others have delegated responsibility for this to private training consultancy companies.

Off-the-job training based on the module system has, therefore, been a major element in engineering craft training and apprentices undergo a total of 36 weeks of training in their first year during which they take two EITB modules. First-year training is, therefore, in transferable skills and is followed in the second and third years of training by more firm-specific skills. In 1986 modifications were agreed in EITB to sub-divide modules into segments, allowing employers to make initial training more firm-specific. EITB also oversees technician and non-craft training in the engineering industry. At the time of interviewing there was no national agreement in the engineering industry on YTS and the scheme was being run on a plant-by-plant basis or through group training schemes. Under the additionality rules which governed the one-year scheme it was possible for companies to obtain YTS funding as a subsidy for training two apprentices taken on in the normal way if they took on three additional trainees. These additional trainees could be in clerical and semi-skilled occupations, the training costs of which are considerably lower than those of craft apprenticeship training. Due to the cost of craft apprenticeship training the EITB has argued for differential funding under YTS for training in engineering craft skills. There is no comparison between the YTS provision for 13 weeks of off-the-job training in the first year of the one-year scheme (a total of 20 weeks in the two-year scheme) with the cost of 36 weeks of off-the-job training in the first year of engineering craft apprenticeship. However, the introduction of the two-year scheme, combined with the dropping of the MSC's stipulation that training should be 'broad-based' rather than job-specific, now means that YTS funds can be used to subsidize apprenticeship training.

The issue most concerning trade unions and, indeed, the Engineering Industry Training Board, has been the collapse of craft apprentice training. Between 1980 and 1982 registrations of first-year apprentices with EITB fell by 50 per cent. The total number of apprentices in training, including those in later years of training, fell from 87 000 in 1980 to 35 700 in 1985 (Dutton, 1986: 35). Though in 1984 approximately 25 per cent of apprentice registrations were YTS trainees, it was still not clear what was happening to trainees at the end of their first year of training; whether they had been issued with contracts of employment from the outset of training or on completion of their first year and whether they were subsequently continuing training or training was curtailed (Dutton, 1986). It was not possible to assess from interviews the extent to which YTS funding and associated trainee rather than employed status had been introduced and whether trainee allowances rather than minimum wage rates had been paid. This is because developments have occurred on a plant basis and higher levels of trade union officialdom have not been involved. By 1986, EITB reported that 9870 young people were undertaking craft and technician training, of whom 2915 were receiving full basic training under YTS (EITB Annual Report, 1987: 6).

The decline in apprenticeship numbers, combined with employers' reports of skill shortages in traditional and high technology occupations resulted in EITB issuing a report in January 1987 outlining the extent of the collapse of training and putting forward proposals for changing the system of financing training within the industry. These included the possibilityof increasing the level of the levy to 0.2 per cent of a firm's payroll and tougher exemption rules.

## The Policy Environment

The major issue affecting craft apprenticeship has been the MSC's objective of replacing time-serving by training to standards. This has frequently been incorrectly represented as an issue concerning the nature of training. In fact the main issue at stake has been that of transition to adult pay rates and whether it should come on completion of a customary length of training or on passing examinations at the end of the training period. As outlined above, modern engineering craft apprenticeships have been introduced with the EITB's module system and though these are by no means universal, insofar as EITB can not monitor training in firms outside the scope of its Industrial Training Order, it has set the standards for training within the mainstream of the engineering industry and for engineering craft training outside it. In contrast, changes in the way in which trainees progress from trainee to adult wage rates have nothing to do with the *content* of training but the *rules* for fixing skilled wages rates. To be sure, training to standards will introduce skill tests on completion of training and there is some basis in the trade unions' concern that this may lead to an acceleration of the training period, a process which has been occurring in any event in the post-war period as the length of apprenticeship has been successively reduced. The consequence of this is that dilution might occur, undermining skilled wage rates or creating differential wage rates, where large numbers of failures occur. On the other hand, not all the outcomes of establishing credentials for achievements in industrial training will automatically be detrimental to trade union interests. Regardless of its implications for wage rates, the concept of 'training to standards' is one that is difficult to reject politically without being seen to be supporting outdated restrictive practices. The different compromises which have been reached in each sector give an indication of the extent to which the nature of production and employment, combined with the structures of joint regulation, have affected trade unions' perceptions of its impact on their members' interests.

In the engineering industry training to standards has been the subject of negotiations between the Confederation of Shipbuilding and Engineering Unions and the Engineering Employers' Federation. The agreement signed between the CSEU and the EEF in July 1983 changed the basis of acquiring skilled engineering craft status from time-serving to the achievement of nationally-agreed standards based on the award of the EITB's Certification of Craftsmanship, that is to say on completing initial training and two EITB training modules. The skilled National Minimum Rate would apply from the time of receiving EITB approval of successful completion of training.

Despite the agreement reached by the CSEU, the AUEW, the major trade union in the CSEU, fought as an individual trade union to resist it, due to the position taken by their National Committee. The reason the National Committee took this position was because the members felt it took four years to train a skilled fitter in the engineering industry and traditionally, favoured a five-year apprenticeship period and later a four-year system. Since the 1983 decision of the CSEU, officials at all levels in the trade union had been in the anomalous position of having to support trade union policy on time-serving in the face of the CSEU position. This was expressed in interviews in the following terms:

> The AUEW has made a dead end stand by opposing training to standards (AUEW).

and

> The AUEW are not parties to the CSEU agreement, which up to four years ago had a four-year apprenticeship. All the other unions in engineering have gone away from time-serving to training to standards. This has caused problems and there are pressures all round because we have been unsuccessful in getting people trained. The EEF says they have got an agreement to train to standards with all other unions and the officials are saying to the national policy body to recognize training to standards as a fact of life. The major detrimental affect has been on the number of apprenticeships being offered to our people and with the rundown in our industry as well this has led to a dreadful situation which is impossible to quantify (AUEW).

In May 1986 after a full day's debate amongst all sections of the trade union a narrow vote changed its position to acceptance of training to standards. The *AEU Journal* reported a speech from the debate: 'The stagnation cannot continue, our convenors are in an impossible position, I challenge you either to escalate or change our position, inactivity is unacceptable. If we cannot bring CSEU to support us, we must change our view (July 1986: 19).' The passing of a motion instructing the Executive Council to co-operate with the required changes in craft apprenticeship training did not resolve issues relating to rates of pay and the monitoring of training. For whilst the monitoring of training is possible in companies within the scope of EITB, this is not true of companies with engineering apprentices outside its scope. The 1983 CSEU agreement made provisions for tripartite discussions with EITB concerning the setting and testing of standards of training in small firms below the EITB's levy exclusion level. In addition, an understanding was reached with the Engineering Employers' Federation that where apprentices were not trained under the new system in small companies the EEF would accept a decision of the trade union concerned as to whether or not the apprentice would receive approved craft status (Training of Engineering Craftsmen, Discussion with Engineering Employers' Federation, 31 March 1983). Nevertheless, concerns remain about apprentices trained outside the engineering industry. When the AUEW National Committee discussed training to standards in 1983, concerns were expressed to George Young and Geoffrey Holland at the MSC about this and the trade union was promised that £850,000 would be provided for EITB to monitor standards of training in out-of-scope companies. Following the 1986 National Committee decision, this possibility was to be re-examined.

Despite the AUEW's acceptance of training to standards, opposition remains to the tying of YTS to apprenticeship. The fact that employers could take on trainees for the first year of YTS and then decide whether to keep an individual trainee on as an apprentice gives no guarantee to the trade unions of the quality of training or on the number of apprentices in training. CSEU policy has been for trainees who have undertaken first-year off-the-job training under YTS to have the normal level of apprentice pay applied retrospectively when they enter the second year of apprenticeship training. The EEF has stated that existing apprentice rates will not be paid in the first year of training because the trainees are not considered to be apprentices until they enter their second year. With the extension of YTS to two years the MSC and EITB have stated that they will be looking to YTS to form the sole source of apprenticeship recruitment to the industry and, with the MSC, have developed a model scheme for this purpose. The AUEW are far from happy with the rates of the YTS allowance (£27.30 in the first year and £35 in the second year in 1986–1987) which they believe are no compensation for existing agreements which pay approximately £40 in the first year of apprenticeship. The real fear, however, is that YTS could result in a two-year apprenticeship on low pay.

Many of the constituent trade unions of the CSEU indicated their concern at the decline in apprentice numbers and are particularly dismissive of the idea that YTS, at least in its early form, could be seen as a substitute for craft apprentice training. It was not viewed as a solution for training in skilled jobs though it is seen as having potential applications in non-craft occupations:

> The TGWU accepts that there are problems with YTS at the sharp end of engineering but trainees can be trained in stores procedures, office work, transport – a whole range of activities which historically do not have an in-built training syllabus or where the existing training syllabus lasts for a short period (TGWU).

Yet, it appears that, given the trade unions' inability to obtain assurances and a commitment from the employers to maintain normal levels of apprentice intakes, some of these outstanding problems will not be resolved in such a way as to make a national agreement feasible. Trade unions, such as the EETPU which do have a national agreement in the electrical contracting industry on YTS are particularly keen to see similar schemes elsewhere, even if it requires making compromises on youth pay rates, if numbers in training can be maintained.

> It's a pity, but the ITB hasn't come to terms with YTS in the engineering industry. At national level the employers and the unions have been unable to reach an agreement. The AUEW has the traditional attitude to apprentice training. The CSEU now has training to standards, that is to say, rates of pay on completion of the course, not on reaching a certain age, but the AUEW National Committee rejected it (This was prior to the May 1986 decision – H. R.) . . . We feel opportunities have been passed aside because of this otherwise we would have more young people in training in engineering – we could have shamed the employers into doing something better than they are currently doing. All the electrical trainees are under the traditional apprenticeship arrangement and there are very few of them. One or two others crept in but the numbers are very, very small (EEPTU).

Whether the new proposals mooted by EITB to increase training activity will result in an increase in apprentice numbers has yet to be seen.

Training to standards and YTS have had different effects for craft training outside engineering. In the chemical industry, for example, an agreement has been reached in the national negotiating machinery on the setting of an exam at the end of each year of apprenticeship training. Though the Chemical Industries' Association wanted the apprenticeship period reduced from four to three years it has remained at four years. There has been a tacit agreement that although training to standards has been accepted as policy, no failures will occur. Since the abolition of the Chemical and Allied Products ITB no records have been kept on apprentices in training, though anecdotal evidence from interviews suggests levels are much reduced. Officials reported that YTS was not widely used, due to overall job losses and that YTS funding was being used to finance existing apprenticeship rather than replace it. There were variations in its applications. Some officials reported that companies had been using YTS and had selected a number of trainees for full apprenticeship training at the end of the first year, with retrospective payment of wages. Other companies have used YTS as a bargaining counter, threatening to reduce apprentice numbers unless YTS trainees are taken on on trainee allowances. Effectively, companies are using the scheme to select their apprentices in the course of a year-long probationary period. In other instances, trade unions have found themselves bargaining over apprentice numbers with apprentices pay rates on the table. This use of YTS has been characteristic of the large companies in chemicals.

At national level the Chemical Industries' Association has put forward proposals on multi-skilled craft apprenticeship training, which is in line with their objectives in national negotiations to increase flexibilities between chemical process operators and craft workers. Though these proposals were under discussion at the time of interviewing, at local level officials reported that multi-skill training was in progress and in the North-West region it was claimed that disproportionate numbers of craft apprentices were being trained relative to process workers.

In general, in these industries, since no national agreements exist on YTS, YTS was viewed as a threat to apprentice training but one which currently affected mainly non-craft groups of workers. Is is supported primarily as a vocational programme aimed at the young unemployed. Particularly in the depressed North-East and parts of Scotland, retention rates were considerably lower than in other parts of the country, with Cleveland reporting only 30 per cent of trainees finding jobs. One official assessed the scheme in the following terms:

> We support it fully because it takes the youngsters off the street. The problem is that there have been a few rogue employers, but the bulk tend to conform to the ethics of the scheme. These are that the kids are there to learn about work and this is a valuable contribution. But experience is that there are more rogue employers than we would like to have seen but this has not been so much the case in chemicals . . . though it has brought us great problems apprentice-wise . . . in theory YTS is about learning about work. In practice it is an excuse for the employer not to take people on. We endorse the scheme, but with hindsight we can say that it was a good opportunity for the employers and they have seized it (AUEW).

### National Agreements on YTS and Apprenticeship in Construction: Main Building Trades

The construction industry is one in which entry into different skilled trades has historically been by means of apprenticeship. Despite criticism of 'traditional' apprenticeship for being based on time-serving, apprenticeship as an institution has changed considerably over the years (Clarke, 1985). In recent times this has involved an increased component of formal training off-the-job at colleges of further education. In the main building trades, for example, training syllabi set by the CITB have been used to determine the content of training since the introduction of

the Standard Scheme of Training in 1974. Rather than being a mono-
lithic, unchanging feature of construction industry training, apprenticeship has evolved with the changing nature of construction work, reflecting the introduction of new materials, changing methods of work and in
some instances, as with scaffolding and heavy plant used particularly in
the civil and mechanical engineering sectors of the industry, the development of curricula because of safety considerations on site work.

Although trade unions, employers and the CITB have been discussing
the introduction of objective tests to replace time-serving for several
years, in practice, many traditional crafts based on the use of specific
materials, have been broken down into their component parts. In the
building sector the apprenticeship period was reduced from five years to
four years in 1965, and in 1974 it was reduced still further, resulting in
apprenticeships lasting between two and a half and four years,
depending on the trade and the acquisition of the CITB craft certificates.
In the construction industry trade unions have supported the introduction
of shorter apprenticeships, and employers have resisted these changes,
apprentices being regarded as a source of cheap labour. Technical
change, combined with the growth of labour-only sub-contracting, has
reduced trade union control of the apprenticeship period and has
resulted in trade unions experiencing difficulties in recruiting apprentices. As the Training Research Group argue:

> Traditionally apprenticeship has served as a means of control by
> craft unions over work and entry into the trade, making less likely
> a surplus which could be used by employers to hold down wages by
> threatening unemployment. In a situation of increasingly frag-
> mented and de-skilled work, however, where such union control is
> being eroded, an artificially long apprenticeship based on time-
> serving principles mainly serves the employers' interests (1981: 13).

Alongside the reduction in the length of apprenticeship has been a move
towards an increasing element of off-the-job training. This reflects not
the end of apprenticeship, but a change in its evolutionary course. As a
bricklayer interviewed by Clarke on on-site training stated: 'They were
just filling up holes in the brickwork and doing bits and pieces – maybe
the odd garden wall; the "marvellous" three year apprenticeship with a
tradesman who has time to train and isn't on bonus is a thing of the past'
(1985: 4). Since 1974, off-the-job apprenticeship training has consisted
of a six-month training and education course for first-year apprentices in
building trades, followed by day-release in the second and third years of
training. It is this scheme which has now been replaced by YTS.

In construction there has been a tendency towards a reduction in the
range of tasks performed by skilled workers trained in the traditional

If we are rational about the NTI we must go along with it, but generally the trade unions' approach to change in apprenticeship has been one of caution or opposition, especially since the pressure for change has come mainly from the employers, the MSC and the Government. A large body of opinion on both the trade union and the employer side in construction remains to be convinced and is hesitant about any change in the traditional apprenticeship system. There is one argument that traditional apprenticeship has stood the test of time, but they don't recognise this as a valid argument. There have been rapid changes in types of building and whilst over the centuries there was relatively little change in building methods, particularly in the second half of this century new materials and pre-fabricated designs have been widely introduced. As a result, some aspects of traditional skills are no longer relevant . . . We have to develop the training system to meet the needs of the industry, which is entirely relevant and standardised (UCATT).

And:

We have reluctantly accepted YTS but we are trying to get the best we can out of it (UCATT).

Whilst there are recognized problems with YTS in construction which require vigilance and enforcement by the trade unions, there is a genuine belief that the scheme can be used to provide apprenticeship training and that it can lead to opportunities for young workers entering the construction industry. Concern that it should lead to jobs rather than unemployment or self-employment in the 'black' economy has underlined the need to use existing structures such as CITB and the apprenticeship committees of the national joint negotiating machinery of the different subsectors to reach agreement between employers and trade unions on the way in which the scheme relates to apprenticeship training and to ensure, by seeking representation on the Area Manpower Boards that only CITB approved schemes receive funding. As one official put it;

There is a problem with all schemes – we need the revamping of the industry otherwise we will have the best-trained dole queue in the world. At the UCATT Biennial Delegate Conference a lad argued that YTS was not a ladder to full employment but a gangplank to the sea of unemployment. Building employers have a problem with workloads but they need skilled people for any upturn in the economy or there will be serious problems. No jobs means that you have disillusioned, frustrated, trained unemployed people (UCATT).

Of course, YTS contributes nothing to the underlying problem of the industry which concerns its workload, cutbacks in public expenditure on large capital projects and the massive growth of labour-only subcontracting. The view is that, used wisely, YTS can retain sufficient skill base in the industry until such time as the workload picks up again. Even so, the numbers of apprentices in training has undergone a drastic reduction in recent years. Clarke estimates that apprentice registrations in the private sector, including carpenters and joiners, electricians, bricklayers and masons, plumbers and glaziers, painters and decorators and plasterers, fell from 66,000 in 1964, to 32,000 by 1973 to 24,000 by 1979 (Clarke, 1985: 2). Table 2.1 shows that since the mid-1970s the volume of training has declined further and numbers of apprentices have not increased despite the massive injection of state funds through YTS. Public expenditure cuts have had disproportionate impact on the construction industry and in May 1977 an informal grouping consisting of the presid-

Table 2.1
CITB Trainees in the Main Apprentice Trades*,
All CITB Trainees, and Local Authority DLO Apprentices

| Year | Main Trainee Trades | All CITB Trainees | DLO Apprentices |
|------|------|------|------|
| 1975 | 69.9 | 79.3 | 8.3 |
| 1976 | 64.5 | 74.1 | 7.7 |
| 1977 | 53.1 | 62.9 | 6.5 |
| 1978 | 54.3 | 65.1 | 6.6 |
| 1979 | 54.5 | 65.3 | 7.0 |
| 1980 | 56.2 | 69.0 | 7.1 |
| 1981 | 50.8 | 60.7 | 6.7 |
| 1982 | 46.8 | 55.0 | 6.6 |
| 1983 | 41.8 | 49.8 | 5.4 |
| 1984** | 41.5 | 49.6 | 4.4 |
| 1985** | 39.9 | 47.5 | 6.7 |
| 1986** | 40.4 | 47.8 | 5.3 |
| Decrease | −42.2% | −39.7% | −35.9% |

* Carpenters/Joiners, Bricklayers, Painters, Plasterers, Plumbers/Gas Fitters, Heating and Ventilating Engineers.
** As at April.
*Source:* Housing and Construction Statistics (CITB) quoted in Rainbird and Clarke (1988: 11).

ents of eight of the major interest organizations in the industry was created to make representations to the Prime Minister. The so-called 'Group of Eight' consists of the National Secretary of the Building Crafts section of the TGWU and the General Secretary of UCATT on the trade union side and representatives of employers' associations and professional institutions. The resort to political solutions for resolving the lack of investment in housing and infrastructure and in generation employment has been taken up in the Labour Party-TUC Liaison Committee's *Jobs and Industry. A New Partnership. A New Britain* (1985) which proposed expansion of public expenditure in construction to create a large number of jobs rapidly in the event of a Labour Government coming to power following the 1987 General Election. A number of Local Authorities have also drawn up job-generating policies based on the expansion of construction work (Brent LERU, 1987).

The extent of unemployment and self-employment in the construction industry can not be overstated. In 1971 approximately 23 per cent of the workforce were self-employed (IER 1987: 70). By June 1987, 410,493 self-employed workers held individual 714 (tax exemption) certificates (IDS Study 396, 1987: 5) but this does not include those self-employed workers who have tax deducted at source, under the '27 per cent off' system. Table 2.2 shows that approximately 50 per cent of the private sector workforce is now self-employed. It is an industry in which very large and very small firms coexist, linked through extensive sub-contracting of work. Particularly in the more labour-intensive sectors, smaller companies shade into self-employment and the informal economy. As an example of the precariousness of the smaller firms in the industry, in 1981 the CITB attempted to increase its levy register by searching for unregistered firms in the membership books of employers' associations and in Yellow Pages directories. As a result, they discovered 52,000 firms which were not registered. A large number of firms were subsequently added to the register, but within a year or so half of these firms had gone into liquidation. There can be no doubt that the growth of self-employment seriously undermines the volume and quality of training (Rainbird and Clarke, 1988). Derek Gaulter, Chairman of the Construction Industry Training Board, has expressed CITB's concern at the lack of on-site training places available for trainees because the decline of direct employment. Furthermore, the industry is beset by the problem of 'cowboy' operators using semi- and untrained people on the fringe of the industry and this poses a serious threat to the quality of work, as well as undermining negotiated wage rates and conditions of employment. As a result of poor quality building work there are 42,000 complaints per annum to the Office of Fair Trading (Construction Industry Training Board, Press Release, 3 June 1986).

TABLE 2.2
Ratio of Trainees to Direct and Self-employed Operatives*

| Year | Self-employed (1) | Directly employed (2) | Total 1+2 (3) | (4) | Ratio 3:4 |
|------|------|------|------|------|------|
| 1970 | 300 | 912 | 1212 | 85.4 | 14.2 |
| 1971 | 328 | 856 | 1184 | 77.5 | 15.3 |
| 1972 | 367 | 861 | 1168 | 82.5 | 14.2 |
| 1973 | 428 | 902 | 1330 | 83.1 | 16.0 |
| 1974 | 427 | 874 | 1301 | 83.7 | 15.5 |
| 1975 | 375 | 820 | 1195 | 79.3 | 15.1 |
| 1976 | 341 | 788 | 1129 | 74.1 | 15.2 |
| 1977 | 325 | 756 | 1081 | 62.9 | 12.2 |
| 1978 | 365 | 750 | 1115 | 65.1 | 17.1 |
| 1979 | 395 | 770 | 1165 | 65.3 | 17.8 |
| 1980 | 375 | 760 | 1135 | 69.0 | 16.4 |
| 1981 | 388 | 678 | 1066 | 60.7 | 17.6 |
| 1982 | 400 | 619 | 1019 | 55.0 | 18.5 |
| 1983 | 409 | 600 | 1009 | 49.8 | 20.3 |
| 1984 | 464 | 585 | 1049 | 49.2 | 21.3 |
| 1985 | 470 | 556 | 1026 | 47.5 | 21.6 |
| 1986 | 487 | 530 | 1017 | 47.8 | 21.3 |
| Change | +62.3% | −42.0% | −16.0% | −44.0% | − |

* Not including public sector construction or business.
*Source*: Housing and Construction Statistics (CITB) quoted in Rainbird and Clarke (1988: 12).

Despite the importance attributed to training under the Youth Training Scheme in the construction industry, there is evidence that some employers continue to train under the old apprenticeship arrangements and do not claim the YTS allowance. In November 1984, *Construction Board News* reported that CITB's Strategic Review revealed that there were approximately two trainees on day- and block-release courses for every three on CITB YTS courses in the first year of the scheme (1984: 3). There was anecdotal reporting of the continuance of day- and block-release schemes in interviews. The fact that in May 1986 *Construction Board News* carried a front page article encouraging employers to claim the £7,000 allowance available for training under the two-year YTS scheme in preference to receiving CITB grants of only

£1,400 for traditional day- and block-release apprenticeship indicates that traditional methods have not been wholly superseded.

Officials' assessments of the one-year YTS were quite positive, due to high retention rates of craft trainees, reportedly as high as 85 per cent, though this was not replicated in the non-craft sector (*Construction Board News*, November 1984: 1). This figure was boosted by the fact that all trainees under the electrical contracting scheme had employed status from the outset of training (see next section). This was combined with the perception that the one-year scheme had not fed the practice of labour-only sub-contracting, though there is anecdotal evidence of firms asking YTS trainees to go on 'the lump' after the completion of the first year.

> As far as UCATT is concerned, one year YTS trainees are not being used for labour-only sub-contracting since a high proportion go on to apprenticeships proper. This is because the YTS craft stream are those who traditionally would have been taken on as apprentices . . . The trainees completing the Building Foundation Training Scheme are those that want to complete their apprenticeship and are unlikely to go on the lump, though this may be different for the two year scheme. Although the MSC proposals are for a broadly based second year training programme this is not on in construction (UCATT).

Despite trade union condemnation of the low level of trainee allowance, there has been little success generally in obtaining 'top ups'. However, progress has been made on the status of trainees on the scheme and the Training Commission of the National Joint Commission for the Building Industry, a committee which deals with apprenticeship indentures, agreed firstly, that the one-year scheme should count as six-months remission towards the period of apprentice training and that the second year of YTS under the two-year scheme should be a part of apprenticeship. (There are some variations in the arrangements which will be illustrated in the discussion of the electrical contracting and the heating and ventilating sector schemes.) Before the two-year scheme was introduced in the autumn of 1986, agreement had been reached in the NJCBI that trainees would be issued with a contract of employment at the beginning of their second year and that they would be paid apprentice wage rates. There is a similar agreement between the TGWU and the Federation of Master Builders, established in the Building and Allied Trades Joint Industrial Council. An apprenticeship registration scheme has been set up under the BATJIC agreement and is built on the model of the NJCBI scheme with some modifications. The registration scheme is monitored by CITB computers. These agreements are endorsed, in the case of the NJCBI, through the Training Commission's local committees which can refuse to grant the six-month remission on the apprenticeship period (as reported in the case of the Direct Labour Organization below) and through the structure of the Area Manpower Boards on which building industry interest groups have actively sought representation. Training schemes which do not conform to CITB standards or which can not offer contracts of employment in the second year do not receive approval or remission of the apprenticeship period. The reason for this is;

> Through the NJCBI we are using two-year YTS to assist genuine employers and not the cowboys and to use it as a subsidy for apprenticeship training. With the change to the two-year scheme the union position is that we don't want trainees to be used as cheap labour. Where employers take on the trainee after the first year of the scheme, they must indenture them, give them the apprentice pay back-dated for six months and top up in the second year. We take this position because at the end of the year the employer must know if the trainee will make the grade . . . Because the first year of YTS training only counts as six months remission of apprenticeship, it means that employers are getting an eighteen-month subsidy for apprenticeship training through YTS (TGWU).

There have been examples of schemes failing to receive approval because they do not confirm to standards, as reported in 'Small builders aim a brick at industry's giant edifice' (*Times Educational Supplement*, 20 June 1986). Furthermore, it is not only building firms which may be refused approval, but also voluntary organizations with a good record on training because they can not meet the requirement to provide a contract of employment for trainees. However, it must be emphasized that trade union regulation of training is only possible where there is strong workplace organization. Whilst the construction unions are able to regulate the use of YTS to some extent through their representation on CITB, on the apprentice registration bodies and the Area Manpower Boards, the industry is not strongly unionized. Its site organization combines with the fragmentation of trade union organization through widespread self-employment and the blacklisting of activists, to militate against effective monitoring of training at the point of production.

### Schemes for the Unemployed

In construction, apprenticeship training is also perceived as being under attack from other schemes which provide temporary employment and contain a training element. Schemes run under the MSC's Community Programme have also been refused approval through the Area Manpower Boards where they have attempted to provide craft training:

We hope the numbers in training will start increasing again because we are afraid that if the present situation goes on we will have people in the future who will say they're craftsmen, who may have a bit of knowledge through YTS and the CP scheme, and who through practice will try and bring themselves up to the skilled level. We had this problem with the dilutees from the six month training courses run at the Government Training Centres. We do have some lads in membership who are dilutees who have brought themselves up to standard, such as bricklayers and joiners, but they are not allround craftsmen. We support CP schemes, but to train labourers not craftsmen (TGWU).

We have had to pick up regionally on the Community Programme . . . They did announce funding for training through the MSC on the Community Programme and some managing agents wanted to set up their own schemes and dabble in craft training. UCATT blocked it. We wanted it to be general operative training on the grounds of its benefit to the individual and the community (UCATT).

The Community Programme has been of particular concern to trade unionists in the construction industry, not only because of the potential for diluting craft training but because of the potential for job substitution. This is particularly serious in view of the percentage of places allocated to building and environmental work. The North West Director of the Building Employers' Confederation (a member of the Greater Manchester Area Manpower Board has commented on 'the ridiculousness of a situation where 26 per cent of Community Programme places are in the building industry with a further 35 per cent on environmental work when skilled building workers and apprentices are laid off' (Society of Civil and Public Servants, 1986: 12).

It is not only YTS and CP schemes which raise concern, but other areas of MSC programmes as well. The Voluntary Projects Programme, aimed at the long-term unemployed have been blocked in construction though they run in other industries.

It is aimed at unemployed people and for basic dole they are expected to undertake construction craft training outside the industry's pay structures and standards . . . There is the 21-hour rule for claiming benefit and attending college at the same time.

This has been a concern of the Building Employers Confederation too. UCATT objected because these people were outside the control of the industry and the industry standards and were thus obtaining diluted standards of training, which just boosts the black economy. This is a problem for UCATT as a union and for reputable employers as well (UCATT).

Though there are serious reservations about the Community Programme, where it is organized through local authorities, it is seen as having some potential benefits for the training of apprentices. As will be seen in the discussion of building training in the Direct Labour Organizations, a major problem has been in finding new build work to train apprentices on, since much of local authority building work is restricted to repairs. Even in the private sector, work in some trades is so limited that there is nothing to train apprentices on. For example, when interviews were carried out in the West Midlands, it was reported that there were no plastering apprentices at all in the region. To combat this, refurbishments and new build work have been sought by the DLOs for training purposes. In Huddersfield, for example, a major local authority-sponsored Community Programme project was rebuilding a large house as a Muslim welfare centre. UCATT had been involved in the approval and staffing of the scheme and it was hoped that it would be possible to get DLO apprentices to work on it for experience of new build work. In fact this model of creating new build work for local authority apprentices to train on started with the Powell House project in Hackney and has subsequently been taken up by other local authority building training departments. An alternative has been to loan DLO apprentices out to the private sector for work experience. Whereas the private sector still has large contracts on which to train apprentices, many of the major contractors are reluctant to take on apprentices in the less prosperous regions because they can not guarantee employment in the region beyond the length of the contract. Unions have had some success in obtaining agreements from companies to place redundant apprentices. A related concern has been that large companies have been using YTS to keep their training schools open, but have not been providing on-site experience, preferring to provide placements with smaller companies.

> The trainees get a grounding in the training school but they are not being transferred to sites. They are placed all over the area in small firms, where anyone is prepared to take them on with only the inkling of a possible future job. We have to ensure that the lads, and the girls as well if they are involved in our trades, have job experience which is meaningful (UCATT).

In fact, the YTS operation in construction is enormous, the CITB managing agency accounting for £84 million in its second year, 1984–1985. Albert Williams, General Secretary of UCATT, has been quoted as saying, 'CITB has done a good job to satisfy both sides of the industry with its approach to the Youth Training Scheme. This will ensure that YTS is positively applied and will safeguard the needs of youngsters' (*YTS Supplement to Construction News*, No. 77, May 1986: i). However, this must be put in perspective. In 1986/7, the main contract for the CITB managing agency comprised £84 million of MSC funding for 19,500 trainees in all sectors, of which about 11,250 were in the building sector. A further £15 million was made up by employers' levy contributions (*Construction News*, May, 1986: 1). As one UCATT regional official pointed out, in an industry employing between 850,000 and 900,000 operatives the fact that employers spend only £15 million on apprenticeship training does not show well in a labour intensive industry.

### Monitoring of Schemes

Given the widespread adoption of YTS in construction, trade unions and employers alike have been concerned that funding should only be awarded to schemes providing training to recognized standards. The issue of training standards has two different aspects in construction: firstly, to ensure that dilution does not occur and, secondly, factors that arise from the New Training Initiative's objective of replacing time-serving by training to standards for building trades. The latter, it should be emphasized, does not concern the introduction of courses where none existed before since, as outlined earlier, CITB has overseen an enormous increase in off-the-job training in colleges since it was set up under the provisions of the 1964 Industrial Training Act. Rather, training to standards concerns the testing of course work on completion of the apprenticeship period and the relationship between this test and the achievement of the full adult pay rate.

The quality of training is ensured in the private sector primarily through CITB. CITB sets the standards of training for the private sector and though outside the scope of its Industrial Training Order, the public sector follows these standards as well. The existence of a body which monitors the standard of training schemes is viewed as important given the nature of the construction industry;

The TGWU would like all training in construction to come through CITB so that we can be sure that everyone getting training and getting grants for training is in organised bodies and pays their dues. This is because the problem in construction is the black economy – Margaret Thatcher has really developed it. It's always been there in construction but it's really developed since 1979 because of Tory policy to help small business. Genuine small businesses have been in demise and the black economy has moved off (TGWU).

So many managing agents run varied courses with titles like 'construction skills' which are not under CITB approval. If the trainees can't get a job at the end then they would try and act on their own or with a pal. The standards in the industry are slipping and this is why we insist that courses must be CITB recognised. The managing agents view is that if they don't get a job then it is 'too bad'. It's impossible for officials to go round and monitor all the schemes and with some of them we wonder what training they're receiving. So we don't know about standards, but if they conform to CITB standards then we have a starting point (UCATT).

The monitoring of standards on CITB YTS schemes takes place through the joint monitoring of courses run in colleges by trade union and employer representatives on the local bodies of the NJCBI. An official involved in these monitoring exercises in the Yorkshire region reported that they had visited colleges in the region and talked to tutors and trainees alike about the schemes that were being run. The quality of training was monitored from the thirteenth to the seventeenth week and it was felt that the standards and the trainees achievements were quite high. From the trade unions' point of view the success of YTS is contingent on the numbers of trainees who are indentured subsequently. He reported that of the trainees he had spoken to on such monitoring visits, 90 per cent had employer sponsorship.

Skills testing creates problems of an altogether different order. Whilst there are objections to the concept of skills testing on the basis that it has arisen as a result of an employer- and government-led intiative, it has been recognised that there are potential benefits to trade unions in accepting an agreed standard of craft work in the different trades if this increases their ability to regulate the employment of skilled labour. This was expressed in the following terms:

With other professions there is a need to pass a test at the end of training, which gives acceptability. I can see no reason why someone working with their hands on a skilled basis should not do the same. If we can regulate the employment of craftsmen and their recognition – for example, only craft-certified craftsmen can be employed on skilled work – this could lead to a move away from malpractices. However, this is in the distant future at the moment (UCATT).

The establishment of skill standards is one issue, but the question of the implications of skills testing for pay is another. Reservations have been expressed that a high failure rate might result in downward pressure on craft rates of pay or an establishment of differential rates of pay for skilled workers who have passed their tests and those who have not.

> We have many reservations about skills testing. We are not opposed to identifying the skills acquired through training but we are concerned that it might result in the reduction of the craft rate of pay if the trainee does not pass the test. We have reservations about this and about who will be the judge (UCATT).

> We are concerned with the pass rate amd what happens if a trainee doesn't pass. Does this mean that we will have to subscribe to the black economy or come to an arrangement about grading structures? UCATT is opposed to grading structures. With YTS the first year of skills testing is coming up and we have to get it right. We only have one shot at it and we could put apprentices off for life if we get it wrong as regards a career in construction (UCATT).

The setting of standards has posed particular problems, not just for CITB but also for trainers in sectors outside the scope of CITB which nevertheless follow the standards of training set by CITB. This is particularly the case with the Direct Labour Organizations building departments of local authorities. In discussing standards testing it is first necessary to establish that methods of certification already exist for establishing standards of competence, as in the case of the City and Guilds of London Institute (CGLI) test. However, to obtain a City and Guilds certificate, the trainee has to pass one practical and two theoretical subjects and under current arrangements a trainee with a distinction on the practical side does not receive a certificate if the theoretical tests are failed. Already some modifications have been made to alter the basis for obtaining the City and Guilds craft certificate. In-course assessment will no longer count as part of the qualification but has been replaced by the practical skills test, which the Training Commission of the NJCBI has agreed to monitor under tripartite arrangements involving trade union, employer and educational interest representatives. The standards testing which has been under discussion in CITB primarily concerns the testing of practical achievements for those trainees who do not obtain the City and Guilds certificate.

Testing was due to start in the summer of 1986. The practical and technical details for the testing of each trade have been agreed through Working groups of the CITB on which the different construction unions are represented. Skills tests are divided into two parts; firstly, a job knowledge test taken at the end of the first year of training to standards set by CITB and the CGLI and approved by the NJCBI. Secondly, a practical skills test to NJCBI standards which is to be taken between six and nine months before the end of training. Testing centres have been set up in the major regions and teams of assesors formed, who have been nominated through CITB and the major interest groups represented on it. The first batch of tests were rejected as it was felt that the standards set were unrealistically high and likely to lead to a high failure rate. A UCATT Midlands regional document of November, 1985 points out:

> There has been lengthy debate on the relationship between the job knowledge test and the practical skills test. Should the youngsters who fail the job knowledge test be allowed to sit the practical skills test? The construction industry is oriented to practical skills and UCATT members on the NJTC have argued that we should not debar youngsters who fail the more academic multiple choice job knowledge test from taking the practical skills test.
>
> But the level of achievement in the job knowledge test will be taken into account with the result achieved in the practical skills test. The practical skills test can be retaken if the candidate is not successful at the first attempt.
>
> This is important because of the wages issue if there is a category of 'passed' apprentices and another category of 'failed' apprentices.
>
> For the same reason, in discussions on the standards to be attained for a 'pass', UCATT has pushed for the test to be one which, hopefully, all apprentices can and will pass (UCATT: 1985).

The problems relating to skills testing in the Direct Labour Organizations are of a totally different nature which reflect the DLOs' underlying problem which is that of the absence of new build work on which to train apprentices. Whilst trade union members in the DLOs recognize that it is important to set a standard which will be appropriate for newly trained apprentices entering the industry, there are problems in setting standards based on apprenticeship training on new build work in the private sector when the majority of apprentices in the public sector are trained on maintenance work. This has particular implications for the amount of practice obtained in different skills, for the speed at which they are performed and for the way in which the apprentice learns to relate to workers in other trades working on the same site.

The skills test is aimed at getting the apprentice to a level at which he is capable of entering the industry. The problem is that there is very little private building going on and where it is there are few apprentices in private firms. Our DLO has only constructed 180 dwellings this year and the problem is that you can't train a joiner or a bricklayer if the only work you have available for them is maintenance. We feel that the test should gear to this but we don't want to see the standards lowered because we don't want cowboy tradesmen. It's a contradiction (UCATT).

Whilst some trades, such as plumbers, can learn their craft in maintenance work, they can not acquire the speeds that are required in construction site work. Though practical training in colleges and training schools can be of high standard, the most the DLOs can provide in site work experience is where miniprojects are set up to teach apprentices different skills, as outlined earlier. Even so, these have limitations. 'If you're not trained on a construction site you can't learn how to relate to different trades. It could be that you could pass the maintenance tests, but not those for working on new builds' (UCATT). These issues are examined in more detail in the following case study of a Direct Labour Organization building department.

## The DLO

It has already been indicated that a major constraint on training in local authority building departments have been cutbacks in public expenditure. Furthermore, as a consequence of the passing of the Local Government Land and Planning Act, 1970, contracts for local authority building work worth over £50,000 have to be tendered for competitively and the DLOs have to show a profit of five per cent on all work. Since 1980 competitive tendering has been extended to repair contracts worth £10,000 or more. There are two main problems with tendering for work. Firstly, in real terms, the amount of work that can be carried out for under £50,000 has reduced since 1970, progressively extending the type of projects which have to be tendered for competitively. Secondly, whilst local authority building departments observe health and safety regulations, pay full tax and National Insurance contributions for their employees and train apprentices, this is not always the case for the companies with which they are in competition. It has effectively restricted training volumes since the cost of training cannot be offset against financial returns. Therefore, whilst superficially competitive tendering appears to offer a cheap way of carrying out local authority building and repair work, there are many hidden costs, which relate not just to the conditions of employment of the workforce and the quality of work, but also to the supply of skills in a locality.

One way in which local authorities have tried to ensure that competition between their own labour forces and firms in the private sector is fair is through the introduction of contract compliance units. These are by no means universal, but in a context in which local authorities are obliged to put work out to tender, it provides a means of checking that *bona fide* firms are given the work and that certain standards in health and safety and wages and conditions of employment are observed.

> Without contract compliance any rogue can get on the council's tendering list. All companies are supposed to have £1 million public liability insurance. A lot of smaller firms go to an insurance company and ask for a cover note. They pay the first premium and forget the rest . . . The small roofing contractors go round all the depots at Christmas with crates of whiskey and cigars (UCATT).

From the training point of view, it is also possible to check that the company is registered with CITB and pays the training levy. Though there is some scepticism concerning what a contracts compliance unit can achieve given the nature of the construction industry, it is neverthless a model which is seen as being capable of guarding against the worst excesses. An example will illustrate what can happen if no contracts compliance unit exists.

Construction is well known as being one of the most dangerous industries from the point of view of accidents and deaths at work. The DLO lost a contract for a central heating job to a local contractor by £2,000. When a senior steward went to inspect the site he found that the contractor was using no scaffolding. He forced them to stop work and put up £3,000 worth of scaffolding. In other words, the DLO could have won the contract. The lifting of building regulations and government policy towards deregulation, as published in the White Papers 'Lifting the Burden' and 'Building Businesses not Barriers' is likely to further undermine the DLOs ability to compete with the private sector for local authority building work. However, the aim here is to examine the environment in which the DLOs operate with specific reference to its implications for training.

In this DLO between 30 and 40 apprentices are taken on each year, including electricians, plumbers and carpenters. The scheme is approved by the trade unions each year. Because of cuts in local authority workloads, they no longer take any wet trades – bricklaying and plastering – because there is no work for them. All apprentices are taken on as YTS trainees and locally there was an agreement with the Building Employers' Confederation that the first year of training on YTS at the DLO training centre would count as six-months remission of apprenticeship. This was unusual because the DLO did not follow the CITB schemes since they had been found to be expensive to run. The apprentice training school nevertheless had a good reputation and apprentices from it had won prizes at the Interbuild competition for three years running. In fact, the training school is run by DLO staff and by buying in teaching staff from the local technical college who do teach CITB approved courses. At the time of interviewing there were only two DLOs with this arrangement for apprenticeship remission and a third, Hackney, which had had a similar arrangement, had recently had it discontinued. Subsequently, this DLO lost its remission too.

The DLO had an arrangement to take on 75 per cent of apprentices trained under YTS on to its permanent staff. UCATT would have liked to have seen more kept on, but the local authority was using the YTS year as an extended interview, taking time-keeping and behaviour into account in the selection process and not just ability. At the time of interviewing (March, 1986) it was not clear what the implications of the two year YTS scheme would be for the DLO. The one year scheme worked in such a way that if the DLO was allocated 30 places and 10 trainees left then the funds could still be used for in-house training. However, under the arrangements for the two year scheme the funding would be lost should a trainee leave. It was not clear what would happen over remission of the apprenticeship period and whether, with six-months remission for each year of training, a four year apprenticeship training would be created. This was subsequently resolved by the NJCBI agreement on employee status and 'topping up' to minimum rates in the second year. However, as indicated above, the DLO lost its remission from the apprenticeship registration period and the number of places approved under YTS was also reduced.

This DLO was currently looking into the possibility of setting up a miniproject on which to train apprentices. An old builders' yard was under consideration for renovation work which would have given the trainees practical experience. With all projects of this nature, schemes could not take away work from existing council employees. It would have subsequently been used by the Conservation Stores (a project run with funding under the Community Programme) who renovate old fireplaces and other items which DLO building workers notify them of when they are taking down old properties.

### Assessing Construction Training

Despite the apparent strength of the tripartite arrangements for overseeing training in the construction industry and the way in which these arrangements are supported through apprentice registration bodies on the one hand through representation on Area Manpower Boards, on the other, the underlying problems of the construction industry are only too apparent. These are primarily reduced workloads and the massive growth of sub-contracting, with conditions of employment outside the industry's negotiated pay structures. These conditions also determine the effectiveness of implementing training policy formulated at national level in trade unions. It is this environment which has resulted in employers' associations and trade unions represented on CITB pushing for the centralization of YTS under the managing agency of CITB in the construction industry and directing of YTS funding wholescale into apprenticeship training. This reflects the CITB view that in an industry in which many employers are unwilling or unable to train, it is impossible for employers to train for the needs of the firm. Training must, therefore, be organized on the basis of the requirements of the industry as a whole, and the training levy, raised on all firms in scope to the board, must be used to subsidize training on an industry-wide basis. In practice, as has been demonstrated, a very large proportion of expenditure on training – more than three quarters of the CITB managing agency – comes direct from the Manpower Services Commission. Moreover, the CITB itself recognizes that it is unable to raise a levy from a very large number of the small firms in the industry and has recently attempted to introduce a more rigorous registering procedure (*Construction News*, December, 1986). Despite this, it is abundantly evident from the quotes from the officials interviewed, that the black economy and self-employment constitute a major restraining factor both on employment and on training in the industry. This is true in the private sector and is increasingly affecting the public sector's ability to train as the DLOs are brought into competitive tendering with the private sector for local authority building and repair work.

From the evidence provided here, it would appear that CITB is able to safeguard, to a limited extent, the skill base of the industry, particularly with regard to craft trades. Despite the high levels of unemployed building workers, some officials interviewed argued that insufficient craft workers were being trained and that this was likely to lead to skill shortages in the event of an upturn in the economy or if a Labour government was returned to power at the 1987 General Election committed to a programnme of major public works to absorb unemployment.

Skilled craft workers would be required to play a leading role in this event. It was argued that neither the CITB nor the employers had the will to do anything about it. General operative training is another area in which relatively little emphasis has been given.

> CITB has a general operative building scheme in its managing agency, but the numbers are minimal. They give the allocations to a few major contractors. This shows a lack of concern for a major employment area in the industry . . . Now many people are doing ground works, road works, drainage, paving and basic scaffolding (erections up to five metres high) using expensive plant and they've never had formal training, or indeed any training at all. The industry doesn't cater for them and this is a serious problem . . . The most effective training of general operatives is Henry Boots. The scheme suits the MSC because they'll take any kid without an interview. This is not a proper industry-based scheme, which is trying to set standards for general operatives in the industry (UCATT).

However, employers' attitudes to training have also to be overcome:

> UK companies' attitudes to training are poor – even the best have poor records. Construction companies' record on the retraining of skilled operatives is nil. The same is true of general operatives. This industry runs on a 'pick it up as you go along' basis (UCATT).

Finally, the building trades have been, *par excellence*, an area of male employment. Though women have been entering some trades it has a predominantly white, male labour force. YTS was intended to offer equal opportunities to men and women and black and white young workers, but the entry of women and ethnic minorities has not been massive. In fact, in the absence of a policy of positive discrimination, YTS reinforces existing patterns of segmentation and discrimination in the labour market (Cockburn, 1987; Pollert, 1986). That these patterns of discrimination should not be challenged has often been justified in the construction industry by the claim by employers, building workers, and trade union members alike, that site work and poor weather conditions make the industry a hostile environment, unsuited to women. Though by no means universal, some of these prejudices are being challenged, partly by the growth of more enlightened attitudes but more importantly, in practical terms, by the realization that the decline in the cohort of school leavers in the 1990s will reduce the numbers of young, white males who have traditionally been recruited into the industry.

## Electrical Contracting and Heating and Ventilating Sectors

Though the majority of apprentices under the CITB's managing agency for YTS come under the scheme for the main building trades, the Building Foundation Training Scheme, which has been examined in the previous section, there are variations within the construction industry on the operation of YTS which relate to agreements reached in subsectoral national negotiating machinery. The aim in this section is to examine the operation of YTS in the electrical contracting sector, in which agreement has been reached in the Joint Industry Board between the EETPU and the Electrical Contractors' Association, and its operation in the heating and ventilating sector, where agreement has been reached in the National Joint Industry Council between the Heating and Ventilating Contractors' Association on the one hand, and the craft sector of TASS (formerly the National Union of Sheet Metal Workers, Coppersmiths, Heating and Domestic Engineers), on the other.

In the electrical contracting industry, the decision to adopt YTS as a means of funding apprenticeship training was affected by two main factors. A major consideration was the massive drop in apprenticeship numbers between 1979 and 1982. In 1979 there were some 4,000 apprentices in electrical contracting but by 1982 this had fallen to a mere 600. However, the impact of this drop was compounded by the fact that electrical contracting has traditionally trained above the industry's own needs and has provided many electrical craft workers for other industrial sectors as well. As Eric Hammond, General Secretary of the EETPU, stated:

> We have always recognised that our industry has a special responsibility because, historically, it has been one of the country's biggest employers of young people through its apprenticeship scheme. Indeed, our electricians were poached by every other sector of British industry, which is why we have always had to train far more people than the industry itself could absorb. That has all changed. No longer are other sectors of British industry taking our electricians – there have been no vacancies. Consequently the intake of apprentices in 1981 was halved and in 1982 it was halved again. Without a new initiative it is clear that 1983 would see only a very minimal intake of young people into the electrical contracting industry. Without some stimulus our apprenticeship schemes would collapse which, in the national interest, is precisely what should not happen (*EETPU Training Bulletin*, No. 1, March 1983: 12).

In interviews, officials stated that approximately 60 per cent of EETPU membership had entered employment through the electrical contracting industry. That is to say, although they received their training in the construction industry, many subsequently left it to take work in engineering and other industries which did not involve site work and provided more stable conditions of employment. This is expressed in the notion that electrical contracting is a 'young man's field' in which few women work and which most leave by their late thirties. This resulted in the perception that, unless apprenticeship numbers were increased, the EETPU could end up as a very small trade union with members just concerned with domestic installation.

The reason the employers gave for the reduction in apprentice numbers was the cost of training, arguing that they could not afford to pay £40 per week for someone who was doing no work. The solution was to use the one-year YTS scheme to increase apprentice numbers and in the first year of its operation there were 2,800 apprentices on the Electrical Contracting Industry Training Scheme. As with the Building Foundation Training Scheme, all trainees follow normal apprenticeship training, which is CITB approved. However, in contrast to the schemes for the building trades, trainees are employees from the start of the training scheme (*Construction Board News*, November, 1984). As in the building trades, the EETPU and the Electrical Contracting Association alike, are actively involved in the monitoring of schemes in colleges at local level through CITB.

A major problem for trade unions with established apprenticeship schemes in accepting YTS schemes in their industries has been the issue of trainee allowances. Though most trade unions have policy positions of seeking 'top ups' to the allowances, in most cases this has met with limited success, mainly at plant level, and has rarely been obtained through national negotiating machinery. The EETPU's rationale for accepting a reduction in apprentice pay rates is a pragmatic one based on the assumption that it is better to ensure that apprentices are trained and receive training to agreed standards than to hold a principled position of insisting on national minimum rates, which may jeopardize training activity altogether. Eric Clayton, Chairman of the EETPU Training Committee argues:

> Most other unions have been preoccupied with wage rates. It is no good negotiating for apprentice pay of £100 a week if you have no apprentices.
>
> Engineering's intake of apprentices has fallen from 25,000 to 7,000 in three years. So an industry employing perhaps 20 times

more employees than contracting has only just over twice as many apprentices. This does not augur well for the future.

. . . If only other unions and industries would follow our lead, then thousands more young people could be given a purpose at present denied them. We haven't just moaned about the level of apprenticeships. We've done something about it (*EETPU Contact*, June, 1985: 10)

Electrical apprentices in 1985–1986 had their YTS allowance of £27.30 per week topped up to £30, with the industry paying the difference. Other employers such as the Ministry of Defence, the local authorities, hospitals and the installation side of the electrical supply industry which are not in scope to CITB but nevertheless follow the standards set by the electrical contracting industry have different agreements for apprentice minimum rates.

Outside the areas covered by the JIB agreement there are no national agreements on YTS relating to electrical apprenticeships and no national schemes. In engineering, where of a total workforce of 2.1 million, the EETPU claims a membership of approximately 80,000, arrangements for YTS only exist at plant level. In 1985–1986 there were some 2,500 YTS trainees in the industry, though not all were in craft grades. The decision of the AEU at its May 1986 National Committee meeting to accept training to standards, thus bringing it into line with the rest of the Confederation of Shipbuilding and Engineering Unions, combined with the extension of the scheme to two years from 1986–1987, may make way for new developments. The same is true of the chemical industry, though the closure of the the Chemical and Allied Products Industry Training Board means that there is now no centralized body holding data on numbers in training nor coordinating training schemes. The Chemical and Allied Industries' Training Review Council, on which EETPU has a seat, has a facilitative rather than a directive role as far as training is concerned. Whilst the Chemical Industries' Association and Imperial Chemical Industries plc have a standards-based training scheme it is not industry-wide. EETPU has argued for standards-based training in the chemical industry, but even though testing on completion of training has been accepted, all candidates pass. Variations in arrangements for testing and the resolution of problems arising from the issue of pass rates reflect the internal politics of trade unions involved in national negotiating bodies for different industries.

Skills testing, as in other sectors of the construction industry, was already being developed before it became one of the MSC's objectives under the New Training Initiative. The 1983 JIB Industrial Determination (covering England, Wales and Northern Ireland) introduced two practical skills tests to the training agreement for the first time. The first is conducted at the end of the first year of apprenticeship and the second on completion of the training period. Apprentices failing their tests at the end of the first year of training do not continue into their second year. The development of skills testing started in 1977 and has been a joint exercise between trade union, employer, educational representatives as well as the JIB and City and Guilds staff under the auspices of CITB. The trade union has emphasised that the acceptance of skills testing by no means attacks the notion of apprenticeship, but it improves its structure, arguing, 'The factor which determines the skills a craftsman has acquired is the standard he can work to. The period of time spent developing these skills is irrelevant' (*EETPU Contact*, June, 1981: 4). Perhaps more than any other craft union, EETPU has embraced the MSC's concept of apprenticeship reform in seeing training not as 'a once and for all times' affair, but as a basic standard upon which later retraining can build, particularly as new technology is introduced or as electricians move from one industry to another in the course of their working lives. (*EETPU Contact*, 1981). The agreement in the electrical contracting industry is open-aged which supports the New Training Initiative's objective of opening up opportunities for adult training. However, YTS funding can only be used for 16 and 17 year olds and the EETPU has been unsuccessful in challenging the MSC on the use of YTS funding for adults.

The situation in the heating and ventilating industry is somewhat similar, insofar as there is a national agreement on YTS and it is the preferred form of entry into the industry even though some employers have continued to recruit school leavers directly into apprenticeship. Here, however, trade union opposition to the introduction of a scheme along the same lines as in the electrical contracting industry resulted in there being no trainees at all in the first year of YTS in 1983–1984. This finally produced an agreement between TASS and the Heating and Ventilating Contractors' Association whereby after the first six months of training, all trainees selected to attend the specific heating and ventilating craft course in the second six months of YTS would be guaranteed employment in the industry as apprentices and would receive additional money from their employers to bring their pay up from the level of the YTS allowance to the tax or national insurance threshold, plus the refunding of the first £3 of travel expenses. In the second year of training the YTS allowance of £35 per week is enhanced by the employers to the current rate of pay applicable to second year apprentices. The acceptance of YTS funding has resulted in some alterations to the training content of the first two years of apprenticeship, but whichever method of recruitment, the trainee subsequently goes on to complete a four year apprenticeship. At local level, there is a system of area committees with tripartite representation of employers, trade union and educational interests to monitor apprentice training programmes.

As in the building industry, heating and ventilating is 'plagued by cowboy operators' and a major concern has been to prevent partly trained people entering the labour market. Trainees entering the industry undertake a course of training leading to examinations in the City and Guilds of London Institute Heating and Ventilating Craft Certificate, the content of which has been recently revised. In Scotland trainees take the equivalent SCOTVEC examinations as well as a practical skills test. (*Construction Board News. Supplement*, May 1986: ii)

## YTS and Non-craft Occupations

In this section the impact of YTS on training in non-craft occupations will be considered with reference to chemicals, engineering and food processing. To some extent the distinction between craft and non-craft occupations is an artificial one and underlies considerable differences between different types of occupational training and socialization amongst non-craft workers. Amongst clerical grades, such as those in which APEX organizes, qualifications, for example, in secretarial and accountancy skills, may be acquired externally to the company in the general education system as a prerequisite for entry into specific occupations. Training will also take place on-the-job, and it may be possible for additional qualifications to be taken on a part-time basis through technical colleges. Similarly, there has been a longstanding demand amongst trade unions organizing process workers in the chemical industry for their jobs to be regarded as skilled (*GMBATU Chemical Industries Bulletin*, no. 139, February 1982: 6) and historically recruits to these grades have received formal training, including day-release for study in colleges. In the food processing industry there are indeed many jobs which have required little or no formal training. This is particularly true of casual workers, who receive short induction programmes including company rules and health and safety aspects but who have otherwise been reliant on supervision by other workers to acquire the skills required for their jobs. The absence of formal training off-the-job does not necessarily imply that no formalized training is received: for example, in one food processing plant at which a shop steward was interviewed (reported in Chapter 4) new employees undergo a three-month induction period under the supervision of a training manager during which they learn how to operate different aspects of the production process. YTS trainees in this firm additionally attended a course in food technology at a local technical college.

In the industrial sectors considered in this section, non-craft occupations have been most affected by the introduction of the YTS scheme and trade unions organizing in these areas have been most subject to the contradiction of supporting the introduction of systematic training, but of opposing the low level of trainee allowances with a particular concern with the exploitation of young people. These are occupations in which, historically, young workers have received short initial training programmes on entry into employment or in which training has been organized informally and on-the-job. Ironically, it is in these occupations that trainees would stand to benefit most from the introduction of formal training programmes if it was not for other aspects of YTS which undermine its legitimacy as a training exercise in the eyes of trade unionists. These centre principally on the low level of the trainee allowance, the lack of employment contract and the fact that trainees may and have been used as a substitute for adult labour, paid at negotiated wage rates. Trade union resource centres have drawn attention to other aspects of the scheme which are sources of disquiet for trade unionists; namely the massive allocations of YTS funding to private training agencies which do not provide work experience themselves and sub-contract trainees to small firms, which are frequently non-union (Trade Union Resource Centre, 1984 and 1986). Therefore, YTS is contentious both because it undermines negotiated wages and conditions in unionised workplaces and exploits young people in workplaces which are outside trade union control. Many officials interviewed are involved in approving YTS placements in their capacity as full-time officials and, in some cases, as members of Area Manpower Boards, but these are not seen as adequate safeguards.

Considerable anger was expressed in interviews at the way in which young people were being exploited and abused through the scheme.

It is the most abused so-called training scheme that exists. Paid for by the Government, at no cost to the employer, so it is cost-free. It gives employers an opportunity to illustrate their willingness to help unemployed youth and minimise the angry feelings of the present generation who will be the workers of tomorrow. It has the added bonus of giving them the opportunity to have people on the premises who are fit, dextrous, agile, who have energy and ability. They can employ people post-YTS direct from a grossly low pay level and give them a small increase and give them the impression that they're being generous (GMBATU).

In engineering the membership is exceedingly worried about the collapse of apprenticeship and it comes up at every conference. This is because, on the one hand, members' sons and daughters can't get work and, on the other, because the future of the industry is in question if there is no trained workforce. This is a very strongly felt issue and there is almost contempt for the attempt to say that YTS in some way or another is a substitute for standard training programmes. We're not talking here about time-served programmes . . . YTS is viewed as a stop-gap measure with tinges of cheap labour. The membership can't understand the pressure for dilution when there is such a surplus of young workers who need training and would benefit from it (GMBATU).

In a number of interviews, concern was expressed at TUC and labour movement support for the scheme and the contradictions this placed on members who opposed it.

The GMB supports YTS, even with all its flaws and warts there's nothing better . . . but problems with dealing with normal industrial employees are intensified when you get to YTS. Family people take note that YTS takes kids off the dole queue and think that this is better than them being on the streets. The issues of youth unemployment and what YTS does are very diverse and it is difficult to come to a conclusion. We are torn between opposing aspects. We don't want the kids bored and vulnerable on the streets but we don't want them exploited and damaging hard fought for terms and conditions of employment. We don't want them losing their self-dignity because of the exploitation and we don't want them casualised (GMBATU).

It is precisely these kinds of contradictions which the local press is so good at exploiting when trade union members refuse to accept YTS placements in their own workplaces in order to defend their own jobs. Several officials mentioned how 'powerful, simplistic arguments' had been used by the press to vilify trade unions for appearing to deny opportunities to young workers.

The majority of trade unions interviewed have policy positions of seeking to obtain improvements for YTS, mainly through seeking 'top ups' to the trainee allowance and on obtaining full contracts of employment, either in the course of the scheme or on its completion. A major concern had been for stewards to monitor that trainees were indeed supernumerary to staff requirements and not doing productive work. Despite these policy positions, success has been limited and has been almost exclusively obtained at company level, reflecting the power of local union organization in the workplace. In some instances, trade unions have prevented companies from taking on YTS trainees on the grounds that if the companies can not pay the 'top up' to the minimum wage rate and can not give a guarantee of employment to permanent staff, then they should not be recruiting trainees. This is a practice that APEX has evolved in the Coventry area through a local district committee structure. It has effectively resulted in a boycott of the scheme in sub-managerial clerical grades in the engineering industry in the locality in contrast to a national position of support for it.

However, these observations should be tempered by the fact that several officials reported that there were very few YTS trainees in these industries in their localities because companies were making employees redundant and closing down plants. For example, the TGWU in the West Midlands reported little involvement of YTS trainees in grades they organize in in the engineering industry, and that their main concerns had been with trainees in retailing. In the same region the GMB reported one large engineering company taking on over 100 trainees through its managing agency, all of which were placed in small, unorganized factories with 5 to 10 employees each. As a consequence, the opportunities for union monitoring and negotiation of improvements were minimal. In chemicals in the North West the GMB reported that they were not happy with the scheme, but that the intake of young people had been very small over the previous five years as the major companies had been shedding jobs. TGWU reported that in the chemical industry ICI had taken on a number of YTS trainees, divided between process operators and craft apprentices and had taken half into permanent employment at the end of the year, backpaying the difference between the allowance and the corresponding rate under the national agreement. The remainder were made redundant. There are obviously regional differences even within the same industry; in the South-East the TGWU reported few YTS trainees in food processing because companies were reducing staff anyway and had trained, experienced staff, mainly women, they could draw on in the event of an upturn in demand for products. Moreover, ready trained, adult workers do not pose the same safety problems with moving parts and machinery as young, inexperienced workers. In the West Midlands, the GMB reported that YTS was widespread in food processing, though the main sectors affected were retailing and hotel and catering. This confirms the experience of other trade unions.

Though strictly speaking outside the scope of the present study, it is useful to examine briefly trade union experience of YTS in retailing because it is this experience which conditions policy responses at national level to the scheme. TGWU, GMBATU and USDAW all reported experience of YTS in retailing. Apart from a general concern that young people are being exploited through the scheme, there are specific concerns about trainees being required to work under conditions which the terms of YTS do not allow. Anecdotal evidence from USDAW indicates that in retailing;

> Trainees work nights and Saturdays, they have even been asked to work Bank Holidays. Attempts to stop this through the MSC have brought the response that if the trainees are happy to do it and they agree to it, why stop them? But there are pressures on trainees if they want a job at the end of the training period. Sponsors in work placements have it all ways. The trainees are not employees but they are manipulated as though they were. They won't release them for day release courses or for block release in busy periods such as Christmas and Easter and the sales periods. This is justified in terms of 'they'll get experience of peak trading times in the retail trade' (USDAW).

USDAW has been one of those trade unions which has given support to YTS on the grounds that if the scheme is rejected in unionized workplaces, then the youngsters are more likely to be placed in non-unionized workplaces where they have no protection (*Labour Research*, 1984). Within the trade union there is disagreement on the extent to which the scheme should be welcomed for introducing training where none previously existed, with possible beneficial spin-offs to adult workers, or has set training back by dropping the ITBs' commitment to long-term adult occupational training with short-term objectives aimed at young people.

A number of trade unions have opposed YTS from the outset and these have been reported in Schnack and King (1986) and Eversley (1986) amongst others. If national trade unions and their rank-and-file members have been reluctant to accept the one year YTS scheme then this has been intensified with the extension of the scheme to two years. For trade unions such as USDAW it raised questions relating to what two years of training in retailing could be for, beyond an extended process of induction into companies. Moreover, in a low pay sector, the attractions to the employer appear to be in the low level of the training allowance rather than more intensive skill training. In 1986 resolutions to withdraw from YTS were narrowly defeated at the national conferences of USDAW and APEX. The resolution at the APEX conference calling on the trade union to press the TUC to abandon cooperation with the scheme registered 37,840 votes against boycotting the scheme as against 32,910 in favour. This result was particularly significant in view of the fact that Roy Grantham, the General Secretary, was the new chair of the TUC's Employment Policy Committee which is responsible for decisions relating to support of YTS (*The Guardian*, 6 May 1986).

## Conclusion

From the preceding review of youth training arrangements it is clear that the implications of YTS and the New Training Initiative's Objective of apprenticeship reform vary greatly from one sector to another. This reflects variations in existing forms of training, its relationship to national negotiating machinery and the existence or otherwise of effective tripartite training structures. Eversley's point that YTS appeared to offer different things to different organizations and interest groups within the trade union movement is borne out by the heterogeneity of its implementation in the four industries concerned, with the consequence that trade union responses to it vary as well (Eversley, 1986: 201). In this context, it is not surprising to find that there is no single coherent response to YTS and other aspects of the New Training Initiative. Policy towards it has not overcome the conflicting aims of defending members' jobs and conditions of employment on the one hand and defending young workers from exploitation as a source of cheap labour, whether in unionized or non-unionized workplaces.

The NTI objective of apprenticeship reform (and, indeed that of adult training) is clearly linked to YTS through its effects on youth wages and has been perceived by employers as such (Rainbird and Grant, 1985a: 61). Even if the New Training Initiative had not existed, there are strong arguments for supposing that mass youth unemployment in the context of the wider employment policies and anti-union legislation of the Thatcher government would still have constituted a threat to the gains achieved by organized labour, both in its knock-on effects on wages and its threat to trade union organization. The question remains, why was the reform of apprenticeship so central in these policy objectives and why was it articulated in terms which represented it as an out-moded time-served system rather than a modern training system based on a large component of off-the-job training? There is no simple answer but the context of attacks on the statutory training boards and trade union involvement in their tripartite structures must be one element in the explanation. The government's perception of trade union vested interests and restricted practices as a restraint on management's right to manage, must also be another. However, if the central concern was indeed industrial training, then an attack upon apprenticeship in this context which had the aim of relinquishing joint regulation of wages and conditions relating to the apprenticeship period has evidently not had the desired effect of increasing the numbers in craft apprentice training.

Finn (1986) has argued that the Manpower Services Commission has been extremely effective in taking on policies of the trade union movement and reworking them in ways which do not necessarily serve their original objectives. This is particularly true of the Youth Training Scheme, since the opening up of training opportunities for all young workers has long been an objective of the labour movement. However, the context in which the scheme was introduced, its underfunding and reliance on private training agencies for training and small employers for work placements have combined to make the experience of it far from the egalitarian, quality scheme that might have been hoped for. Though some concessions were won by the TUC on the most obnoxious aspects of the scheme (Keep, 1986) continuing support for it and involvement in the tripartite structure of the Manpower Services Commission have not clarified an analysis of it as a training scheme, as a scheme for the unemployed or as a scheme which has wider ramifications for workplace organization and the exploitation of young workers over which trade unions have limited control. It is true that the Area Manpower Boards, to which schemes are sent for approval at local level have trade union representation, but demands for the AMBs to have executive powers (Centre for a Working World, 1986) are a clear indication of their lack of power over the schemes. Despite the existence of the tripartite structure of the AMBs they have neither the resources nor the powers effectively to monitor the scheme in the interests of trade union members. The exception is where other structures exist, for example, in the case of apprentice registration bodies and the tripartite structure of CITB for trade unions in the construction industry. In effect, trade union participation in what is essentially the administration of the scheme, legitimizes a programme which many rank and file unionists and young people find unsatisfactory.

Neither the trade union movement, nor indeed opposition political parties, have articulated a clear alternative to the Thatcher government's policies in the field of youth training. This is not to say that the need for a political alternative has not been articulated and indeed unemployment and the lack of competitiveness of British industry have correctly been perceived as the underlying problems. Nevertheless, confronted by mass unemployment and schemes that are presented as having a training content, the cynical use of the term 'training' to denote socialisation into low job expectations has not been seriously challenged.

# 3

# New Technology and Training

## Introduction

In recent years it has been recognized that training is no longer a once-and-for-all times phenomenon which a worker receives on entry into employment, that will last throughout his or her working life. The speed of technological change, combined with an assumed need for greater labour flexibility means that now and in the future workers will be expected to adapt and/or change their jobs continuously in their lives. Training is expected to be pivotal in this process. In this chapter, I shall examine trade union perceptions of the training opportunities offered to workers to retrain and update their skills when new technology is introduced in the workplace. I shall also consider the extent to which trade unions themselves have sought training for their members in the context of broader policies towards the negotiation of technological change in the workplace. With youth training, policies towards collective skills may be formulated on a trade or industry basis. Though this is also true of some training issues relating to the introduction of new technology, for example, the introduction of word processors in offices and the applications of electronics to electrical work, there are many instances where the applications of new technology are specific to a particular production process and will be negotiated at plant level. Therefore policies formulated at national level by trade unions must provide members in the workplace with the tools to negotiate a wide range of practical situations.

A close examination of the issues related to retraining in workplaces indicates that it is often difficult to distinguish between trade union responses to the acquisition of skills linked to the introduction of new technology and those related to employer demands for greater flexibility. In this chapter I focus on new technology and in chapter 4 I consider labour flexibility in more detail. In both cases, changes in job content may or may not be accompanied by access to training programmes. A formal training programme may be used to legitimize and recognize new skills in the wages structure. Alternatively, the acquisition of new skills and changes in job content which occur in the absence of formal training may not lead to re-evaluation and regrading of jobs. As such, it may constitute a means of avoiding industrial conflict over job demarcations because there is no formal recognition of new skills. In many of the instances reported here, the introduction of new technology has resulted in the deskilling of jobs rather than up-skilling. Many trade unions now believe that a concern for job design and demands for training when new technology is introduced may help guard against de-skilling.

### Retraining

The expansion of opportunities for adults and, in particular, the updating of the skills of existing workforces, is perceived as a major factor contributing to the competitiveness of the British economy. The Manpower Services Commission has stressed the importance of re-training in the context of contemporary developments in technology as a means of adapting and extending skills:

> rapid changes in technology and the nature of many jobs, coupled with structural changes in the labour force including a decline in the numbers entering the workforce, and changes in patterns of work will mean that future skill needs will not be met by initial occupational training of young people alone. Adults who have already been in the labour market for some years must have access to vocational education and training previously open only to young people entering the labour market. They need the opportunity to adapt their existing skills and to learn new ones to meet demand (MSC, July 1984: 3).

The perception that new technology requires the updating of skills and, indeed, the modernization of the training system is part of this world view. David Young, whilst chairman of the MSC indicated that reform of the training system, which would make it more flexible and responsive, was an essential pre-requisite to meeting 'the skill needs called for increasingly by accelerating technological change' (MSC, July 1984: 2).

In theory, adult retraining, both of the employed and unemployed has been an integral part of the New Training Initiative. Objective Three states 'we must open up widespread opportunities for adults whether employed, unemployed or returning to work to acquire, increase or update their skills and knowledge during the course of their working lives'. In practice, though resources have been allocated to Open Learning (through the Open Tech scheme) and pump priming funds have been available to encourage collaboration between training and educational institutions and employers, the Adult Training Strategy has relied largely on exhortations to employers to train. The Adult Training Strategy's 'Awareness Campaign' launched in the autumn of 1984 was primarily a publicity campaign and was soured by the TUC's withdrawal from its launch, a response to the government's decision to withdraw the rights of trade union membership from employees at Government Communications Headquarters (GCHQ) in Cheltenham. In the absence of bodies with powers to raise a training levy as a means of encouraging training, decisions relating to adult training fall entirely to the employer. Whereas with increased powers, the ITBs might have been able to put into practice a policy for increased adult training, their replacements, the voluntary training bodies, the NSTOs, are committed to non-intervention in their members' training decisions. Their activities extend to developing Open Tech training modules, disseminating information about courses, disbursing MSC funds and, in some cases, developing Codes of Practice aimed at encouraging training, including the retraining of adults. But whether this is sufficient to encourage employers and individuals to make the necessary investment identified by the MSC is debatable.

Historically, British employers have a poor record on industrial training and a return to a market-driven system is unlikely to increase volumes of training. This is of particular concern in a period of rapid technological change since the potential of new technology is most likely to be realized where firms adopt long-term labour force planning and training programmes. A National Economic Development Office survey shows that employers have a degree of choice in the way in which production processes are organized and how jobs are designed. There are high- and low-skill options for the introduction of new technology. Greatest productivity is achieved where new technology is introduced in consultation with the trade unions with long-term perspectives on skill requirements and the appropriate incentives in the wages structure to adapt and acquire new skills. Consultative measures combined with secure employment can contribute to productivity through the workers' knowledge of manufacturing systems. In contrast, the low-skill option, rather than expanding workers' range of skills, avoids training by compartmentalizing tasks which in the short term may result in the loss of potential gains in productivity. In the long term it may create inflexibilities because it will not be possible to add on additional skills at a later stage (NEDO, 1986).

### New Technology Jobs and Skills

New working practices often accompany the introduction of new technology to exploit productivity gains. Trade unions recognize that companies invest in new technology to remain competitive. Their policy is, therefore, not to resist technological change but to attempt to control its introduction and to obtain a share in its benefits through seeking agreements on new technology, disclosure of information and job security. In doing this, a major concern has been to obtain greater involvement in labour force planning, hence a direct interest in matters relating to training and retraining. The acquisition of new skills, frequently at the expense of older skills, inevitably raises the question of reward and demands for regrading. Likewise, where jobs are de-skilled by the introduction of new technology trade unions may have to resist pressures to reduce wages or to make jobs casual. In this respect the issue of skills is centre-stage in respect of new technology since it relates directly to conventional trade union concerns with wages and conditions, as well as to longer-term objectives of industrial democracy.

It is a truism that all technology has at some stage been 'new', however the problem is to focus on specific contemporary developments which have been defined as 'new technology', towards which trade unions are having to develop a strategy in their workplace politics and practice. It is important to emphasize that production processes are being restructured by generalized technological change, rationalization and expansion as well as by new information and communications technologies. As a result, it is extremely difficult to assess the 'effect' of new technology in isolation, without reference to the complex social systems into which it is being introduced. Though it may be possible to analyse the 'impact' of one item of new technology on specific occupations, it must be borne in mind that other organizational and technological factors might also require consideration. Some jobs may be directly affected, with the result that workers may be negotiating around new technology; others may be indirectly affected and decisions relating to its implementtion may not be subject to negotiation and bargaining. A focus on trade union officials' assessments of the impact of new technology on retraining can shed light on processes affecting the labour market in general and some occupations in particular, but tells us little about organizational dynamics which would be best studied through detailed case studies of firms. A thumbnail sketch of a large employer in the food processing industry, based on interviews with an ASTMS steward and official with responsibility for that company will give some indication of the range of issues involved.

## The Food Processing Company

This large multi-national has recently been undergoing a major process of restructuring. It produces mainly food and drink, though it does have non-food lines as well and grew as a result of a large number of mergers. It had had four major divisions in the UK and a number of smaller ones. At the time of interviewing, one division had been sold off in a series of management buy-outs and another was closing down factories and depots, with further buy-outs on the horizon. The company thus has factories on many different sites, producing both finished products and intermediary materials, with distribution networks linked to each division.

Each division has been affected differently by the introduction of new technology; in one division it mainly affected offices, in two more both offices and production and in the fourth half the production lines were cut whilst there was massive investment in updating some of the production lines which remained. At the same time the distribution system was updated with the introduction of microcomputers in the depots linked to the mainframe computer. The site visited contained two factories, a communications centre housing central computing facilities and satellite communications, site services and the commercial offices with group and divisional functions.

In 1979 the company had a long-range plan of selective investment and rationalization. This was implemented through a major redundancy exercise whereby more than a third of the workforce at the site was shed. The reductions in employment have been due partly to rationalization, particularly of product lines which are not mainstream, and partly due to new technology. Thus whilst older plants have been closed down, new investment has been concentrated in a small number of new plants producing main product lines. The redundancy exercise allowed many older workers to leave the company on favourable terms due to their long years of service. Management considered many of them to be unwilling or unable to adapt to new technology and new working practices. A younger, more adaptable workforce remained. Other developments were occurring in the structure of the labour force; the plant had always used a proportion of seasonal and casual labour. However, with the recession and reduced labour turnover due to the existence of fewer employment opportunities in the external labour market, the company had cut back on recruitment of permanent and casual workers. Paradoxically, whereas in the past the nature of the work and the state of the labour market had always ensured a rapid turnover in some occupations, the tightening of the labour market in recession has resulted in the company issuing temporary contracts to reduce its commitment to sections of the workforce which previously had little attachment to it.

The introduction of new technology and new working practices was presaged by changes in departmental structures and in managerial responsibilities. Since 1979 supervisors have acquired additional respons-ibilities whilst the managerial scale immediately above the supervisory grade disappeared. The next level in the managerial structure also acquired additional responsibilities including responsibility for mainten-ance work which had previously been separate from the manufacturing departments. This has resulted in the company requiring greater engineering skills from first line managers, and new recruits are likely to be graduate engineeers or chemists, or mechanical and process engineers. In addition, the fact that further redundancies are on the horizon creates reluctance on the company's part to recruit new workers into permanent jobs especially since the possibilities of job loss from 'natural wastage' are reduced. Some inter-union frictions have developed between the old maintenance and manufacturing managements which are organized by different trade unions but who are now performing the same job.

Managers were selected for the new computer controlled plants from 1982 onwards on the basis of managerial skills rather than knowledge of technical processes. Subsequently, managers, electricians, fitters and operators who were to work the plant spent two weeks undergoing training for the new plant at the company's training college. Before the plant was built they were taught its functional specification. Process engineers, who had commissioned the plant and outside electrical contractors were involved in the training process. Management were concerned that the course should involve both the running of the new plant and the working practices that they wished to see in it.

On the shop floor, electricians received the most training in skills relating to the new technology. With the new plant, there is an electrician with diagnostic skills on each shift in each plant for maintenance work because the cost of 'downtime' in lost production is so enormous. Managers have also been sent on three-day courses so that they can get into the programmes but the electricians have effectively claimed the computer keyboard and modifications to programmes as their skills, although other trade unions would argue that there is no intrinsic reason (for example the danger of working with high voltage electrical currents) why they should claim it as theirs.

The fitters' and sheetmetal workers' work has also changed as negotiations over restrictive practices over the years have increased flexibility in their respective areas of skills. Fitters are no longer accompanied by mates to carry their bags and clean up after them, and have undertaken courses in pneumatics (pipework) whilst the sheetmetal workers now do some fitting work. Both have been negotiated through agreement on security of employment, no enforced redundancies and increased pay.

Though new technology has been introduced in process control and in the offices, homeworking, as in the much-publicized example of Rank Xerox, has not developed to any great extent. There are some people in factory management services who work at home and are connected to the computer by modem, but they are essentially on call to debug problems.

In the office areas, new technology was first introduced in payroll operations. This had the effect of reducing wages of office staff by three-quarters. They have 18 systems covering everything from work in progress to raw materials and as a result managers are not only expected to input information, but also to have access to a greater range of information. In 1982 agreement was eventually reached for managerial staff on the introduction of new technology, introducing new scales and performance appraisals. However, new technology was not explicitly mentioned in the agreement because of the bandwagon effect it might have for other grades. The agreement involved a flexibility clause which created an instrument for negotiating on working practices at a later stage.

Office staff have, of course, been affected by the introduction of word processors and in this company, being a multi-national, satellite communication with subsidiaries around the world. Security has been an issue for staff working in the satellite communications centre, though food processing is an industry which is more security conscious in general terms because of its 'trade secrets' than the brewing industry, for example. Routine line work will also be affected by the introduction of new technology, leading to job loss. The company was under competitive pressure to provide multi-packaging for large retail outlets with the possibility that production-line workers', fitters' and managers' jobs would all be lost if this kind of work went out to contract. Distribution within the company had also been affected by computerization and the depot system had been reorganized.

These organizational and technological changes resulted in a shift in the type of training provision provided by the company. The training department had been physically located in one place with numerous instructors who could be called out to any manufacturing department. The department served the whole site and up until the mid-1970s, with recruitment of permanent and seasonal labour, they were taking on about 50 people a week. The main form of training was a week's induction course in the training department itself. In the early 1980s the decline in the number of new starters resulted in greater stability in the labour force as the large transient labour force was reduced. This meant that there was both a reduction in recruitment and a decline in the numbers of leavers so training switched from induction and familiarization towards training and retraining in new technology.

The company uses a system of operator-trainers which allows education and on-line experience to be combined. The main problem with this approach is consistency, and there is a particular emphasis on safety aspects. Operator-trainers get normal pay plus a training allowance when they are training. Particularly since the reinvestment in plant in the 1980s, instructors have to be familiar with the new processes. There are operator-trainers in each plant and they themselves receive a two-day course in training techniques. Manufacturers' courses are also used for specific items of machinery.

In addition to operator-trainers, there are specific courses which are run for example, in forklift truck training which are to ITB certified standards. Craft training in electrical, fitting and pneumatic skills is conducted at outside establishments such as technical colleges. If training is required in the new systems which are specific to the plant the training manager and the systems manager devise a one-off, in-house course. The company is trying to increase the range of skills of craft workers in order to achieve multi-skilling. Fitters had been sent on electronics courses and it was anticipated that cross-flexibility would be achieved through training.

Management training for all divisions and all sites is conducted at the company's own training college and includes both formal and informal training. A large proportion of the courses offered are in general management skills and since it is a separate profit centre, spare capacity is offered to other companies.

Although management uses videos for some training packages (e.g. on hygiene, safety, the state of the business, information on new developments) the training department regards this as education rather than training. The department was looking at 'open learning' packages, though none had been adopted. It was felt that the current system of 'sitting next to Nellie' was effective.

## New Technology and Training

The example of the introduction of new technology given above, is one in which the company has given consideration to the skill needs of sections of the workforce and has invested in training. However, overall the volume of training it conducts has decreased alongside the numbers of new recruits it has taken on. Without more intensive study of the establishment, it is impossible to make an assessment of whether the introduction of new technology resulted in specific jobs being upgraded in skills or de-skilled. Changes in payment structures do not necessarily reflect job content. Whilst this company invested in training when new technology was introduced, this is not always the case. A survey conducted by the GMBATU on the introduction of new technology in 25 workplaces in the food industry found that little or no training was offered to workers. Management preferred to settle for restricted job design creating boring and monotonous jobs, and potential inflexibilities in the workforce at a later stage. The report argues:

> (Lack of training) would tend to suggest that either the new technology is very simple to operate, or it is not very different from the previous technology, on the other hand, it could suggest that employers are underestimating in this area. It most certainly suggests that many employers are not gearing up their labour forces for the future requirements of new technology. It would also suggest that many employers, far from seeking a flexible and experienced workforce, are not prepared to spend the money on training and instead are content to settle for very narrow job boundaries which separate basic operation of machines from process control (GMBATU, 1984: 9).

This survey found that on 50 per cent of occasions, stewards considered that the introduction of new technology had a major impact on skill levels. On 35 per cent of occasions it led to increased skill requirements and in 14 per cent of cases led to de-skilling (1984: 8). Despite this, in 23 per cent of cases no training was given and in 17 per cent of cases only basic instructions on the job were given, stewards describing this instruction as 'very little' , 'minimal' or 'limited' (1984: 9). The report goes on to argue:

> Shop stewards should involve themselves in the design of jobs of those needed to operate new technology. They should be aware of the boredom factor which was mentioned by one workplace. They should seek proper training courses so that our members are not seen by employers as mere spectators or button pushers, but instead are workers who understand the process and how technology controls and assists it. Job satisfaction and job enrichment must be seen as a key priority, and proper training is the only way to secure and enhance it (1984: 9).

Within the food processing industry there is variability in the application of new technology. New equipment is often customized to each workplace, and so the impact on jobs and labour force organization will vary enormously. The GMBATU survey indicates:

> In general terms, the common features are computerisation, microprocessors, automation and centralised control. The extent of these features varies widely from workplace to workplace, largely because of a variety of factors. For example, some processes are more susecptible to the introduction of this machinery, while in other instances the employers have not yet committed the investment necessary to upgrade their existing machinery (1984: 3).

This demonstrates the unevenness with which new technology is being introduced, and the fact that the full range of applications is far from complete. Although the survey evidence suggests that the changeover to new technology is only just starting, labour force planning appears to represent no more than *ad hoc* responses to immediate problems rather than a long-term strategy.

The view that relatively little training takes place when new technology is introduced was echoed by officials from other trade unions. USDAW emphasized the absence of long-term labour force planning in the food and drink industry and the fact that even when the ITB was operating, employers organized training on the basis of a short-term assessment of skill needs. APEX, likewise stated that there was little, if any, formal training available and that employers appear to believe that 'so-called "on-the-job" training is optimal because it enables training to take place while people are producing'. The trade union argues for more training and joint union-employer involvement in drawing up programmes leading to recognized qualifications. They emphasize the need for training in transferable skills in the principles of new technology (e.g. in word processing) rather than short courses run by manufacturers which are machine-specific.

Even in a more skill-intensive industry such as engineering, officials reported little evidence of long-term planning for skills. Similarly, a survey of 500 AEU members funded by the MSC, reported that though many engineering companies encourage retraining when new technology is introduced they do not give it much support. Although most of the AEU members were in favour of new technology, a significant proportion claimed they had received little or no training in new skills. Many of those that had, said it was of poor quality. Sixty-nine per cent of respondents also thought that their foremen and supervisors lacked the necessary skills to handle the technology whilst a further 43 per cent claimed that their supervisors had not received training in the new technology (*Engineering Training Today*, January 1988: 2). Officials from AUEW/TASS view new technology as a continuous process of adaptation affecting all grades of their membership. The trade union supports retraining programmes but claimed that they were virtually non-existent. It views Open Tech and the concept of an employer-led training strategy with scepticism:

> By saying employers should determine training means none will be done and everyone knows this. Who is the Government trying to kid? Some forward-thinking employers are thinking about adult training but the majority find it cheaper to poach. TASS condemns the MSC for going through the motions on adult training (AUEW/TASS).

Likewise, the AUEW claimed that little training is on offer when computerization is introduced and that it was difficult to convince employers of the benefit of training in new technology skills:

> They take the attitude of 'devil take the hindmost'. They've been converting craftsmen to technicians without us knowing it and we want to ensure that there is a sharing of the benefits of new technology. We are not getting a return for our members when new technology is introduced . . . Some employers are offering new skills and the AUEW is running courses. Even though this is being done, our members are not getting a share of the benefits (AUEW).

In a similar vein, EETPU considers the introduction of electronic controls of machinery the most important factor affecting members' jobs in engineering but felt electricians were being thrown in at the deep end and were expected to learn through trial and error. Members feel they need specialist training to commission and maintain equipment and felt there was a need for broad-based training in the general principles of new technology, rather than the narrow-based training provided by equipment manufacturers. Many companies are reluctant to send their members for training even on short externally-run courses.

The dearth of training in new technology skills provided by employers has resulted in a number of trade unions developing their own training courses in electronics. EETPU was the first to develop these short courses and opened a training centre at Cudham Hall, Esher, in 1980. Short courses in electronics, electronic logic systems, programming and microprocessor interfacing are run. The college also has mobile instructor units so that courses can be provided in plants and in 1985, the trade union extended its training facilities to regional offices. The courses provided have been successful with both members and employers and so provision has expanded. There are obvious advantages to members if they can upgrade their skills and their employability by attending. Whilst other trade unions continue to take the view that training is the responsibility of the employer, AUEW and the craft sector of AUEW/TASS are now also involved in organizing electronics courses for their members.

### The Effect of New Technology on Jobs

Trade unions recognize that there are positive and negative effects of new technology on jobs, and invariably stress the need to seek the positive benefits in negotiations. The GMBATU survey, for example, found that 10 per cent of the workplaces surveyed had seen a spin off in the form of the creation of new departments or new product areas. Whilst a number of sites reported speed-up of lines, decreased manual control and more boring work, others noted that it made the environment cleaner and safer and had allowed expansion. Whilst on 60 per cent of sites fewer workers were needed, in 32 per cent of cases labour requirements remained the same or increased. Strong workplace organization and joint negotiation enables trade unions to press for the more positive benefits of new technology.

The impact of these contradictory processes are summarized in a TGWU publication:

> If technological improvement means that workers are retrained and re-employed, well and good. If it means that long working hours can be cut so much the better. If it means that the strain of work can be lessened, and holidays lengthened, then change can be welcomed.
>
> But if technological change means redundancy and unemployment; if it leads to a smaller number of people working long hours for a good wage while millions are left idle: if in fact there are no benefits to the mass of workers involved but only higher sales and higher profits for the firm, then technological development must be treated with utmost caution (TGWU, 1979: 4).

New technology does not present an either/or situation as the quotation suggests, but both processes are occurring simultaneously. Some workers, particularly those with higher-level skills, may enjoy improved conditions of employment, greater job security and, by becoming more flexible and acquiring new skills, arguably become more skilled. Others are still employed but are finding their work de-skilled and degraded. But undeniably, new technology introduced in the recession has been a contributory factor towards massive job losses and this, combined with the casualization of large sectors of the working population has resulted in both a degradation of work and a de-skilling process through loss of skills at the societal level.

What, concretely, are the technological innovations that trade unions are currently confronting and, in the economic recession, how are these combined with demands for increased labour flexibility? What, in particularly, distinguishes this technology from earlier generations of technology which requires a new response from organized labour?

Many trade unions point out that technology has always been changing because where production is geared to the realization of profit, manufacturers must continually improve production methods to compete in the market. In its pamphlet, 'Microelectronics: New Technology; Old Problems, New Opportunities', the TGWU argues that earlier inventions such as the steam engine, the petrol engine and the electrical motor all resulted in dramatic changes in methods of production and distribution which, in their time, meant 'closure for outdated plants, the migration of the workforce and the uprooting of communities' (1979: 3). However, in the past there were brakes on the speed of change as a result of the immense costs of new investment. In contrast the distinguishing feature of microelectronic technology is that it is extremely cheap. Not only is it cheap, but it is highly adaptable and has a wide range of applications. In the same way, an APEX publication considers microelectronic technology to be distinctive insofar as 'it is flexible, instantaneous and can be rapidly modified to perform a wide range of tasks with very little human effort. It is reliable, it is available from many competing sources; it is growing at a rapid rate and most important of all, it is cheap'. (APEX, 1980: 3). The TGWU pamphlet continues:

> A microprocessor costing only pounds can now do the work of hardware costing thousands of pounds, so companies will find it easier to make investments in microelectronics. On top of that, microelectronics can be applied in just about every working situation: not just in factories, but in offices, warehouses, shops – everywhere that people work (TGWU, 1979: 3).

The pamphlet then lists the main applications of microelectronics to different areas of work. These are: in manufacturing, where assembly lines are already automated, microelectronic technology can programme machines to do one particular task 'quickly, effectively, endlessly' thus reducing the need for production workers (1979: 7). In assembly work, microprocessors will affect both products and production processes. For example, numbers of components will be reduced as microprocessors are designed to replace separate parts, whilst machines can be programmed to perform a range of tasks:

> Many processes will be affected by micro-electronics: measuring and weighing; filling and packaging; quality control; sorting; batching; welding and spraying. Microelectronics will have a definite effect on even such skilled operations as machining. Machine tools can be instructed electronically to machine delicate parts, using sensors and measuring equipment. Numerically controlled machine tools have already been introduced, and the microprocessor generation of these will soon be a common feature in many factories (TGWU, 1979: 7).

In continuous process plants as in the steel, food processing and chemical industries, microelectronics can be applied to testing, temperature and pressure controls, stress analysis, continuous casting and the monitoring of power consumption. Maintenance work, in particular is likely to be simplified by microelectronic circuits. Outside immediate production processes electronics can be applied to design work, materials handling and office work (TGWU, 1979).

Manufacturing companies change the skill composition of their labour force both by introducing new technology and by changing the way in which goods are produced. In fabrication shops in the engineering industry, new technology removes the need for tool changes, a highly-skilled job. The computer can be programmed so that the speed of production of pressings is increased considerably. Steel plates are fed into the machine which feeds out completed pressings and human labour is only required for taking them off and stacking them. Instead of employing workers on guillotine operations, manufacturers can buy direct from the steel stockholders, who provide steel plates already cut to size. If enough customers do this, economies of scale enable the stockholders to invest in automatic machinery, thus making sub-contracting not only more attractive from the point of view of reducing fixed costs, but cheaper than production on site.

Similar developments are occurring in sectors of the food industry. For example, a large retail chain which had a national depot for preparing meat lines for its retail outlets decided it was too expensive to re-equip and modernize the depot. In future, 'boxed' beef and lamb lines will be bought from an outside supplier. New technology means that meats can be prepared and prepacked at the abattoirs whilst the wholesale operation has been radically changed alongside the loss of skilled butchery jobs in retail stores. A GMBATU official in the Midlands argued that jobs were being designed in such a way as to require minimal training:

Work which requires training, skills and higher pay – management have eradicated it with machinery and new technology. Investment has been made in areas where skill was, with the aim of de-skilling . . . this is guided by the 'general worker' philosophy. De-skilling means low pay and it is the exceptions to the general worker which creates the pressure towards higher pay (GMBATU).

The engineering industry is, of course, affected by the continuing recession, though some sectors are more buoyant than others. Redundancies have occurred, but this is the result of reorganization not just the introduction of new technology.

There is redesign of jobs and there are fewer moving parts now, so fewer people to work on them. There are changing attitudes to layout and design . . . Many companies have increased turnover per worker dramatically (AUEW).

A major factor affecting the interfacing between production and design has been the development of computer-aided design (CAD) and computer-aided manufacture (CAM) and computer-numerically-controlled machine tools (CNC). Whilst enhancing the individual toolmaker's job by taking on part of the design function, it decreases the overall demand for skilled toolmakers. An AUEW official wryly commented, 'For the unions, new technology doesn't provide any members. New machine tools don't pay membership dues, attend meetings, get sick or take holidays.'

### Broader Processes of Technological Change

There is a tendency to consider technological innovations as phenomena which have an impact on social relations in the firm and as requiring higher or lower levels of skills, fewer or greater numbers of workers. The impact or potential impact of new technology on manufacturing processes can, therefore, be assessed, and in related areas of office work, accounting, warehousing and distribution. However, it is the application of new technology to accounting methods, both relating to stock control and labour requirements which are of particular interest, given managerial job objectives of increasing labour flexibility, and this is nowhere more relevant than in the construction industry, where site organization of the industry, combined with the variability of production have resulted in the application of new technology to the design process, to accounting and the organization of site work. This affects the way in which labour is organized and the structures of control in work.

Campinos–Dubernet has characterized recent developments in the labour process of the French construction industry in the following phases:

> In the 1950s . . . the construction industry also attempted to increase labour productivity, and this at a period when the scale of sites was growing. They tried to introduce serialisation, a stabilised labour process, off-site fabrication in factories with fixed work posts. This left only foundation work and erection and finishing on the site. This was the period of heavy prefabrication. It failed however both for technical and economic reasons . . . In the early 1960s most firms in the construction industry returned to the 'on-site mixing' and the use of shuttering systems which were more flexible and better adapted to site variability, to the types of construction and their location. However . . . the external variability remained considerable (1985b: 4).

The major innovation brought about by the introduction of new technology as such, has been in the way that computerization has enabled management to take account of the variability in the production process by speeding up stock-taking and reducing the amount of time required to deal with the enormous amount of information generated by the labour process.

Computerization allowed contractors to increase flexibility of labour and stock. Though Campinos–Dubernet distinguishes a minority tendency in the French construction industry in this latter period towards increased use of Taylorized work methods (the division of jobs into separate tasks under centralized management control), she argues that the majority tendency was towards the delegation of control to site management, with control exercised through budgetary constraints (1985a: 8). Hence the major technological factor affecting production has been the increase in off-site production and pre-fabrication, combined with a fragmentation of the labour process through labour-only sub-contracting and increasing use of specialist sub-contracting. This is confirmed by Clarke for the British construction industry:

> The most important feature of the post-war situation for building labour was the decline in the traditional 'wet trades' of bricklaying, plastering and painting with the growing use of concrete, steel frame and plasterboard . . . This was compounded by the 1960s and 1970s with the great extension in the mechanization of site work (for instance through new types of dumpers, hoists and cranes) and increased use of prefabricated components . . . What is now most marked in the construction labour process is the

increase in composite processes (drylining and suspended ceiling fixing, to cladded and curtain walling, to flat roofing) and in the intensive use of new materials (from plastics and aluminium to heavy breeze blocks to, of late, asbestos) (1985: 5).

The overcoming of problems of variability through the use of computerization and the fragmentation of the labour process through its division into specialist functions lends itself to payment-by-results systems. The effect of these processes on skills in the industry were noted in interviews:

There is more pressure in the South-East of England for skills to be broken down into separate entities than elsewhere, but the influence is spreading. For example, with suspended ceiling companies. Traditionally ceilings were constructed in timber by joiners but with new materials limited skills are required. The skills are learnt with the emphasis on speed and the workers pass themselves off as specialists. These methods lend themselves to payment by results schemes which is another attraction to the employer (UCATT).

The link between working practices and techniques of production is indicated in the following statement:

Specialist sub-contracting does tend to further break down the traditional craftsman's job, but there are differences in working practices in different parts of the country. In England you might see a newspaper advertisement saying a contractor was looking for first and second fix joiners, as well as roofing joiners and framework carpenter/joiners. A joiner in Scotland wouldn't know what they were talking about. Twenty years ago a joiner/carpenter would be expected to undertake all types of work such as joist floors (the 'first fix'), erect a timber roof and complete the fittings to a home. Some squads now work only on roofs because they can increase their speed and their bonus payments (UCATT).

Some sectors are more capital-intensive than others; civil engineering, engineering construction and offshore construction generally are more capital-intensive than the building sector.

In the offshore construction industry more powerful lifting facilities are changing the way production is organized. Bigger modules for oil rigs can now be built onshore; the oil rig stands in a jacket and office, accommodation and workshop modules are built on top. This has resulted in an increased proportion of the work being done onshore. In the same way, in the heating and ventilating sector there has been a move to welding rather than traditional jointing methods (flanging and screwing). This makes installation easier but not repair and maintenance. On the manufacturing side, sheet metal workers are finding CNC machines are increasingly being used in their work and in pipe-setting many pre-fabricated materials are prepared on CNC machines and just assembled on site.

It is not only in the construction industry that generalized technological change combined with new technology is changing labour processes. The TGWU stated that in sectors of the engineering industry it is automation which has had the greatest impact on operative and semi-skilled areas. That is to say, members' jobs are displaced by machines, leading to redundancy and unemployment. Where automatic controls are being introduced, training has been given to both experienced and younger employees, but the numbers of semi-skilled workers has been cut enormously. Similarly, in the food and drink industry, changes have taken place as the result of the introduction of new plant and the speeding up of production lines. In the drinks industry firms have been replacing the miles of roundabouts and conveyor belts that used to be found in factories, by palletization. On the distribution side of the industry, the draymen's jobs have changed with moves from bottled to canned beers and from the large 54 gallon hogsheads to smaller metal casks. The old hogsheads carried traditional beers which have to be treated gently so as not to disturb the sediment, whilst modern pressurized beers which are transported can be 'bounced around' in their metal casks.

New technology has an indirect effect on jobs in distribution, where it affects ordering and accounting but may only marginally affect the work of the driver delivering the goods. In the same way, with warehousing functions, workers in the warehouse may have no direct contact with new technology themselves, but the use of information technology may affect the way they work.

In all production processes, the areas most susceptible to the introduction of new technology are those concerning the handling of information. It is in the areas of warehousing, retailing and mail order that the Taylorization of routine clerical work is occurring, as computerization cuts out the thinking parts of many jobs. In a real sense, managerial control is extended and work de-skilled by separating conception from the execution of work tasks. This process is explained in the USDAW New Technology Pack (Manufacturing and Packaging Section):

In the past machines worked faster and faster. They could DO more than a man could using his own unaided labour; but machines couldn't make choices about WHAT they did. They could only vary what they did at the command of a human operator. They couldn't do the equivalent of THINK! Computers have changed all that. Because they can COLLECT, STORE, PROCESS and ANALYSE information they are now capable of doing the thinking part of a job. *And they can assemble often enormously complex information and analyse it far more quickly than the human brain* . . . New technology replaces BRAIN POWER while other previous changes replaced muscle power (USDAW, nd: 2–6).

When this capacity to handle information is combined with machinery, then the physical and often the thinking part of jobs is removed. An USDAW official commented:

Warehousing functions are now more mechanical. There are robot pickers going round warehouses and people only stack the shelves. Robot pickers are certainly going to be developed in the future and there are already examples of where they have been introduced.

If this is integrated with laser beam checkouts in retail outlets and bar codes on every item then, in a real sense, jobs will be de-skilled and degraded.

Work is becoming totally de-skilled . . . for example, the cashier's job used to be a grade higher than a general assistant, but with laser beam check-outs . . . you don't need skill to pick up a can of beans and wave it over the beam. There are pressures from the employers to degrade the checkout operator's job.

In these areas, the application of new technology does not entirely remove the demand for labour, but the problem lies in the quality of the job that remains.

There are still jobs for USDAW members but they are unskilled and low paid . . . We don't have craft union concerns. We are concerned with what job will be left after new technology is introduced rather than whose job will be taken (USDAW).

### Office Work

The application of micro-electronics to data processing and handling in offices has a major impact on white-collar jobs. It is difficult to assess the impact on overall numbers in employment, but an impressive number of occupations are likely to disappear or undergo radical change in the near future. These are, in the office sector; postroom workers, typists, secretaries, invoice clerks, filing clerks, shipping clerks, stores clerks, insurance clerks, sales clerks, stock clerks, progress clerks, data preparation staff, cashiers, telegraph operators, warehouse workers, draughtspeople, computer operators, programmers, accountants, supervisors, administrators, junior and middle managers; in the service sector TV repairers, telephone repairers, meter readers, proof readers, compositors, library assistants; in the production sector, light electricians, machinists, mechanics, inspectors, assemblers, operators, material handlers (APEX, 1980: 2).

A number of trade union publications (TGWU, 1979; APEX, 1980; USDAW, nd) have pointed out that women's jobs, in particular are likely to be affected by new technology. This is true of routine assembly and packaging jobs, but more importantly, in clerical areas where women predominate. It is here that the potential for increasing labour productivity and managerial control is considerable due to the labour-intensive nature of office work. The same publications indicate that without trade union initiatives towards the training and retraining of the workforce whose jobs are affected by new technology, de-skilling is a real threat.

The handling of information in office work is an area affected by micro-electronic information-processing capacity. White collar jobs in offices are affected in two main ways. On the one hand there are those that are becoming 'technologically outdated' and on the other hand, there are those that are dramatically transformed by new technology. White collar workers organized by APEX in the engineering industry, 'sub-managerial staff', are affected in different ways. Within this group there are people like comptometer operators whose work is being replaced by computers. Progress chasers' and auditing clerks' jobs are disappearing since the first computer systems are usually introduced into these areas. Likewise, ASTMS reports that with managers taking responsibility for inputting exceptions to normal wages (e.g. holidays, sickness, etc.) into the computer, wages staff have been drastically cut.

The most universal area of change in the office area is that of word processing. The health and safety aspects of Visual Display Units have been widely publicised; (APEX, 1983; TASS, 1985) but the replacement of typing by word processing also has far-reaching implications for the nature of the work. For example, there may be less emphasis on speed and the aesthetic qualities of the work as formatting functions are taken over by the word processor. Accuracy and speed become less important as the job shifts towards editing and correction functions.

In manufacturing companies, a considerable amount of routine clerical work is disappearing in areas relating to the ordering and distribution of parts. In the past, customers used to ring in, order a part and this was then dispatched. Now the technology exists for the customer to speak direct to the computer, which orders and dispatches the part.

> Rationalization goes hand in hand with new technology. Whole business systems are being changed and more centralized control exercised. It does affect staff because people are no longer needed to fill in forms in triplicate and to do accounts. Mergers and takeovers between companies mean that clerical areas can be more easily rationalized so that work in different sections isn't duplicated (APEX).

The AUEW also emphasized that a number of factors are involved, including reorganization, rationalization and new technology. With powerful computers, multi-site companies are able to centralize functions such as pay and maybe even production control on one site and simply send the information to other sites when it is needed.

Apart from workers whose jobs are directly affected by new technology there are changes for managerial and supervisory staff. APEX expects that there will be a reduction in numbers of people with supervisory functions with the reduction in employment and the automation of clerical work through computerization. With centralized control management can keep track of work in progress without the need for first line supervision. This is confirmed by ASTMS' view of developments in food processing, for example, where their members work in quality control, the retrieval and dissemination of information and the management of stock control. For ASTMS members in food processing the problem has not been one of job loss, because supervisors, managers and foremen are needed whatever the numbers employed in particular departments. Problems identified by ASTMS relate to the simplification of members' jobs by the rapid treatment of information and the difficulties of acceptance of technological change by older members, particularly those over 50.

## Policies towards New Technology

A major policy objective with respect to the introduction of new technology has been for trade unions to obtain agreements on new technology, job security and disclosure of information. To this end model clauses have been drawn up, new technology action packs published and courses organized for trade union activists (see Bamber, 1988 for a review). Leaving aside for one moment the effectiveness of such measures, it is important to emphasize that the aim has been to draw the introduction of new technology into collective bargaining concerns because of its effects on employment and on occupations. Though many of the early agreements concerned security of employment, APEX in particular has found that these agreements have not been able to counter tendencies towards de-skilling unless training and job design are also considered under the terms of the agreement. Therefore, access to training and trade union involvement in job design are increasingly issues that are raised by trade unions in negotiations on new technology and that requires new sorts of expertise in the trade union movement.

A number of trade unions stressed the importance of early discussions on the introduction of new technology so that members could be prepared and adapt. However, it was argued that employers often buy machinery and only think about operating it and maintaining it at a later stage. More forward planning is needed. In response to questions in the GMBATU survey (GMBATU, 1984) stewards reported that agreements on disclosure of information had been obtained at 28 per cent of the sites surveyed, on new technology at 8 per cent of sites and on job security at 16 per cent of sites. Despite the absence of formal agreements in the majority of cases, stewards nonetheless reported that informal discussions and *ad hoc* negotiations had taken place in practice in two-thirds of instances. The report notes that in terms of preparation for negotiations in this area only 40 per cent of stewards had attended GMBATU or TUC courses on new technology. This indicated the need for the education of stewards in the bargaining aspects of new technology, especially given the fact that at 56 per cent of sites employers planned to install more new technology within two years.

A number of trade unions have emphasized the importance of obtaining training for all members in areas affected by the introduction of new technology. TASS for example presses for all drawing room staff to receive training when computer-aided design (CAD) is introduced in the design area.

> We take the view that if we don't get involved in training and technology, technology will control us. We felt we needed an input. Our main philosophy is that we are not frightened of new technology . . . our members design and build it . . . and we have reached agreements in salaries for those who train and upgrade their skills. We also have agreements on payments for academic qualifications such as HNC, ONC and BSc. They are standard rates plus, but they are not universal (TASS).

The GMBATU report argues that if new technology is introduced in the absence of training, boredom and monotony can be a problem for members if their jobs are very restricted. They call for proper training. (GMBATU, 1984: 9).

APEX also raises training and job satisfaction as issues arising from the introduction of new technology, arguing the case for workers' involvement in job redesign as a means of creating more challenging and interesting work which more fully utilizes members' capabilities. Moreover trade union representatives should press for the retraining of the maximum number of staff and all employees in affected departments to minimize friction between those on new equipment and related staff. These should include general appreciation courses provided at educational institutions and not just manufacturers' courses (APEX, 1980: 47).

The problem with trade unions involving themselves in job design and job evaluation relates to the fact that in the past they have been unilaterally imposed by management. Trade unions advocating involvement in them are not advocating evaluation exercises carried out by consultants at management's behest, which may reinforce existing divisions in the labour force, but are calling for a process of joint trade union–management projects. APEX strategy towards job design has evolved due to the failure of early agreements to include issues of job satisfaction and a perception that, particularly in office work, Taylorization has been brought in on the back of new systems. In analysing new technology agreements negotiated by the membership since 1979, only two were found to include clauses on job design and one of these was at the trade union's own office headquarters. They have subsequently published two documents on job design arising from the work of their Office Technology Working Party (APEX, 1980 and 1983), aimed at translating 'a body of abstract material into concepts and language understandable to non-experts' (Holroyd, 1985: 5) and including checklists for job evaluation exercises. The objective is to combine workers' and managers' experiences of the jobs and working practices with the aid of a facilitator to provide a new job design which will benefit both employees and employer. Whilst APEX recognizes that the publication of the documents has not led to any new initiatives, there is now a session on job design in every national, regional and area educational programme. The trade union maintains that the weakness of the technology agreements struck in the 1970s lies in their concern with discrete systems and items of equipment whereas now and, increasingly, in the future, trade unions will have to give consideration to systems as a whole. Whilst new technology agreements which incorporate job design constitute an important arm of trade union strategy towards new technology, they are only one aspect. APEX believes that though it may be possible to achieve progress in individual workplaces on job design, the Conservative government's aggressive approach to trade unions is not conducive to the joint regulation of new technology. Social planning, industrial democracy, national and local enterprise boards, issues which have been raised in TUC policy statements are all essential to creating an environment in which the benefits of new technology accrue to workers and management alike. This is echoed by other trade unions:

> tremendous steps forward must be taken towards full participation by the workforce, through their union channels, supported by procedural rights and substantive agreements, extending collective bargaining to corporate investment, manpower training and the adoption of new technology (TGWU, 1979: 14).

The emphasis, therefore, is in establishing procedures for negotiation at the point of production as well as for creating sources of expertise to benefit workers.

## Conclusion

In this chapter I have demonstrated that the trade unions examined in the project have positive attitudes towards training as a means of increasing the skills and bargaining power of their membership. However, the evidence from the interviews suggests that relatively few workers are offered opportunities to update their skills when new technology is introduced. This is largely due to the fact that decisions relating to retraining are made by individual employers and despite official encouragement to retrain through the Adult Training Strategy, there is no effective mechanism for encouraging firms to do so. Retraining arrangements are, therefore, made in-house rather than at industry-level. Some employers clearly are putting resources into retraining and, insofar as they relate to the updating of skills and technology and do not form a major threat to demarcation between jobs, are welcomed by trade unions.

New technology can increase or decrease skills depending on its applications and managerial decisions which affect job design. With training, jobs can be broadly defined and workers' adaptability and discretion increased. However, the evidence presented here, suggests that in many instances, new technology is introduced in such a way as to reduce skill requirements. A large number of jobs are disappearing or being radically modified by it, whilst information processing has the potential to make labour accounting more precise and in this way make increasing use of casual labour. The growth of more casual forms of labour is likely to reduce training volumes still further, both of young people entering the labour market and any commitment to retrain adults. In this context it seems that in the absence of powers to compel and encourage companies to train or a major investment of public funds in quality training, both the quantity and quality of training are likely to continue to decline.

# 4

# A Flexible Workforce:
# To Train or Not to Train?

## Introduction

Until recently, continuing training or retraining referred to two distinct phenomena: managerial and supervisory training in the firm, and schemes for the unemployed and ex-services personnel in the external labour market. The importance currently attributed to the retraining of employees in general in competitive strategy marks a significant break with previous perceptions and practices. In Chapter 3, the role of training was considered with respect to the introduction of new technology. In this chapter, training in the context of broader objectives of achieving labour flexibility is considered.

Flexibility is itself an ambiguous concept, which has different meanings according to the context in which it is used. On the one hand, workers' flexibility involves the use of skills in such a way as to exercise autonomy over the labour process, and as such constitutes a means of empowerment. On the other hand, employers' flexibility to deploy labour may result in increased control, casualization, de-skilling and the dispensibility of workers. There are indications that in the labour market as a whole, there has been an increase in casual forms of labour, which partly reflects shifts in industrial structure. Within firms, employers have been requiring workers to adopt more flexible working practices, which may or may not be introduced through training programmes and may result in the upgrading of skills or de-skilling. The extent to which this increases or decreases workers' autonomy will depend on local circumstances.

Upgrading and de-skilling are social relationships rather than empirically measurable phenomena. They refer not only to subjective experiences of work, but also to the value placed on particular skills realized in the wage relation. It is not inconceivable for individuals to experience de-skilling, but to find their skills upgraded in the wages structure. Alternatively, they may feel that their job demands an increased level of skill which is not financially rewarded. Cockburn (1983: 121) has argued that an element of skill is also constituted by workers' collective organizations insofar as trade union strength in the workplace determines the value of different kinds of labour. The latter is particularly significant in the context of employers' moves to increase flexibility between jobs, since British trade unionism has developed on the basis of trade rather than industry or political affiliation.

## Flexibility and Training

The nature of contemporary changes in the labour market and employment practices has been widely debated and will not be discussed here. (See for example, Atkinson, 1985; European Trade Union Institute, 1986; Incomes Data Services 1986; Osburg, 1984; Piore and Sabel, 1984; Pollert, 1987). The aim here is to establish the issues that are confronting trade unionists in their workplaces, and in particular what the implications of flexible working practices are for training and trade union policy. If, as Piore and Sabel argue (1984), the mass production paradigm is now being replaced by 'flexible specialization' in which product range and quality supersede volume as marketing objectives, this has implications for both job design and training. Mass production lines based on Taylor's principle of a series of limited work tasks, require relatively little training and workers' are not expected to exercise much discretion in their jobs. In contrast, where product runs are smaller, workers need to be more adaptable. Whilst empirical studies support the view that small batch production and flexible manufacturing systems do have the potential to increase workers' autonomy over their work (Friedman, 1977; Campbell and Warner, 1986), the precise way in which new production methods affect the organization of work, the design of jobs and the skill structure of the workforce has yet to be established. It may not necessarily lead to the reclaiming of craft skills as Piore and Sabel argue, whilst productivity gains may well result in job losses. Cross, an advocate of multi-skilling, argues that 'significant reductions in factory operating expenses have been achieved even in those cases where few redundancies were declared. For example, a traditionally manned plant with the typical departmental empires with managerial and other demarcations can, with the full adoption of an integrated and flexible organization, reduce manning levels by 20–30 per cent' (1985: 41). Not only can improved productivity, brought about by flexible working practices, result in redundancies, but in combination with other employer initiatives such as moves towards greater identity with company performance, single-union deals and 'no-strike' agreements, it can be viewed as an attack on trade union organization itself. Furthermore, it is questionable whether the types of flexibility demanded of all grades of worker from the unskilled to the skilled result in the upgrading of skills and increased work autonomy as Piore and Sabel suggest. They neglect job losses which inevitably accompany productivity gains on this scale and exclude the detrimental effects this policy may have on ancillary workers and others not identified as being in the 'core' labour force.

In the UK the concept of the flexible firm has been put forward by writers such as Atkinson (1985). It is presented as a radical break in recruitment and employment patterns. Based on research carried out at the Institute for Manpower Studies, his work is prescriptive rather than descriptive of employment trends. He himself recognizes that 'Research suggests in practice relatively few UK firms have explicitly and comprehensively reorganized their labour force on this basis . . . those managers who want to grasp permanent, medium and long term advantages recognize the need to formalize practices within a policy framework of some kind' (1985: 28). Atkinson dichotomizes employees into a core and a periphery. The core, he argues, is functionally flexible in the sense that it can perform a range of different production tasks, whilst the periphery is numerically flexible and dispensable. He links the concept of core workers with core production functions, whilst peripheral workers are more likely to be employed in ancillary activities. The training implications of this model are that the supposedly secure core workers will be highly trained and that their pay will reflect this. By contrast,

> by definition peripheral groups only supply skills which can readily be found on the external labour market. The more discretionary elements in the job, and the more specific the skills involved to the needs of the firm then the more likely it is that the job will appear at the core . . . conversely 'plug in', low discretion jobs in support or ancillary activities are likely to appear at the periphery (1985: 28).

It is interesting to note that Atkinson classifies trainees on government schemes as part of the disposable, peripheral labour force.

Apart from employers' strategies towards increasing workers' flexibility, the state itself has played an important part in increasing labour flexibility through deregulation. It has done this through changes in employment rights and social security legislation as well as through a determined attack on trade union organization. Therefore, state policy towards training and the labour market is an important element in increasing labour flexibility.

The European Trade Union Institute argues that flexibility essentially entails the loosening of labour legislation and the weakening of trade unions.

> An important part of the 'flexibility debate' in those European countries where it has achieved a certain momentum has been the extent to which such joint regulation of the use of labour within companies should be abandoned and replaced by management control. The goal of some advocates of 'flexibility' has become not just the removal of legislation regulating the use of labour at company level, but the fundamental weakening of trade unions' ability to represent their members' interests and take action to advance them (1986: 100).

Whilst, as the report points out, this is not a strategy pursued by all employers, in Britain, in particular, deregulation, small business exemptions, privatization, small business supports and anti-union legislation contribute to create a climate in which greater flexibilities in labour deployment can be achieved.

Perhaps one of the most crucial questions regarding labour flexibility is the extent to which the deregulation of the labour market itself undermines training and de-skills. The shifting of risk to employees whether they are self-employed, work on temporary contracts or work for sub-contractors is the opposite strategy to that of vertical integration of interests which is a characteristic of company strategy in a period of growth (ETUI, 1986). Though as a short-term strategy it may be effective in cutting labour costs, in the long term this may not be the case. Where there is labour insecurity, turnover and absenteeism will be higher. There will be little company loyalty or pride in work, both of which have implications for the quality of products. Moreover, since firms are less likely to invest in developing the skills of the more casual sections of their workforces, and have no interest in training 'indirects' then this has long-term implications for job design and the labour process. If jobs are performed by people readily recruited on the external labour market then these jobs must be designed to take this into account. The same report points out that the reduction of labour costs by making labour more dispensable is a short-term defensive response to recession. A long-term strategy for growth must be one of investment in new technology and in increasing the flexibility of the labour force by increasing its skill level. Flexible labour practices, based on limited job design and low-level skills will in the longer term create inflexibilities and a labour force which has low-level, inflexible skills.

Of course, there is evidence that some higher-level skills are now being performed by workers on short-term contracts, on a consultancy or on a self-employed basis. That is to say, not all non-standard forms of contract imply low-level skills. However, insecurity of employment is not conducive to a stable supply of these skills and whilst companies may wish to economize in the recession, failure to build up their own skill base may put them at a disadvantage when the economy picks up. Though there are short-term savings for companies in adopting the strategy of labour flexibility, in the long term efficiency may be prejudiced. Osburg argues,

> the dominant factor in long-term productivity growth is, however, the development and implementation of new technology and methods of production. The gains to be made from the efficient allocation of existing resources are quantitatively much smaller than the gains in dynamic efficiency which are produced by the continual development and diffusion of more productive new technologies. The primary requirement for the implementation of new technologies is not flexibility of movement *between* firms, rather it is the flexibility and co-operation in the use of labour within firms (1984: 32).

Flexibility is closely linked to the question of the introduction of new technology. But to argue that new technology *requires* a flexible labour force is deterministic. There is an element of managerial choice both in the technology acquired and in the structuring of work tasks. Evidence suggests that the productive potentiality of new technology is best achieved through the creation of a highly-skilled, flexible workforce in a climate of negotiation and consultation (NEDO, 1986). This may mean a degree of decentralization and greater discretion for individual workers over the work they perform, though as Campbell and Warner (1986) show, management may try to reassert control through tighter supervision. The low-skill option may result in skill inflexibilities in the workforce which may not only affect future managerial decisions in the choice of machinery but also the design of new machinery upstream.

Finally, demarcations between jobs in factories, frequently designated as 'inflexibilities' have been regarded as forms of job control exercised collectively by different groups of workers (Hyman and Elger, 1981). Though commonly regarded as trade union creations, their existence in non-union plants suggests that they are the product of management decisions regarding the organization of production which are subsequently defended by the job holders. Though increasing flexibility may be viewed as an attack on job control, this does not mean it is an irreversible attack and that trade union controls will not also be established over new structures of work organization.

## The Extent of Labour Flexibility

As indicated above, there has been considerable debate generated by the concept of flexibility but it is not easy to ascertain the extent to which it has been implemented either as an *ad hoc* response to the recession or as a coherent managerial strategy. In this section, the views of the trade union officials interviewed will be examined to see the extent to which flexible working practices are affecting members' jobs and skills.

### Casualization

To turn firstly to the development and extension of casual forms of labour in the recession and its implications for skills it is first necessary to establish the extent to which there has been a qualitative change in the nature of employment. Many of the officials interviewed reported increases in the use of casual labour and in particular its extension to jobs and sectors of employment in which it had previously not existed, or in which it had become part of a regular pattern as opposed to a short-term response to particular labour shortages. Many expressed their concern not just at the deterioration in conditions of employment and its implications for trade union organization, but also in its effect on the skill content of their members' jobs. Others recognized that it was often the already de-skilled jobs that tended to be casualized. In this way existing patterns of segmentation in the labour market and social inequality are intensified.

A major feature noted particularly amongst women workers has been the absolute and relative growth of the number of part-time workers. An important feature of the pattern of part-time working is that the average numbers of hours worked is decreasing, and many part-time workers now fall outside employment protection legislation. In addition, service sector employment is growing relative to manufacturing and so part of this trend reflects shifts in industrial structure towards sectors which are characterized by lower levels of full-time employment and poorer pay and conditions.

Part-time work has always been characteristic of the service sector, particularly personal services and in retailing. In manufacturing part-time work has been linked to shift work with women working morning, afternoon or twilight shifts. A qualitative change facilitated by developments in information technology has been a move to individual negotiations with the employer on part-time hours geared to the family commitments of individual women. Particularly in the service sector and in retailing, rather than working part-time shifts a woman works hours that are tailored to her individual needs. Under the guise of allowing more individual freedom, the worker develops a privatized relationship with the employer. These isolated workers are difficult to organize in trade unions because of the hours they work and the individual's perception that the trade union has nothing to offer in terms of negotiating on collective conditions of employment.

Several officials interviewed, particularly those in general unions representing large numbers of female workers, made reference to the growing use of part-time hours. Though some were more sceptical on the extent to which increased part-time working could be applied to specific industries without increasing the costs of supervision, monitoring and training, others perceived it as a widespread and efficient practice for the employer.

> Employers see the female workforce like a tap to be turned on and off. They have a very short-sighted approach to work patterns and there has been a wholesale transference from full-time to part-time work, the economics of which revolve around the teabreak . . . It is now possible to maintain a steady rate of effort throughout the period this way but quality is not being taken seriously and the workforce is divorced from the product – a pair of hands divorced from the brain. The GMB views it as a form of de-skilling. The process of using part-time workers has been around for a long time now but new technology is intensifying it. The workforce used to physically handle the product but now they mind the machine and deal with things when they go wrong (GMBATU).

Effort levels and managerial control can be increased by the use of part-time labour:

> The employer realizes that the majority of work is down to menial tasks requiring minimal training. This opens up another rich pasture – you can meet the peaks and troughs in the order book not by overtime, possibly by lay-offs, but because of the low level of skills required you can do it by taking on part-timers – women – and temporary workers . . . in one local company . . . there are 300 employees, the majority work four or five hours a day. There's a high energy factor on these short shifts because fresh groups are always coming in and you don't meet the troughs in effort curves. They've overcome even that! They work like the clappers because they get rid of them if they don't and so productivity increases. Crucial to this are the opportunities for management to simplify

every job. You reduce the mental and physical effort and reduce the need for training (GMBATU).

If the de-skilling of jobs is a feature of part-time employment, then this is also true of temporary work. There are industries which have traditionally had a strong element of seasonal work, especially where the product is perishable. However, officials reported that in some parts of the food industry, workers who used to be retained over slack periods, no longer find this to be the case. In this instance the pattern appears to be one of employing a body of workers the year round and taking on seasonal workers – usually married women – in the few months of peak labour demand.

A more disturbing development is the growth in the numbers of workers who fall outside the mainstream of labour law (Leighton, 1986). Officials reported that temporary working rather than being a short-term solution to peaks in demand, had become a more permanent feature of employment practices in some companies. Two examples from the Midlands illustrate this. One company has been taking on employees on 12-month contracts with the stipulation that they must then leave the company for three before being re-engaged. This practice is designed so that the employees do not start to feel the company has obligations to them and also means that many employment benefits which are cumulative, like redundancy, or have qualifying periods such as maternity leave, sick leave and holiday pay, are not available to them. They are dispensable and the company is also able to cut down on some of the related costs associated with the wages bill. Another practice reported was that of recruitment for periods of 12 weeks only, with the worker being dismissed on the Friday and re-employed the following Monday. In this instance the employer evades the law which stipulates that the employee must be provided with a written statement of terms and conditions of employment within 13 weeks of being taken on. Thus, there is no job description, no fixed rate for the job, statement of hours of work, holidays, sick pay or pension rights. These examples compare with usage of 10-month 'supplemental' contracts by Control Data (Leek, 1985). Due to trade union attempts to influence their operation in a redundancy situation, the company introduced new contracts which specified that the supplemental contract required the worker to provide work for the company 'as and when required'.

A further method of increasing the variability of labour costs is to sub-contract certain areas of work. This is a long-standing practice, but officials reported shifts in the range of functions that were being put out to contract, often replacing directly-employed labour. Sub-contracting may concern ancillary activities, the production of certain components or skills and expertise which are not required on a year-round basis, or are of a 'one-off' nature (for example, the installation of a new plant). In the four industries under consideration, sub-contracting is widespread and in construction is particularly well-established. Outsourcing of components and sub-contracting of ancillary services are significant in the other three. The 1984–1985 GMBATU survey of wages and conditions in the chemical industry found contractors working in canteens, in office cleaning, security, transport and building maintenance. Only 13 of the 62 establishments surveyed had no sub-contractors. At 22 plants the trade union had a policy of insisting that all contractors should be members of GMBATU or other relevant unions.*

The TGWU reports that transport, in particular, has been affected by increased use of sub-contracting. Many firms are no longer employing their own fleets because of the expense of maintaining managers, mechanics and record-keepers in the offices. This usually means that the firm's own drivers are made redundant and the fleet sold. Some drivers may be re-employed on a self-employed basis or as employees of a sub-contractor. There are spin-off effects for other trade unions such as the AUEW when maintenance staff serving the garage are made redundant.

The AUEW reports that the issue of sub-contractors has been a frequent cause of local dispute, often reaching the headquarters conference stage. However, the position of only accepting sub-contractors if they are trade union members is essentially a rearguard action, since by the time sub-contractors are operating, it is too late to fight on behalf of directly-employed members at the plant.

Sub-contracting poses specific problems for trade union organization, relating to its effect on negotiated wages and conditions of employment. Sub-contractors may not be party to agreements which stipulate minimum wages and conditions and may thus undercut wage costs. Several officials reported cases of members being made redundant and then being re-employed at the same plant but working for a sub-contractor. Trade unions may insist that sub-contracted workers are unionized and receive agreed rates of pay, but the extent to which they are able to enforce this will depend on the effective control trade union organization exercises over the supply of skills. It is easier to enforce with some occupational groups than it is with others. With the building trades, where a third of all workers in the construction industry are self-employed, it is extremely difficult to exert effective control over sub-contractors. Some local authorities have set up contract compliance units to monitor conditions

---

* I am grateful to GMBATU for allowing me to see this unpublished material. The numbers of establishments with sub-contractors in each category were as follows: canteen – 22, office cleaning – 31, security – 15, transport – 21, 'other' – 2.

of employment and the observance of legal requirements by private firms doing council building work but this is essentially a defensive mechanism established to protect the Direct Labour Organizations from unfair competition when tendering for council work.

## Flexibility Between Jobs

Whilst so far the contractual flexibility of the labour force has been discussed, there is also ample evidence of moves towards greater flexibility between jobs in the sense of the reduction in demarcations between occupations. Company-specific skills currently being developed contribute in a different way to the dynamics of plant bargaining power than those of skills that are transferable between firms. With transferable skills the bargaining power of the workers possessing those skills exists by virtue of the fact that there is a market for those skills outside the enterprise. With company-specific skills bargaining power may be increased by the lack of replaceable skills on the external labour market.

Evidence from the interviews suggests that flexibility is being introduced for all grades of work from the skilled to the semi-skilled and unskilled. In some instances it is taking place through programmes of formal training, in others through informal learning on the job. Trade union officials in the Midlands reported that changes had taken place on a plant by plant basis without the trade unions making a proper response. These developments had occurred entirely on the employers' initiative and often with no recognition in the payments' system of the new skills acquired or changes in tasks performed. Particularly amongst the unskilled and semi-skilled workers in the region, these new skills were imposed and not recognized, even where higher-level skills were being employed. Two main issues have emerged: firstly, that fear of unemployment has been a major factor in the acceptance of new working practices, especially where it has been imposed rather than negotiated; secondly, that the changes that have been made are not once-and-for-all changes but the beginning of a new way of working whereby constant changes of work tasks will be the expected pattern. Employers appear to be seeking 'a general worker philosophy whereby all workers are general and flexible' (GMBATU). GMBATU officials in the Midlands with responsibilities for engineering and food processing argued that what is currently happening is merely a development of more flexible attitudes towards changing job definitions and boundaries, which serves as a preparation for a major assault on craft skills and demarcations at a later stage. Where agreements have been reached on flexibility it is also the case that they are establishing principles for constant change in job definitions. The Incomes Data Services Report on flexibility states that despite the interest generated by flexible working practices, so far it is only enabling agreements which have been negotiated and most employers admit that the process of achieving full-scale flexibility has only just begun (1986: 1).

Constant changes in unskilled and semi-skilled work tasks put tremendous pressures on workers to adapt, and this is especially onerous for older workers:

> Companies rely on the fear of the workers that if they don't adapt and exhibit flexible attitudes and abilities of their own then they are ripe for selection for redundancy. Incredible pressure is being placed on those of 45 and 50 who dread what's happening and the indications suggest that older people are accepting menial tasks to avoid being trapped by constant changes of semi-skilled jobs. Janitorial jobs are at a premium . . . The car industry is setting the pace, where mobility, flexibility are a state of the art. At the same time, the monotony and boredom of screw driver assembly work is tremendous because the skills are so watered down (GMBATU).

In many cases the skills required to facilitate this job rotation have been acquired without the benefit of a formal training period. Though some companies operate a system of 'operator trainers' whereby workers are given an extra allowance when they teach another worker their own skills on the job, in many instances new skills are learnt by one operator teaching another with no formal recognition of this teaching role. In some instances this has led to disputes over payment. In this context, it is extremely difficult for workers acquiring new skills to obtain pay rises or regradings.

Although the indications are that flexibility amongst unskilled and semi-skilled workers is being imposed and not recognized, there are some examples where increased flexibility has been welcomed by trade unions as a progressive move in the interests of the health and safety of the workforce.

### 'Quality Foods'

'Quality Foods' is a small factory established 11 years ago employing approximately 200 workers which produces pre-cooked frozen meals for a large high street shopping chain. It used to be a small family concern but is now owned by a major food manufacturer.

All the workers belong to a single trade union, GMBATU, which organizes maintenance staff, stores and production workers, supervisors and their assistants. The majority of workers are women, though the maintenance staff are men. Amongst the production assistants the men do the heavy work, but otherwise there is complete transferability between jobs.

Up until five years ago, there had been clear job definitions and demarcation lines at the factory. Production workers worked on the track and there were also skilled chefs who cooked and checked quality. With the reorganization, the same production methods are being used, but the production-line workers are now doing part of the chefs' jobs as well. As a result, the skilled areas have been reduced, whilst production workers have taken on additional skills and have become more flexible. There is now total mobility between jobs.

The impetus for flexible working practices came, in this instance, not from an employer initiative but in response to health and safety problems. Much of the work involves the repetitious cutting, skinning and jointing of poultry in cold stores which caused tenosynovitis (TSV) and carpal tunnel syndrome. At one point 22 per cent of the workforce was unable to work because of arm complaints. The Volvo principle was initially applied as a means of rotating work so that workers on the day shift worked at their own speed on the entire process of preparing the poultry. This was eventually abandoned because even with increased job variety production-line workers were not moving on to other low risk jobs for TSV, such as packing. Furthermore, opposition developed to this method of working amongst the night-shift workers who were reported to have a different culture to the day-shift workers. As a result a system of complete flexibility of jobs, was developed so that workers rotated between 'high' and 'low'-risk jobs.

When the health risk was first identified the frying and packing areas were considered to be low-risk jobs. The cutting lines, which account for the main body of the factory, had quite a few high-risk jobs and some people could be boning off legs all day long in the cold rooms. Since there were too few low-risk jobs to put disabled people on, they reached an agreement with the firm that 10 places would be kept for TSV sufferers. Once they had 10 people on low-risk jobs on the frying and packaging lines if an eleventh or twelfth person went down with TSV, then the disabled person with the least amount of time in the company would leave. A physiotherapist comes in twice a week and decides with the people with arm complaints what they can and cannot do. For example, they might go home or they might go on a low-risk job. The arrangements for job rotation have to be strictly followed since prolonged periods on high-risk jobs are detrimental to healthy people. A consequence of this is that all production workers have to be able to do all jobs on the cutting line, and these are the most difficult jobs, as frying and packing are considered to be relatively easy.

To obtain this flexibility between jobs, training was required. There is a three-month training period for new workers with one month spent off the line. A training officer retrains existing staff if they feel they need updating on particular aspects of the work. Even before flexible working was introduced, workers were taught all the jobs on the line. Now, if a worker is off for more than four weeks, through industrial sickness or for another reason such as maternity leave, they have to undergo a rehabilitation programme, which eases them back into the line over a four-week period.

Currently, each rota lasts 40 minutes before jobs are changed around. Efforts have also been made to reduce the numbers of high-risk jobs through automation. For example, there is a machine which chops the chickens in half and takes the wings off and another which shapes the fillets. None of these innovations resulted in redundancy, though it is possible that new workers who might have been taken on, were not. More recently, the skinning job was mechanized, but its introduction, whilst reducing one risk, increased the risk on two other jobs and resulted in 18 cases of TSV.

Though the trade union initially welcomed the introduction of flexible working to solve the problem of wrist injuries, it effectively created another in the process. Job rotation reduced health risks on the production lines but the additional skills that the line workers took on have not resulted in increased pay. The only jobs which could be included in the rota were jobs which were more highly paid, but the company has refused to award them additional pay for taking on semi-skilled work. Although the range of job content has increased, from the trade union's perspective the result has been de-skilling.

In this example, flexibility presented no potential threat to inter-union relations since the entire workforce belonged to one trade union (GMBATU). However, on multi-union sites, changing job definitions, particularly where this involves workers becoming more transferable between different occupations, raises issues of spheres of influence and can place a strain on inter-union relations. It is not without significance that the major agreements on flexibility have been reached on greenfield sites and have often been combined with single union or single-site negotiations.

### Flexibility on Multi-union sites

It is first necessary to underline that flexibility in this area has several different meanings in practice and in its implications for trade union policy. Firstly, there is flexibility in the peripheral areas of a skilled trade, which may involve a fitter, for example, doing some minor electrical work or an electrician doing some of the fitter's job. In fact, developments in this area have been widespread and do not pose problems for trade unions organizationally. Moreover general unions and some of the craft unions, who would argue that their members have always been 'all rounders', would see it as a means of enhancing skills. So, despite employers' complaints of craft inflexibilities, there has been considerable movement in this area, and 'demarcation as it was understood and practiced in the 1950s and 1960s has long been fading away under the combined pressure of recession, new technology and competition' (IDS Report, 1986: 9). Changes in the peripheral areas of craft skills are very different to the major changes that are currently being called for and which are embodied in the concept of 'multi-skilling'. Otherwise known as 'skill exchange', 'third streaming' or 'dual trading', the jobs of distinctive crafts are rolled up together so that one craft worker can equally do the job of another trade. Compared to the concessions made in peripheral areas of craft skills, the impact of multi-skilling is more far-reaching, and there is greater dissonance between what it might mean for the skill content of individual jobs and its consequences for organizational identity. Significantly, in a country in which trade unions have organized on an occupational basis rather than by industry or political affiliation, multi-skilling opens up a hornet's nest of potential disputes by undermining the distinctive occupational basis of particular trade unions. This is as true where it affects relations between craft unions as it is between craft and general unions, which is particularly the case in the chemical industry where multi-skilling combines process and maintenance work.

### Trade Union Views on Multi-skilling

Multi-skilling is a prime example of an issue which at surface level appears to be about training and acquiring new skills, but which at a more profound level is about the changing organization of work and shifts in the balance of power between trade unions and the employers and in relations between trade unions. Before discussing the extent of its existence in the different industries, and trade union perceptions of its implications for their members and for themselves as organizations, it is first necessary to put multi-skilling in the context of the recession: the massive job losses which have occurred as companies have restructured, and the employer offensive against the trade unions which has been facilitated and supported by anti-union legislation introduced by the Tory government. Therefore, in this context, training which is likely to lead to vast increases in productivity, job losses and further erosion of trade union power, will be resisted.

> Flexibility is linked with the employers' offensive . . . the climate is wrong for discussing it . . . Their general attitude is that the unions are down, unemployment has cowed the workforce and they can put the boot in with impunity (GMBATU).

> New skills and new technology have to be used. The unions accept this, but they are concerned about the rate of introduction of new technology. The human element in production is becoming increasingly dispensable. Old activities are disappearing faster than new ones are generated . . . We fear that if it is not regulated then the future will be bleak for the job expectations of many people. This has resulted in the national unions' reluctance to take up a stance on multi-skilling because training means the elimination of the human element. Job losses in chemicals have been massive . . . This job reduction has coincided with the highest level of production ever. This indicates the extent of the problem in accommodating new training. The trade unions have been remarkably accommodating because their members are being dispossessed. Whereas business accepts every advance in technology because it has to compete for markets (AEU).

There is also a real fear that multi-skilling can lead to de-skilling, if it is not subject to joint regulation. This is evidenced in derogatory references to 'all-singing, all-dancing craftsmen', 'glorified handymen' and 'men for all seasons' expressed by many trade union officials. Although multi-skilling may require retraining, this does not necessarily mean that craft workers' existing range of skills will be fully utilized or that a deep knowledge will be acquired of the new skills. That is to say, multi-skilling is viewed as combining skills but on a shallow level. Some trade unions suggest that those claiming that it increases the skill content of jobs are doing a public relations job on behalf of their own members. This also happens where one trade union argues that its own members are more capable of taking on new skills than those of other trades. Multi-skilling has been resisted not just because it causes redundancies and represents an assault on trade union organization, but because it leads to de-skilling:

> Multi-skilling is not limited to retraining. Resistance to it is due to the craftsman's view that he wants to retain skill (not just craft pride) and multi-skilling is about de-skilling . . . The employers' associations wanted to impose multi-skilling, but so far this has not been taken up by employers. TASS would oppose the imposition

of multi-skilling since it has nothing to do with training and skills but with taking away the rights of workers (TASS).

Although multi-skilling poses a threat to an individual worker's skills through the possibility that it will lead to de-skilling, it also poses a threat to collective identity, by undermining the distinctive occupational basis of the different trade and craft unions. Though the development of multi-skilled workers on greenfield sites poses no direct threat to existing union organization on that site, since the workforce is a *tabula rasa* as far as inter-union relations are concerned, it nevertheless poses an indirect threat insofar as companies in the same economic sector are in competition with each other and must also take advantage of productivity gains from the introduction of multi-skilling. Where companies are introducing multi-skilling it is often accompanied by single-site or single-union agreements, which themselves cause problems for inter-union relations where sites are unionized. In other instances some trade and craft unions have lost negotiating rights even if they have not lost representational rights. Where formerly distinct jobs are combined, it poses problems of a different order. For example, if there are redundancies which categories of workers will be made redundant? When skills are combined, which categories of worker will show the greatest aptitude for acquiring the new skills and have preference for retraining? Which of the existing skills is most essential to the new production methods? Which are the most appropriate trade unions to represent the future workforce if some lose negotiating rights? Competition for members can increase conflicts between trade unions and opportunism, combined with a willingness to accept no-strike deals, increases divisions within the trade union movement as a whole.

> The changes didn't bother us in the past, but the new plant is more sophisticated and computer-controlled, and this resulted not so much in conflict but in abrasions with other unions which didn't exist before. This is intensified with unemployment and the recession. We are finding inter-union rivalry quite intense in many places and it is severely straining the sense of brotherhood in the movement . . . The employers' philosophy is one of pleasing the biggest groups rather than the smaller ones. In chemicals this means pleasing the process operators (AUEW).

Ideally, trade unions need to respond by acting together, by reaching agreement on spheres of influence and by amalgamation.

> It has been a significant move for the trade unions to accept some degree of skill-sharing between previously isolated crafts. Some unions are terrified of the prospects of going too far, not just

because of how it may affect their members' interests, but also how it will affect the future of the unions. These problems arise because we can't amalgamate as quickly as the rate of change is forced upon us (AUEW).

Of course, the trade unions are most likely to be able to sort out the division of the remaining jobs amongst themselves in a situation in which they are consulted about proposed changes and the modifications to jobs occur through a process of negotiation. However, evidence suggests that a number of employers have been trying to impose multi-skilling and agreements have been reached in several cases only under the threat of a partial or total closure of plants. This was the case in Shell Carrington, an example which will be reviewed in more detail shortly, and at Babcock Power's Renfrew works where agreement was eventually signed between management and the nine unions on the basis that if it was not agreed within 48 hours then 1000 people would be out of work (IDS, 1986: 4).

To what extent, therefore, is multi-skilling an issue in each of the industries within the remit of this project? It is a peripheral concern in construction where some small employers and local authorities have been pushing for it. Rather than rolling together different craft skills, new construction techniques and the use of specialist sub-contracting have been tending to break down existing craft skills into their component parts. Employers are indeed increasing the flexibility of the labour force in construction, but this is through increasing its contractual flexibility rather than through increasing the range of tasks performed by the different trades. This can largely be ascribed to the industry's continued dependence on craft skills and the variability of the labour process in site work (Campinos–Dubernet, 1985a and b). Multi-skilling is an issue for trade unions organizing in food processing, engineering and chemicals, though to differing degrees. Some trade unions argue that it will potentially affect all industries.

The extent to which trade unions perceive multi-skilling as an issue is a reflection of the distribution of their membership by industry and by occupation. In some sectors, e.g. petrochemicals, safety considerations mean that flexibilities in certain types of welding and jointing work are out of the question because they threaten standards of work. The extent to which multi-skilling become an issue is also a reflection of the extent to which flexibilities established with other trades (organized by other trade unions) are perceived as having potential to dilute skill or to dilute bargaining power *vis-à-vis* employers and other groups of workers. This was expressed in statements such as:

Blurred lines of demarcation have never been more relevant than they are now. We have to make sure that shop stewards don't sell their souls and the principles of the union. We mustn't allow unskilled people to perform skilled jobs. This is to protect the interests of the union as a whole (AUEW).

and

The aim of the employers is at de-skilling and to give part of our work to mechanical craftsmen to keep the peace . . . Some of the agreements haven't been to the long term advantage of our members so we are developing a policy to make sure that it doesn't lead to de-skilling but to the acquisition of increased skills (EETPU).

As a result, the numerical importance of a particular occupational category, its ability to take on new skills and the implications of this for grading structures take on a new salience.

There is, of course, a regional dimension to changes in working practices which it is not possible to develop here to any great extent due to the limitations of the project. Historical work on the definition of skilled work has shown that the bargaining strength of particular categories of worker within local labour markets have been crucial in determining skilled rates of pay (Wood, 1982) and anecdotal evidence collected in the course of fieldwork suggests that differences on a regional basis, for example, between large batch and small batch production, grading systems for different types of skills, the balance between production and maintenance work, could determine trade union responses to demands for increased flexibilities between trades.

Employers in a number of industries have been raising demands for multi-skilled craft workers particularly in the maintenance area (Cross, 1985). This is partly in response to the introduction of electronic control systems which mean that the nature of maintenance work requires more diagnostic skills, but it is also due to inefficiency in maintenance work, recognized by the trade unions themselves, where several trades perform different parts of the same repair job, involving considerable waiting around. Employers are seeking different solutions to this issue. One is for production workers to be increasingly involved in the day-to-day maintenance of machinery. A further solution is for different craft workers to be organized into teams which work together, thus decreasing waiting time. Finally, there is the possibility of creating multi-skilled maintenance craft workers. Though some craft unions argue that the cost of a five-year multi-skilled apprenticeship is not attractive to employers, there have nevertheless been changes in apprenticeship training which make it possible for workers to acquire limited skills in a number of different trades. The Engineering Industry Training Board for example, has recently broken down its module system into smaller components with a view to increasing employers' choice of combination of skills.

In the engineering industry, discussions have been held between the Engineering Employers' Federation and a sub-committee of the Confederation of Shipbuilding and Engineering Unions on working practices since November 1984. At the annual conference of the CSEU in June 1986, the sub-committee reported that negotiations would continue towards a specific framework of agreement at national level containing mutual concerns from either side to be implemented at domestic level as appropriate to the local circumstances of the establishment (IDS, 1986: 4). In return for a reduced working week, CSEU members were prepared to agree, in broad terms, to flexibility of labour and the efficient use of human resources, amongst other things, though the sub-committee itself does not have the authority to conclude an agreement and it would be subject to further discussion amongst the constituent trade unions. In the Midlands, it was reported that multi-skilling is 'bubbling on the surface, but hasn't really broken through in a big way yet' (EETPU). It is an issue characteristic of large companies rather than smaller ones and it is here that the employers themselves have created a division of labour which has resulted in demarcation lines between jobs. Though it has been fashionable to blame trade unions for demarcation boundaries, Incomes Data Services notes 'at Mars, which has no trade unions, the company found that many of the engineering demarcations which in other companies are often blamed on the AUEW were in fact operating. Management practice and older technical needs have combined to create demarcations, as much as trade unions protecting jobs' (1986: 10). In smaller companies people work in a different fashion and tend to be 'all-rounders'. In small jobbing shops, for example, everyone is on the same rates of pay and bonuses so the introduction of multi-skilling does not affect earnings in the same way as it does when it crosses the jobs of different grades of worker. Moreover, changes in working practices are more easily accommodated on an informal basis rather than through formal negotiating procedures at this level. At British Leyland, with the introduction of new technology at the 'New West' plant, two-trade maintenance work became a major managerial objective. Yet because of the strategic importance of the maintenance force, management considered the formal abolition of demarcations through negotiations to be a course of action that was too risky to take. Rather, a piecemeal erosion and redefinition of maintenance organization occurred through allocating different trades to on-line maintenance teams to particular machines. Scarbrough comments, 'The cleverness of two-trade allocation was that it employed the new technology of the BIW process as a mediating factor between formal demarcations and operating efficiency: the maintenance needs of the production process rather than trade job controls effectively determined the on-line workers' behaviour. It therefore eliminated the need for a direct confrontation over demarcations which a more formal approach might have required' (1984: 12). Not surprisingly, it was the experience of negotiations at British Leyland and Talbot, which prompted the EETPU to create a national vetting system for agreements on flexibility.

The majority of trade unions recognize that multi-skilling will be widely introduced in the future in the industries studied in this project but the extent to which it is perceived as imminent or as a threat depends on the industry and on its impact on inter-union relations. Whilst skill-sharing between crafts is occurring in the maintenance area in the food processing and engineering industries, as yet flexibilities between craft and non-craft workers are only being introduced in the chemical industry, and even so this is principally amongst the major companies. The Chemical Unions Council was reported as 'having their horns locked with the CIA and ICI over multi-skilling' in chemicals (TGWU) when interviews were conducted in 1985. The issue is not seen as being a straightforward adaptation of payment systems to increased skill levels through the introduction of new increments but a 'whole new ball game of rolling jobs together'. The trade union position was that major concessions must be granted if working practices were to change. This was expressed on a number of occasions by trade unions organizing in chemicals;

In the grey areas of flexibility the AUEW has a great deal of sympathy. For example, if a fitter takes off a valve, he slackens off four bolts and finds an electrical connection. He sends for the electrician. He slackens the screws and wires and then they need the rigger to lift things out. A welder then has to come . . . and there's a lot of waiting involved. If the fitter can take out an electrical element, do the rigging and burning, that's all right so long as it's within the scope of his capabilities. The same is true for an electrician. If they need a little bit of training then we would go along that route.

The other extreme is the all-singing, all-dancing craftsman – multi-skilling. We could see process people taking over part of skilled jobs and we would see this as de-skilling. You could argue that some parts of skilled jobs are not very skilled at all, but we view skill as a whole, not as a series of parts. The same is true of the manager's job (AUEW).

The potential increases in productivity are also recognized:

> The 'in' word of the 1960s was 'productivity'. Now it is 'multi-skilling' or 'skill-exchange' and even 'third-streaming'. They are rolling up jobs and training people so that, for example, an electrician and a fitter could do both jobs. The combination of existing jobs will do away with assistance. Process workers will repair machines, that means they will combine process and maintenance activities. The unions are not taking a Luddite approach but we take the view that new types of agreements are needed to enshrine these new ideas. These agreements need to reflect a substantial increase in earnings and rewards for acquiring expertise and training and putting them into practice in new types of jobs. We also want guarantees of no redundancies otherwise it will just be a demanning exercise (TGWU).

Though discussions have mainly taken place at national level, there are considerable pressures to enter negotiations at local level:

> Ultimately the employers are looking for craftsmen who are 'men for all seasons' but this has its limitations. This impinges on the GMB area. In the last five years employers have been seeking to bring changes whereby process workers would do maintenance work and where necessary a maintenance craftsman would be able to do some aspects of process work. Both have to have training. The GMB is not prepared to go along this road, but we are not burying our heads in the sand. Not until there has been a national agreement with ICI on multi-skilling will we allow there to be a local agreement (GMBATU).

Yet whilst national officers of all trade unions placed an embargo on local discussions with employers on multi-skilling there is tacit recognition that a national agreement is impossible given the implications for inter-union relations. Whilst the formal position of no local discussions is maintained, there is evidence that a number of companies have attempted to start them and it may be that some of the inter-union issues can only be resolved at plant level. Whether the national trade unions can rely on the employers not to overstep the mark, is a different issue. A similar situation exists in the food processing industry, where developments in flexible working amongst maintenance workers is proceeding on a plant by plant basis. However, the competitive pressures are not the same in food processing as those in chemicals.

## Multi-Skilling in Chemicals

In chemicals multi-skilling is a live issue and the trade unions have been under pressure for a number of years, both in national negotiations and at local level, to grant concessions on flexibility. The issue was brought to a head in the 1980s by conflict at Imperial Chemical Industries and by the setting up of the Shell/Esso gas liquids plant at Mossmorran, at which multi-skilling had been introduced through recruiting workers for jobs outside their main areas of competence. Whilst Mossmorran is a greenfield site and presents no inter-union problems as a result of abolishing existing demarcations or removing existing negotiating rights, it nevertheless raises issues of concern for the trade unions. Firstly, it was a non-unionized site and it was not yet clear whether the companies would retain this status or whether they would seek a single-union agreement. More importantly, because chemical companies compete in an international market in which other countries, for example Saudi Arabia, benefit from cheaper feedstocks, then increased productivity at one plant in the sector has ramifications for others which compete with it. Whilst the trade unions recognize that flexibility will spread to other plants in the industry in the coming years, they perceive the need to protect jobs, earnings and trade union recognition rights. They argue for changes in working practices through agreement rather than by imposition. The general trade unions, in particular may be in danger of being squeezed out of the industry by the raising of skill requirements (*Financial Times*, 27 December 1984). Multi-skilling in chemicals illustrates the industrial relations implications of training activity carried out in the name of 'up-skilling'.

The basic problem in this industry is that employers are seeking to introduce multi-skilling on a piecemeal basis through local level discussions with the trade unions rather than through a national agreement. ICI, for example, has been trying to introduce new working practices on the basis of the existing Weekly Staff Agreement, dating from 1969. The company claims that the agreement recognizes the continual need for changes in working arrangements as determined locally and after discussion on each site (*Financial Times*, 27 December 1984). However, the Signatory Unions Committee has placed an embargo on local discussions until national guidelines have been agreed for changing the existing wages structure and job evaluation scheme. The trade unions base their resistance on the fact that the existing agreement accepts that changes in working practices can only take place if all parties to the agreement agree them and this is not the case. The management argues that technological changes affect each plant differently. New working practices and changes in job definitions cannot be determined from a common starting point and need to develop gradually over a number of years at the local level. That is to say, they are not seeking a once-for-and-all change in working practices but to establish a basis for continual change. This situation is mirrored in negotiations with the Chemical Industries' Association, the employers' organization for the industry.

Despite the insistence of the national trade unions that no discussions should take place on new working practices at local level until national agreements have been reached, local officials have reported that their members are under considerable pressure at local level to enter discussions on multi-skilling. For example, in one instance, ICI plant supervisors had been invited to discuss the working practices of people working under them, though no concrete proposals had been put before them. In another ICI plant, de-manning and reorganization had resulted in a built-in requirement for temporary labourers and contractors. Some maintenance workers who had been displaced had been offered process work and this raised the suspicion that the company might be introducing multi-skilling through the backdoor, in the sense that someone with this background would be ideally placed to do a combination of process and maintenance work.

All the officials interviewed with responsibilities in the chemical industry considered that multi-skilling will eventually be introduced and thought that it would be brought in by agreement rather than imposed. They recognize that it is an issue in the 'majors' rather than in smaller companies, and that some employers are pushing vigorously in this area because they are forced to by economic circumstances. By contrast, 'the clever ones with no need to panic are watching what is happening and picking out the best' (ASTMS).

Of course the problem with a development which is likely to lead to job losses in opening up access to training and thus to skills which were previously claimed by specific occupational groups, is the potential it opens up for conflict over membership and spheres of influence. Particularly where employers are pushing for single-union or single-site agreements alongside changes in working practices, suspicion and distrust between trade unions may undermine solidarity between workers. This distrust has been expressed on a number of occasions; general unions viewed the motives of craft unions with suspicion; craft unions argued that their members in the maintenance area were better equipped to take in aspects of process workers' jobs than vice versa. Trade unions representing maintenance workers saw employers wanting to please process workers as the largest group in the industry and thought the opportunities presented to process workers to increase the skill content of their jobs might make them more willing to reach an agreement on working practices. By the same token, craft unions saw themselves in competition with each other for claiming multi-skilled workers as their own:

> The employers' philosophy is one of pleasing the biggest groups rather than the smaller ones and in chemicals this means the process operators. Normally you would find one maintenance worker to every three plant operators. In the new chemical plants more is being demanded of the general operators and they are using higher skills. The employers' reaction has been to pressurise craft unions to relinquish the more menial aspects of craft jobs to enlarge the process operators' jobs. This has been occurring at a quickening pace over the last fifteen years. The AUEW has been suggesting to employers that it is more sensible to train a craftsman with existing traditional skills to operate the plant he maintains than perpetuate existing conflicts and the upgrading of the operators (AUEW).

Since employers are testing the ground on multi-skilling and many officials perceived their membership to be under pressure to enter local level discussions on multi-skilling, it seems appropriate to examine in detail the agreement reached at Shell Carrington.

## Shell Carrington

'A working culture turned on its head' was how the *Financial Times* described the agreement signed in July 1985 at Shell Carrington. In the context of threatened closure of the plant an agreement was eventually reached whereby the 1250 strong workforce was reduced to 480 and literally every demarcation was 'swept away' with the introduction of new working practices and a massive training programme for those being retained. Though the trade unions had no negotiating role in the agreement, they eventually signed it. As the *Financial Times* points out, the changes in working practices are not, in themselves, novel. What distinguishes Shell Carrington from Mossmorran where similar practices have been introduced is the fact that 'flexibility far beyond the more common limited flexibility within craft groups has been brought into a relatively old British manufacturing site with a deep-rooted, tough and sophisticated, though non-militant, union culture' (*Financial Times*, 7 August 1985). A TGWU official commented that if Mossmorran, a greenfield site, is equivalent to developments at the Rupert Murdoch's *News International* plant at Wapping in the printing industry but on a larger scale, then the significance of introducing new working practices at Shell Carrington is 'as if Murdoch had got a breakthrough on Fleet street with the EETPU doing SOGAT jobs'. The Carrington Technicians' Agreement, which ran for 18 months from October 1985 meant that all non-management jobs would be incorporated into a new single-status technician structure. Teams of technicians operate and maintain the four plants on the site alternating between four months on shift work and two months on maintenance work. Though some specialists remain, for example, on computers and pumping equipment, the company expects every plant technician to be sufficiently skilled to perform 80 per cent of craft work across traditional craft trades. By completing two skill modules, over a period of 12 to 18 months, technicians will be promoted to a senior technician category. The only limitation to performing a job will be where the skills required are outside the individual's competence or where safety considerations require specialist skills (IDS, 1986: 41).

Restructuring at Carrington has involved a changeover from a three- to a two-tier structure of the workforce. Formerly, it was made up of the following occupations: production operatives, craft operatives, a middle layer of staff including administrators, clerks, typists, accounts department staff. On the technical side there were laboratory technicians and drawing-room staff plus the supervisory staff who made up the interface between the management and the shopfloor. Management consisted of chemists, accountants, the personnel department and senior management. The new structure has involved the merging of the middle and bottom tiers of the workforce. The tip of the white-collar work has gone into management whilst the remainder has become single-status technicians, who include the shopfloor. This was facilitated by changes in recent years in management structure. Functional divisions, for example, between engineering maintenance, project and technical services departments and special administrative services were simplified as a precursor to changing the structure of work tasks on the shopfloor.

What were the conditions for the introduction of flexible working practices at Shell? Firstly, the plant was under threat of closure and, a trade union official commented, 'in these days of complete plant closure, to save one-third of the workforce seemed an achievement' (TGWU). Secondly, Shell was prepared to buy the workforce out of its former practices and Carrington technicians now have the highest rates of pay of any industrial workers in Britain. There were three salary scales in 1985; Scale I starting at £14,000 per annum, Scale II at £17,000 and Scale III at £20,000 for a 37-hour-week. Thirdly, redundancy terms were generous for those made redundant and furthermore, a redeployment unit was set up with a trade union resource of six full-time shop stewards and four managers working on an unlimited budget for 18 months. The TGWU *Herald* reported in September 1986 that 85 per cent of the 500 workers made redundant had been found jobs through the redeployment unit, partly through the advertising of their skills and partly through the collation of job vacancy data. Retraining had also formed an arm of the redeployment strategy whilst placements overseas in the chemical industry in Saudi Arabia had been particularly successful.

As far as training is concerned a modular training programme has been undertaken on-site with the co-operation of local technical colleges. Workers can now obtain certificates of competence in mechanical and electrical skills. There are also two- and three-day modules that can be taken in the basics of rigging, pipe fitting, mechanical fitting, instrumentation electrical work, lagging and forklift truck driving. The Chemical Industries' Association and the City and Guilds of London Institute (CGLI) have collaborated to produce a new chemical technician certificate, which is a halfway house between a mechanical qualification and process operator training. This certificate may link in to more advanced qualifications at a later stage.

The homogenization of working culture, brought about through extensive training programmes has nevertheless brought with it important modifications to the concept of 'tenancy rights' to jobs.

> The Company explained that each job in the new Carrington had been assessed to determine the extent to which it was fundamentally the same or different from a position in the old structure. The vast majority of the jobs were fundamentally different and therefore no employee had any 'tenancy rights' to fill them. Everyone on site was eligible for these *new* jobs and the Company intended to appoint people on the basis of the best person for the job (IDS, 1986: 41).

Since technically, after retraining, any shopfloor worker will be capable of doing any job, management can afford to choose people in a redundancy situation on the basis of criteria such as enthusiasm for the job and work discipline rather than training in a specific trade. In practice, during the redundancy exercise, workers were asked to vote on the package before they knew if they would be retained or not and no one group of workers had greater claims to retention than others on the basis of existing skills.

If these have been the conditions for the introduction of multi-skilling in a plant with a tradition of trade union organization, what then, have been the results for the workforce? For individuals, certain benefits have been attained; pay has been increased, there is an extended guarantee of job security, new skills are being acquired. Yet for the trade unions the removal of all demarcations and the ending of separate collective agreements has ramifications for them as organizations which have yet to be fully tested. There is now only one site agreement for the trade unions which retain negotiating rights, though in the process three of the seven trade unions which formerly had them have lost them. Naturally, there is bitterness amongst trade unions which have lost negotiating rights, as well as potential problems ahead for those that have retained them.

> They are all in one melting pot. Agreement exists but normal demarcation lines have been taken away and everyone can be a member of any of these four unions. This has really put the cat amongst the pigeons . . . The temptation is for each union to say they're the appropriate union . . . The problem for the unions is sorting out the population that remains (ASTMS).

If there is, indeed, a more exciting future ahead for individual technicians without the artificial constraints of craft barriers, then for trade unions as collective organizations the problems posed relate to spheres of influence over the remaining, homogeneous and inter- changeable workforce.


**Trade Union Response to Multi-skilling**

The trade union position in national negotiations with the CIA and ICI has already been outlined in an earlier section. If Mossmorran was a first off in the chemical industry for the introduction of new working practices on a greenfield site, then the significance of Shell Carrington, must be as a learning exercise in how to approach new working practices in a multi-union site for the trade union movement as a whole. Shell, as argued earlier, has been forced to experiment with new working practices, by economic circumstances. Other companies whose situation is more stable can afford to watch developments and learn from experience. Trade union officials reported that in early 1986 representa- tives from companies throughout the chemical industry had been taking a keen interest in Shell and had been on visits to the site.

Largely because of pressure in the majors, but particularly in ICI where the company is trying to push through local discussions on the basis of the existing Weekly Staffs Agreement, shop stewards have been demanding training from their full-time officials in the concepts employers have been using. As a result, a number of one-day courses have been run on trade union responses to employer initiatives on flexibility. The TGWU, in particular, has been arguing that trade unions should not believe that employers will stop making demands for flexible working if they are resisted and recommend that suggestions should be tested out and examined in detail. This needs to be done in full co-operation between process and craft unions. The existence of flexibilities within the craft maintenance force through productivity deals and concessions on pay is viewed as a precondition for further developments towards full-scale flexibility between craft and process work.

If the employers are watching developments within the industry on flexible working practices, then the trade unions would be wise to do likewise. In early 1986 BP Chemicals in Grangemouth was widely anticipated to be the next site of a major flexibility agreement and in the summer of that year agreements were concluded with the TGWU, craft and staff bargaining groups on a two-year pay and productivity deal leading to a reduction in demarcations, group working arrangements and 300 job losses. Central to the agreement was the widening of job tasks through an extensive programme of training whereby process workers would undertake some maintenance work and craft workers would undertake some process work. The company argued that the main principle of the training was to expand 'principal jobs' rather than to create an all purpose refinery worker through a three-stage skill development programme linked to pay increases (IDS, 1986: 3). A corollary of increased skill levels and flexible team working amongst the directly employed workforce was the contracting out of ancillary functions, namely cleaning and gardening, with no limitations on the contractors working patterns and a commitment by all employees to co-operate with the contractors.

## Conclusion

In this chapter, measures leading to the increased flexibility of the labour force have been examined, with particular reference to their implications for training. Three major developments have been noted; increased use of casual forms of labour, flexibility between tasks achieved through training and flexibility between tasks achieved without training. Whilst casualization is perceived as a threat to trade union organization and conditions of employment, this is rarely articulated as an issue relating to job design, de-skilling or training. The problem therefore, is one of organizing casual workers or seeking, through trade union action or political means, methods of improving their conditions. In contrast, where flexibility affects direct employees who are trade union members, it is not simply an issue concerning skills, with or without access to training, but one which relates directly to trade union organization itself. Training, therefore, is not a neutral phenomenon with an unambiguous outcome. On the contrary, it is introduced into existing sets of social relations. It concerns collectivities of workers, who may be organized in different trade unions. It is subject to negotiation not only between workers and management, but between different groups of workers. Therefore, major initiatives in increasing the flexibility of the labour force, particularly where this involves the removal of demarcations are viewed cautiously since they involve increases in productivity, on the one hand and job losses, on the other. The evidence presented suggests that as yet, full-scale multi-skilling across trades has only been achieved in sectors of the chemical industry, involving major investment in retraining. Increased flexibilities have been achieved by employers in food processing and engineering across a range of grades though not necessarily by means of formal training programmes which make explicit the acquisition of new skills.

Many trade union officials reported casualization, job losses and de-skilling rather than the existence of training programmes enhancing skills. Employment legislation, aimed at reducing workers' rights, is unlikely to result in increased security of employment and employers' investment in skill training. On the contrary, disposability of labour is based on the assumption of low-level skills and low discretion jobs which may have implications for the way in which goods are produced and their quality. It may be realistic either to assume that training for these jobs is non-existent, or to expect that it will be provided by the state through the education service or by training schemes. In this case, real skill training can scarcely be expected since this is a preparation for employment in a specific job. On the contrary, low-level skills and socialization into the work ethic are more in order.

# 5

# Training as a Policy Issue

## Introduction

Trade unions in general are supportive of training for their members since it opens up opportunities for making jobs more interesting, improving pay and increasing the bargaining power of labour. Whilst some unions, particularly the craft unions have long had a tradition of organizing around skills training, this is not the case for unions organizing in non-craft occupations. This may be because qualifications are received through the general education system or are not subject to collective bargaining, as in the case of the white-collar unions or because historically little training has been provided in the grades in which they organize, as in the case of the general unions.

In Chapter 2 the industrial relations agenda of the Youth Training Scheme was discussed and, in particular, how it interacts with existing training arrangements in each sector. In order to understand the dynamics of training policy, it is useful to make a distinction between the quality and content of training and how these may be negotiated through the institutional structures of training, and bodies which are concerned with their ramifications for wages and conditions of employment. In her study of print workers, Cockburn differentiates between struggle about skill and its value. She argues, ' (t)here may be collective struggle *over* skill, but it is not necessarily *about* skill. It is about the value of labour power and control over production' (1983: 121). The more closely that skills learnt through training are related to collective bargaining over pay and conditions and the claiming of particular types of work, the more likely it is that policies towards training will be coherent.

The extent to which trade unions effectively and coherently represent their interests on different training bodies is largely a reflection of the occupational categories they organize and the organizational structure of the trade union itself. These dimensions are set out in table 5.1. Though many of these dimensions are the same regardless of the policy

TABLE 5.1
Factors Affecting the Representation
of Training Interests

1. *Coherence of strategy*

| | |
|---|---|
| centralization of decision-making | devolution |
| homogeneity of membership | heterogeneity |
| specialization of training policy function | generalization |

2. *Relevance of representation of interests*

| | |
|---|---|
| formal training period | informal or no training |
| transferable skills | firm-specific skills |

issue, the question of the type of qualifications required for entry into occupations is of particular salience to training policy since trade union memberships are differentiated according to the length and types of training members receive on entry into an occupation.

From the table it is possible to hypothesize that, for example, craft unions with a centralized decision-making structure and a relatively homogeneous membership would have greater coherence in policy towards training than a general, multi-industrial union with a devolved decision-making structure serving a heterogeneous membership. The type of training received on entry into employment – formal or informal in transferable or firm-specific skills – affects the relevance of participation in different bodies and the extent to which accountability and the communication of decisions is significant to the membership at large. These distinctions do not imply that general and craft unions have totally different approaches to training policy, since the process of amalgamations between trade unions means that unskilled, semi-skilled and skilled workers are to be found in them all. However, the formulation of a coherent training policy is more likely where trade unions or sections within them represent relatively homogeneous occupational groups and where these groups undergo formal training to obtain their skills. This is more likely where skills are transferable than where they are specific to the firm. The position of white-collar unions is slightly different since although their members may have relatively skilled and/or well-paid jobs, their qualifications may be obtained through the general education system as well as through training in industry.

The coherence of training policy is also affected by linkages between curricula and qualifications negotiated in training bodies and the wage bargaining structure. This relationship is particularly important where completion of recognized training courses or periods of training triggers increments in wages. Under the traditional apprenticeship arrangements, new wage rates were triggered off by completion of the apprenticeship period. This has now been modified by the acceptance of trade unions that adult wage rates will be awarded to apprentices when they pass skills tests on the completion of training.

Having outlined the factors which affect the occupational labour markets in which trade unions operate and attempt to control through different strategies, it is most appropriate to consider each of the nine trade unions in turn. It should be stressed that the trade unions interviewed do not just organize in the four industries covered in this project, but others as well and whilst the information presented here will be true for these industries, there may be considerable variations in other industries with different employment structures, methods of work organization and training infrastructures. Furthermore, it is acknowledged that the process of amalgamation between trade unions has resulted in the incorporation of smaller craft unions and white collar sections into general and multi-industrial unions, and that the craft unions themselves have opened membership to non-craft workers. Consequently, this account does not discount the fact that sections or trade groups within some of the trade unions concerned do not organize on the same basis as is indicated here, which will reflect employment conditions and the state of the labour market in those sectors.

## ASTMS

This inquiry was concerned with ASTMS policies in the food processing and chemical industries. In general ASTMS is not concerned with work-related industrial training since the majority of its members are managers who, once trained, are generally not retrained though they do tend to be sent on refresher courses to update their knowledge. Though the trade union has its own training college at Bishops Stortford, this is concerned primarily with industrial relations training for activists and stewards and not industrial training. Industrial training does concern ASTMS and it has a longstanding interest in it but not as an issue directly affecting its own membership except those who are trainers and training advisers themselves. As a consequence training is not a separate policy area with clearly defined responsibilities. Each national officer has responsibility for a specific industry and training may come into this general responsibility.

This does not mean that ASTMS does not have or historically has not represented its interests on training bodies. The trade union had seats on FDTITB and on CAPITB before they were abolished and is currently represented on the non-statutory training organizations in chemicals and food processing, CAITREC and FMCIT, by national officers with responsibility for these industries. However, it was reported that policy objectives on training are reached through informal consultation with colleagues in different industries rather than through formal policy-making structures. As one national officer put it, 'it was all *ad hoc* and not formalised'.

In general, policy is formulated through the Annual Delegate Conference. The trade union holds national policy positions, for example, it is opposed to the low level of trainee allowance on YTS and so it supports a policy of 'topping up' to normal youth wage rates. Despite this, YTS does not impact on ASTMS members in the same way as it does on other trade unions, since it does not affect them directly. Their members who are trainers try in managerial terms to improve the position of the trainees, with emphasis on obtaining full-time employment for the trainees after the completion of the training period.

ASTMS opposed the closure of the ITBs from both the point of view of the effect it would have on training and from the point of view of defending their members who worked on the staff of the ITBs (there were ASTMS members on all of them apart form the Distributive ITB). The trade union perceives the closure of the ITBs in food processing to have resulted in training taking place on a company by company basis and not on an industrial basis. Companies train for their own needs and their are no cross-industry modules which set standards or have validity outside individual companies. The trade union takes the view that the heterogeneity of the industry was a strong argument for retention and sees training activity as having been splintered by the closure of the ITBs, and most of the NSTOs as ineffective and underfunded. ASTMS has a seat on FMCIT, which is considered to be the only active NSTO in the food industry and the only one to welcome trade union participation. The view is that in food processing the government's criteria for abolition had not been met (i.e. that satisfactory voluntary arrangements did not exist prior to the winding up of the ITBs) and that the decision to abolish, though phrased in terms of the bureaucratic inefficiency of the Boards, was based on political opposition to state interference in industry and the government's support for a return to the operation of market forces in training matters. ASTMS believes that a series of statements by the MSC and at the CBI conference at Harrogate indicate that there is dissatisfaction with voluntary methods and that statements by Sir Richard O'Brien indicate that a return to more formal methods of ensuring training takes place are on the agenda.

When the FDTITB was closed down the trade unions on the Food and Drink Economic Development Committee of NEDO pressed for an EDC monitoring role over training arrangements. This led to the setting up of a committee of employers and trade unions to monitor arrangements for training, though the papers were restricted to members. It was opposed by some employers' associations but was supported by some major companies. This Employment and Training Committee produced a document on productivity and the need for greater competitiveness in the period preceding the winding up of the ITBs. The trade union side took the position that their members should not be involved in accepting measures to increase productivity unless there was a reasonable set of rules, a 'code of practice', on job security which could be adopted by trade unions, employers and the government. This resulted in the publiction of a document 'Code of Conduct on Employment Security', in 1984 which lays down that there should be adequate notice of lay-offs and opportunities for retraining to counteract productivity gains made to the employers' benefit. Interviews at local level indicated that agreements on job security with clauses on retraining of workers in ASTMS grades had been successfully negotiated with some major companies.

In chemicals, it is harder to obtain a national overview of trade union policy on training which is partly a reflection of the closure of CAPITB, partly a reflection of the policy of decentralization of training activities actively pursued by employers in the chemical industry. This is a function of the local self-help groups, or Chemical Industry Training Organizations (CITOs) set up by the NSTOs of the chemical industry employers' associations – principally those of the Chemical Industries' Association, the Association of the British Pharmaceutical Industry and the Proprietary Association of Great Britain under the umbrella of the Chemical Industries' Training Review Council (CAITREC) – and the employers' strategy of seeking changes in working practices through local agreement rather than through national negotiations. Though ASTMS has a seat on CAITREC, at the time of field work the national officer nominated had not yet attended a meeting and was unable to report a view on its effectiveness. As in the food and drink industry, the plant or company bargaining unit culture of the trade union and the fact that jobs are not comparable across industry combine to make training a plant or company issue. It does not constitute a policy area which is generalizable across the industry.

## AUEW/TASS

TASS is a trade union which, since its origin as the Association of Engineering and Shipbuilding Draughtsmen in 1913, has had a high profile on training and has had a history of supplying technical notes to its membership to enable them to increase their skills. It recognizes that a skilled membership increases its collective bargaining power by virtue of the skills it controls as well as the individual's ability to improve job security and career prospects. The trade union takes the view that skills of the labour force constitute an important national resource. This perspective is illustrated in documentation issued at the time of the Westland crisis in early 1986 when the national position (not, incidently, supported by the Westland workers themselves, see Overbeek, 1986) was that the European bid for the helicopter company should be supported on the grounds that skilled workers and technical expertise would be best safeguarded by retaining European rather than US control of the company (TASS, nd.).

TASS policy towards training is in line with the trade union's general policies which place it on the Left of the trade union movement, which are supportive of state intervention in industry, selective import controls, the growth of industrial democracy and a strong role for the trade union movement in both economic planning and training policy. This political orientation is evident on a wide range of policy issues, and extends to the removal of professional barriers to job progression, support for equal opportunities policies and a recognition of the need to unify the trade union movement across traditional barriers between craft, general and white-collar grades as indicated in its claim to be the trade union 'for all staff in the engineering and allied industries and services'. Though in practice this aim has not been achieved as amalgamation with the AUEW was called off in 1985 it has been the basis for a series of amalgamations with a number of smaller craft unions since 1981 (see *Financial Times*, 29 May 1985). In 1986 and 1987 discussions were under way on amalgamation with ASTMS (*Financial Times* 11 March 1987, 16 April 1987; *The Guardian*, 8 May 1987) which had the potential to create a major political bloc on the Left of the trade union movement as opposed to one based merely on industrial sector.

The significance of training to the wider political and industrial policies of TASS is clearly stated in Ken Gill's introduction to the pamphlet 'TASS on Training':

Every trade union is interested in the training of its members and future members. For TASS, however, training has always been of very special concern. As the Technical, Administrative and Supervisory Section of the Engineering Union, the pay and status of our members is to a large extent directly determined by the acquisition of skills and knowledge. This in turn depends on what is available to them. Since its inception in 1913, TASS has organized not only trainees but also trainers and has itself devoted substantial financial and human resources to the dissemination of technical information to its members. In recent years, TASS's growing female membership has reinforced and augmented its campaign for real equal opportunity for women in careers in engineering. As higher and higher placed engineers have come into TASS membership, TASS has become more and more involved in breaking down the archaic attitudes prevailing in top British management and in the engineering institutions which prevent the full development and promotion of engineering workers from the 'shop floor' to the very top. Most importantly the existence and progress of TASS depends upon a healthy British economy and a healthy British engineering industry – both of which depend in part upon the quantity and quality of real training in Britain. That is why, at a time of real crisis for training and an unprecedented degree of misleading by Government, TASS offers its analysis and views for the future. We have a right to be heard. (TASS, 1982: Preface).

Arising from its general political outlook as well as its organizational base in the engineering industry (arguably the key to the health of manufacturing industry in general) TASS policy on training is both coherent and comprehensive. A full statement of policy on training has been made in the publication 'TASS on Training', the main arguments of which can be summarized as;

1. Employers train for their own needs and statutory training boards are essential to develop the quantity and quality of training required in the national interest. Unions have a major role to play in training policy and implementation at all levels.
2. British training inferiority is due to lack of resources devoted to training.
3. Even with high levels of unemployment there are skills short-ages. Skills bottlenecks can be expected especially in sections of engineering introducing new technologies when the economy comes out of the recession.
4. Labour force planning and economic intervention are essential to the full utilisation of the nation's human resources and require training to be organised on an industrial basis.
5. Training should be a continuous process with no artificial barriers to progression.
6. Positive action is required to eliminate discrimination.
7. Trainees must not be used as a cheap labour substitute.

8. The State must guarantee the completion of apprenticeship training.
9. Trade union education should form part of vocational preparation and training.
10. Training is needed in managerial, supervisory and commercial skills.
11. The training systems of other countries, including Scandinavia and the socialist bloc should be studied, recognising that each system has developed out of a distinctive industrial culture, with the priority of catching up with the resources devoted to industrial training elsewhere.
12. TASS supports the TUC's policy of 'Training For All' but regards the Youth Training Scheme as 'work preparation for all' and should not be considered as the basis for the future industrial needs of the nation (TASS, 1982: 3).

TASS is categorical that the cause of high unemployment and the crisis in the training system lies in lack of investment in industry and in human resources and not in the inadequacies of the training system as it existed prior to the abolition of the ITBs. It argues:

> Never before has there been so much talk about training – and so little constructive action. Education may – if the nation can afford it – be an end in itself. Vocational training is not. Memorising the Latin verses of Horace may possibly beautify one's life. Learning coil winding theory is only beneficial if one is going to make use of it to earn a living . . . Whilst a small percentage of the UK's obscene level of unemployment may be due to training inadequacies, training – of itself – is not a cure for unemployment. Full employment will only be created by the correct economic policies, by investment, by manpower planning, by creativity and by skilled, enterprising and progressive management in both public and private sectors. People can be trained for these functions but training alone will not produce them. (TASS, 1982: 4).

Whilst TASS welcomes the Youth Training Scheme like it did the Training Opportunities Scheme before it as a measure for getting young unemployed men and women off the streets, it does not view it as providing industrial training:

> TASS welcomes any measure which, even temporarily, cuts unemployment and helps prepare young people for work but neither YOP nor YTS can make any significant contribution to the development of the operators, technicians, technologists and

administrative staff which the UK will need in the 21at century – if Britain is to survive as an industrial nation. To allocate one billion pounds per annum to such schemes and call it money spent on training is downright misleading (TASS, 1982: 4).

This view was echoed in interviews:

> YTS is a fraud on young people which is mainly concerned with massaging the unemployment total. This is not the view of the TUC but TASS lost the argument in the TUC and has to go along with its policy . . . Our subjective view on the quality of YTS is that it is inferior to a year's apprenticeship training which it is supposed to be exempted from. The MSC knows this but there is a conspiracy of silence. EITB sought differential funding for engineering YTS but the Government and the MSC refused it. This sets the seal on the inadequacy of the two year YTS . . . On YTS we go along with EITB attitudes reluctantly, so do the employers. Both realise that YTS is an inadequate level of funding (TASS).

Eric Winterbottom, former deputy General Secretary of TASS has forcefully voiced the trade union's overall view of the New Training Initiative in the following terms:

> The Government's New Training Initiative is a bogus prospectus. It requires superhuman gullibility to accept it as a genuine attempt to improve training provision in the country . . . the government's so-called training strategy is nothing more than industrial relations gerrymandering, involving an attack on wage levels for young workers; the curtailment of skills training to the narrowly perceived needs of the employer; an attempt to absolve employers from contractual obligations and the observance of agreements; the exclusion of trade unions from the defence of young workers' rights; and a further unscrupulous 'cooking up' of unemployment statistics (Greater London Training Board, 1984: 17).

In publications the government's support for employer-led training has received searing criticism:

> Adult training is a joke because there is none being done. The closure of the Skillcentres was a move in this direction. By saying that employers should determine adult training means none will be done and everyone knows this. Who is the government trying to kid? Some forward thinking employers are thinking about adult training but the majority find it cheaper to poach. TASS condemns the MSC for going through the motions on adult training (TASS).

and

> Trade unions have a vital role to play in the formation of training policy and practice. Those employers who do train (unfortunately a declining number) seek to train *for their own needs*. Trade unionists, on the other hand, want their members' training to be as broad as possible to enable them to get promotion or to get jobs in other firms and in other technologies (TASS, 1982: 4).

TASS is strongly supportive of apprenticeship, notably the modular training system of the EITB established since 1966 which forms part of the accepted training system for both craft and technician apprenticeships. It has been highly critical of the 'wilful ignorance' of the nature of modern apprenticeship shown by many politicans and media commentators in discussions around the New Training Initiative. It made a major contribution to the report 'Outlook on Training' prepared by the TUC/CBI/ITB Review Body through the participation of Ken Gill, TASS General Secretary. This laid the basis for the New Training Initiative, published in May 1981. 'TASS on Training' describes the series of events leading up to the decision to abolish the ITBs in the following terms:

> These documents initiated a massive consultation exercise with TASS and other unions, employers, educationalists, local authorities, etc. Carefully drafted written and verbal evidence was produced, all of which has been largely ignored by Mr. Norman Tebbit who became Secretary of State for Employment in September 1981 . . . Meantime, a quango-bashing campaign had been launched in the media, largely directed against ITBs. A most irresponsible document *ITBs: Why They Should Be Abolished?* was issued by the Conservative Party's Centre for Policy Studies. Although disowned by employers, its theme that trade unions and the state should play no part in training persists as part of British reactionary culture . . . (TASS, 1982: 6).

TASS's own position strongly critical of the unilateral determination of engineering training by employers, arguing for a strong trade union role. This is argued not just on the basis that employers' train for short-term needs, which invariably fall short of industry-wide requirements and that they train in firm-specific skills rather than transferable skills, but also on the basis that trade unions themselves are repositaries of considerable expertise which has a major contribution to make towards the definition of training objectives.

The wide social and political perspectives of a trade union such as TASS enable it to make special contributions in the Training field.

Examples include TASS's membership of tripartite bodies such as ITBs, MSC, Equal Opportunities Commission, Commission for Racial Equality and local and regional committees, as well as trade union based associations like the Confederation of Shipbuilding and engineering Unions, Trades Councils, TUC and its regional committees, European Metalworkers Federation, International Metalworkers Federation, ICFTU and WFTU, the Labour Party at all levels, etc. (TASS, 1982: 13)

In fact, TASS has engaged in a range of training interventions on the basis of which it claims to have successfully recruited into membership many thousands of men and women (1982: 12). These include the evidence it submitted to the Committee of Inquiry into the Engineering Profession, 1979–1980, chaired by Sir Monty Finniston (the Finniston Report), in which it argued for an integrated framework of education and training for all levels of worker within the engineering industry, from manual apprentice to chartered engineer. It has addressed itself directly to the longstanding concern with the low status and pay of professional engineers in British companies (TASS *Electronics Bulletin*, No. 2 nd) arguing that strong collective organization of professional and technician engineers is the only way to win improved salaries and status rather than a statutory Engineering authority recommended by the Finniston Committee (Eaton and Gill, 1983: 118). Furthermore, it has linked the low status of engineering as a career to artificial professional barriers to employee development. It has expressed particular concern for opening up opportunities for women in engineering through training, publishing 'Negotiating for Equal Opportunity for Training' in January 1979 which was subsequently incorporated into 'New Technology: a Guide for Negotiators' (TASS, 1982: 13). It maintains that trade unions themselves have a vested interest in the promotion of managerial and supervisory training:

> Contrary to the image portrayed by the media, collective bargaining exists for the avoidance of costly strikes, though the right to strike is essential to the defence and advancement of employees' conditions. Many strikes, however, are actually caused by the lack of managerial competence on industrial relations matters. Too many managers – and TASS has many thousands of managers in membership – are appointed without any preparatory training whatsoever, least of all in industrial relations (TASS, 1982: 13)

The coherence of TASS training policy relates, on the one hand to its concentration of membership in the engineering industry and its historical development as a trade union organizing skilled technical and design workers. Furthermore, its political outlook, which leads it to argue for import controls, government support for research and development, industrial democracy in firms and a central role for trade unions in economic policy, is based on a positive evaluation of the skills of the workforce as a major national resource. This leads it to differentiate sharply between industrial training and schemes for the unemployed, and to perceive that the collective bargaining issues concerning training are concerned primarily with conditions of employment during training.

TASS was strongly critical of the proposals to abolish the ITBs and at the 1981 CSEU conference, registered its total opposition to closure. It also argued for the retention of the industrial training committees serving the members of affiliated trade unions. It has also criticised cuts in UGC funding to technological universities (AUEW/TASS *News and Journal*, August 1981). When the decision to abolish the ITBs was announced, TASS Deputy General Secretary, Eric Winterbottom commented, 'the EITB may have escaped the axe, but the government intends to use the garotte instead by cutting off its funding of operating costs from March next year. Mr Tebbit clearly puts quango-bashing and penny-pinching above the need to catch up with our competitors in vocational training and education (AUEW/TASS *News and Journal*, December 1981: 6).

Despite the government's decision to retain EITB, it continued to be under threat from employers' associations and individual large employers. At the end of 1983, 13 large engineering companies including Ford, Plessey, GEC and Vickers approached the Secretary of State to argue the case for abolition. Though the Engineering Employers' Federation did not join this call it did set out detailed recommendations for the reform of the Board, which were subsequently accepted and which resulted in EITB giving greater emphasis to training in new technology skills and the recruitment of more specialist staff. This change in emphasis was welcomed by TASS, amongst other trade unions with seats on the EITB board, with TASS claiming that it had been pursuing these types of reforms for years, and that the failure of EITB to diversify its programme beyond craft and technician training had been due to employer opposition.

In summary, TASS is vocal in its support for industrial training, especially in high technology skills, and views its interventions on training as a major strategy for recruitment amongst workers in a wide range of occupations within engineering. Its commitment to new technology training has been demonstrated in the setting up of an Electronics Panel within the trade union in 1985 and the publication of an Electronics Bulletin. It has been quick to highlight underinvestment in the skills of the technical workforce, lack of government support for research and development, and higher education, as well as the disincentives to technical training created by the low pay and status of the engineering profession. Ken Gill, the General Secretary has argued, 'training and retraining should be regarded as a fixed overhead, like paying the rates . . . (engineers) are especially important as new technology changes the face of our industries. Engineers are a precious national asset, and it is economic madess to ignore their educational needs' (AUEW/TASS *News and Journal*, March 1985: 1).

Not surprisingly, the the designation of responsibilities for training within the trade union reflect the priority attached to it as a policy issue. There are officers with specific responsibilities for training, both within the main section of the trade union and in the craft sectors, based on the training concerns of the craft unions which have amalgamated with TASS since 1981. However, inside the union, interests are organized through industry committees rather than through the different sectors. In early 1986 the first meeting of the Heating and Ventilating Advisory Committee was held and proposals were afoot to set up similar arrangements for engineering construction and offshore construction as well (though the latter presents considerable organizational problems given the dispersion of the industry and transience of the labour force).

In the main section of the union an Assistant Secretary has responsibility for training and has a seat on the board of the Engineering Industry Training Board. There are three committees dealing with training: the Youth Committee, concerning the recipients of training, the Industry Committee, which is concerned with policy attitudes, and the Technical Committee which is concerned with the detailed content of training. Policy on training is formulated formally by the annual Representative Council. In addition to the Assistant Secretary, the National Secretary for the Patternmakers' craft sector has a seat on the board of EITB, and the National Officer for the heating and ventilating craft sector has a seat on CITB. The trade union is also involved through the lower levels of the committee structures of the ITBs. Seats are also held on the voluntary Shipbuilding Training Agency though the structure is more like that of a local association than a national body. At the time of interviewing, seven officers had seats on Area Manpower Boards. Though TASS is represented on the Economic Development Committees of NEDO, such as the Industrial Electrical Equipment EDC, it was reported that training only arose in discussions there as a peripheral issue. It is also represented on the craft committee of the City and Guilds of London Institute and the Business Technician Engineering Council and whilst members have seats on the boards of governors of colleges, responsibilities for representation are arranged locally.

## APEX

APEX is a union organizing primarily amongst clerical and managerial staff. Although it recruits across a wide range of industries, the bulk of membership is in engineering and a majority of members are women in sub-managerial grades. (Eaton and Gill, 1983: 304–5). Because new technology has an enormous impact on the office jobs that many APEX members perform, the trade union's Office Technology Working Party has been prominent in producing a series of publications on health and safety and job design related to the introduction of new technology and these include a consideration of training (see Chapter 3). Apart from this focus, the trade union's major training concern has been with YTS, since the areas in which APEX recruits do not have industry-wide established initial training programmes. Despite this, in interviews the decline of clerical apprenticeships was mentioned, and examples given of companies in which they pertain or used to pertain. With the extension of YTS to two years, APEX has the objective of seeing the reintroduction of clerical apprenticeships, examined and certified to existing qualifications such as BTEC, RSA and CGLI, rather than through the creation of a new qualification, linked to YTS, which has no wider validation.

As a result of its orientation to YTS, APEX has been particularly concerned with developing a policy response for TUC consultations on training, in particular in relation to the Review of Vocational Qualifications, the Adult Training Strategy and on the implications of the recommendations of 'Competence and Competition' for workplace representation. However, it is not only the occupational structure of the trade union which takes it in this direction, but also the position of its General Secretary, Roy Grantham, who was both a TUC Commissioner on the Manpower Services Commission and, since 1986, the Chair of the TUC's Employment Policy Committee which is responsible for decisions relating to support for YTS. Therefore, despite the relative coherence of the policy response to MSC and YTS at national level and the identification of the trade union with a position of support for the MSC programme, there is nevertheless division within APEX over continuing support for it. At the 1986 Annual Conference a resolution calling on the trade union to press the TUC to abandon cooperation with the scheme was narrowly defeated (*The Guardian*, 6 May 1986). The aim here is to examine the trade union's official policy in this area.

APEX supports YTS on the grounds that it is preferable for trainees to be placed in unionized workplaces where representatives can monitor the progress of the scheme than in non-unionized workplaces where they are more vulnerable to abuse and there are no trade union controls. For many members there was no training before the introduction of YTS, so it is regarded as an improvement insofar as it does introduce systematic training for the first time for some grades. The APEX position is to encourage representatives to seek YTS placements in their work-places, but on trade union conditions. APEX has issued guidelines for negotiators and a model training agreement, covering all types of training, not just for YTS trainees. YTS supervisors are trade union representatives and members are involved in programme review teams, organised by APEX two years in advance of the MSC's requirement to do so. APEX's main aim is that the trainees should get jobs at the end of the scheme, either in the company where they have been trained or elsewhere, but retention rates of trainees vary considerably by region. The trade union has some 50 schemes on file.

At the time of interviewing it was not clear what the implications of the extension of YTS to two years would be and APEX was concerned with such issues as the numbers of places to be offered, the implications of Approved Training Organization status and whether it would result in trainees receiving recognized qualifications. An APEX press release (15 July 1985) expressed a guarded welcome to the proposal to extend the scheme to two years, arguing that support was conditional on its voluntary nature and expressing concern, on the one hand, at inadequate monitoring arrangements and at the low level of trainee allowance, on the other.

Internally, APEX has two national officers who share responsibility for training, the Education Officer and the National Official for the food processing industry. The Education Officer's responsibility is for trade union education and training programmes and industrial training comes into this brief. Most officials of the trade union have responsibility for training in the companies they represent and because the trade union receives so many requests for approvals for YTS and Community Pro-gramme schemes, this responsibility is designated to officers even where their own members are not directly involved. A working group which drew up the guidelines for YTS and the model agreement met over a two year period between 1983 and 1985. Though it had been discontinued, in 1986 its reconstitution was under consideration. Day-to-day responses to the MSC are an administrative matter and the General Secretary and the Education Officer report back to the Executive Council of the trade union on decisions that have been made. Policy formulation takes place through debate at Annual Conference, and training had been on the agenda every year since 1983. Decisions made at conference are amended between conferences by the Executive Council as the General Secretary takes action and reports back to it. The trade union attempts to respond to all requests from the TUC to comment on MSC proposals circulated to it but always able to, due to the short time-scale allowed in which to develop a response.

APEX opposed the closure of the ITBs and was actively involved in the campaign against abolition. APEX has no seat on the EITB though a national officer has been involved at sub-committee level. They have a seat on the voluntary FMCIT in the food processing industry but argue that the financial incentive to train no longer exists in the absence of a levy mechanism. Apart from that, APEX has a seat on the Employment and Training sub-group of the Food, Drink and Tobacco EDC, on the City and Guilds Policy Committee on Education and Training, on the Computer Studies Committee of BTEC as well as members on the Area Manpower Boards. At local level officials and lay members sit on governing bodies of colleges.

## AUEW

The training issues facing the AUEW relate to two main areas: firstly, the retraining of existing members and secondly the initial training of new or potential members. The former is essentially an industrial relations issue, which may take the form of additional training of the existing workforce which relates to the introduction of new technology or new work processes, in which case the trade union has an interest in seeing new skills acquired by members rewarded in the pay structure. In chemicals and in engineering, multi-skilling and new working practices have been the subject of national negotiations with employers' organizations and these issues have already been discussed in Chapter 3. Policy towards initial training hinges on the defence of the apprenticeship system, and whilst the trade union is seriously concerned by the massive drop in engineering apprenticeship training in the years since 1979, it also has to contend with the threat of dilution and the lowering of youth wages posed by YTS. In particular, the government's policy of introducing training to standards has caused divisions within the union as it became isolated within the CSEU in continuing to oppose the achievement of full adult pay rates on completion of training. The decision of the National Committee to accept training to standards at its May 1986 meeting marked a recognition that its existing position was no longer tenable, though the decision was passed on a narrow majority.

> We would like to see, having come through three years with a war existing between the unions and the AUEW, and between the employers and the AUEW on the training system in engineering –

and the conflict is now concluded, we want to get down very seriously to discussions with the EEF, the EITB , the MSC and the CSEU to make a greatly improved system (AUEW).

The AUEW's conference decision which brought it into line with CSEU policy was partly prompted by a recognition within the union that if it failed to come to terms with YTS then other trade unions with a more pragmatic approach towards the scheme would be the beneficiaries in terms of recruitment of new members.

The major issue confronting apprenticeship training in engineering concerns the relationship between apprenticeship and YTS. There are no national agreements on YTS in engineering and schemes have been negotiated at establishment level. There is no overall national picture on how the schemes operate in practice though evidence collected for the EITB in one locality suggests that YTS funding has been used to support training under the additionality rule of the one-year scheme, though companies in general have continued to use existing apprenticeship training and pay the National Minimum Time rates on a wage for age scale (Dutton, 1986). AUEW issues the TUC guidelines on YTS to negotiators and generally follows TUC policy of pressing for 'top ups'. However, it was not known how successful this policy had been at establishment level.

One of the main concerns arising from the acceptance of training to standards is the implementation of training standards in companies out-of-scope to EITB. Companies in-scope and EEF-federated companies are not generally viewed as problematic for the implementation of training to EITB certified standards, though the AUEW has argued that money should be made available by the MSC for the monitoring of training standards in companies over which EITB has no remit. This applies particularly to smaller companies which are exempt from paying levy by virtue of their size as well as companies outside the engineering industry which train in engineering craft skills. This is a particular concern in sectors in which the ITBs have been abolished and replaced by voluntary training arrangements.

The introduction of segment training raises further issues of concern for apprenticeship training. In 1986 EITB approved the breaking down of the module system into smaller segments so that employers could effectively make apprenticeship training more company-specific. The segment system will also facilitate adult retraining. AUEW does not wish to see the reemergence of 'company-trained' apprentices and argues that monitoring is required if segment training is not to take place at the expense of core skills.

Traditionally the President of the AUEW is responsible for apprenticeship and has a seat on EITB. In the period between the death of Terry Duffy in October 1985 and Bill Jordan's election to President in April 1986 this responsibility fell to the Executive Council member responsible for YTS. Bill Jordan's appointment to EITB was subsequently announced in June 1986. Within the trade union, Executive Council members have responsibilities for industries and training comes into this remit. The AUEW has no specific training committees though an Executive Council member could write a report to the Executive Council if a specific issue arose. Policy is formulated by the National Committee which is made up of 120 lay representatives who meet annually. District Committees also discuss training policy.

Externally, AUEW is represented on the CSEU Recruitment, Training and Retraining Committee, though there have been difficulties over the AUEW's minority position on training to standards. Members of the Executive Committee sit on the different committees of EITB, for example, the committee looking at segment training. At local level officers sit on the training committees of EITB, on company training committees, on the boards of colleges, the EITB directly sponsored training schools and the Area Manpower Boards. AUEW contributed to the discussions in the Gauge and Toolmaking EDC of NEDO which led to the introduction of two courses leading to a Master Gauge and Toolmaker certificate in 1985. Outside the engineering industry representation varies according to training bodies in existence and bargaining structures. For example, in chemicals, AUEW does not have a seat on CAITREC, although it has been involved in discussions with the CIA and other craft unions on the future of craft apprenticeship training in chemicals. Whilst the trade union is represented, for example on the Electronics EDC, Japanese penetration of the market rather than training is the main concern.

AUEW provides industrial relations training for members, both independently and in conjunction with other trade unions and the TUC. An Executive Council member is responsible for the Education sub-Committee which runs the education programme. Some are general courses for stewards, whilst others are industry-specific. A new development within the brief of this sub-Committee has been the organization of industrial training for members in the form of the Engineers 2000 courses in electronics and robotics. Electronics courses are also run with the EETPU at its industrial training college at Cudham Hall, Esher.

## EETPU

The electricians' union, EETPU, is one that sees its policy towards training as integral to its identity as a trade union committed to the philosophy of the 'new realism' in industrial relations. Its interest in single union and no-strike agreements and its notoriety gained from its involvement in disputes such as *News International* at Wapping (Bassett, 1986) are to be found alongside a pragmatic approach to the Youth Training Scheme and the provision of training in electronics and robotics for members which has no parallel in the trade union movement. Eaton and Gill (1983) comment that EETPU offers a package of services to members more on the lines of a friendly society than the collective defence of interests more traditionally associated with trade union membership. Certainly the trade union's approach to training bears this out; it is part of a package designed to enhance members' skills and individual bargaining power, which at the same time serves as a vehicle for attracting potential new members. The centrality of training to EETPU strategy is best indicated in the internal structures of the trade union which are concerned with training. To date, the EETPU is the only trade union to have a training representative structure on a par with the health and safety representative structure in other trade unions.

It could well be asked why EETPU has such a highly developed and coherent policy towards training. There are a number of explanations. Firstly, the jobs of electricians are enormously affected by the impact of electronic and technological change. This is combined with the fact that the electrical contracting industry has traditionally trained a large proportion of electricians, well above its own requirements, and it was in response to the reduction of training in electrical contracting that EETPU struck a deal with the Electrical Contractors' Association on YTS which involved accepting a reduction of youth wage rates on condition that numbers of apprentices in training were maintained, as reported in Chapter 2. Therefore policy towards training is motivated by a concern, firstly, to maintain the numbers of new members entering the organization and secondly, by ensuring that members are well placed to claim jobs requiring new technology skills through attendance at courses run by the trade union. This strategic view of training has been explicitly stated in EETPU publications:

> If we are successfully to face the challenge presented by NET (new electronic technology – HR) then training is a key factor. Without a positive attitude, new work will be taken up by other groups of workers and without the appropriate training, maintenance elec-

tricians will not be able to claim this work as theirs simply because they will not be able to do it . . . Electronics represents a natural progression for the electrician . . . but despite this distinct advantage there are relatively few people able to cope with NET in all its forms. This shortage effectively means that the present situation is unique in that it is ready made for electricians to considerably improve their position relative to more traditionally based crafts (EETPU *Contact*, September 1980: 4).

The training representative structure is part and parcel of this aggressive approach to the claiming of new technology skills, and is not only intended to raise awareness amongst members of the significance of claiming new technology skills:

> Training representatives would encourage the better use of manpower availability, avoid de-skilling, promote youth training, adult training and retraining.
> Training representatives would promote the policies of the EETPU in new technology and industrial training, further expand our powers of influence to existing and potential members and provide a marketing force for our own technical training facilities (EETPU *Training Bulletin*, March, 1983: 8).

Technical training at the trade union's college at Cudham Hall, Esher, which has now been extended to mobile instructor units and courses run at EETPU offices in a number of localities, is seen as means of attracting ordinary members and reinforcing their commitment to it in an industrial rather than militant sense.

The main policy-making body in the EETPU is the Executive Council. Its other duties include carrying out policy, ratifying agreements and integrating the work of full-time officials with the national policy of the trade union. It may also participate in pay negotiations. (Eaton and Gill, 1983: 135). Meetings take place monthly and Executive Councillors are elected by postal ballot for a five year period of office. Because it was felt within the trade union that the Executive Council would be unable to specialize on training, especially with the advent of YTS, a separate sub-committee was set up, the National Training Committee, which was presented with proposals on training, including a structure for dealing with training matters and free union membership for trainees in the Transitional Training Section. The latter is computerized so that trainees can be contacted on completion of their years' free membership period with a view to taking out full membership.

The Training Committee formulates policy on training and 15 Divisional Training Officers are responsible to it. Training Representatives in companies coordinate with Divisional Training Officers who are full-time officials based at EETPU Area Offices. The responsibilities of these regional officers include expanding EETPU's technical training courses into the divisional structure of the union, arranging company in-house training courses, and utilizing EETPU premises and other locations for organizing courses. Area offices are taking increasing responsibility for organizing industrial relations training, in particular for newly-elected training representatives, for shop stewards and for health and safety representatives (EETPU *Training Bulletin*, No. 3, February, 1984). Since March 1983 a Training Bulletin has been published, with the aim of 'explaining the current schemes coming into operation and how we, as a union, meet the challenge this represents' (EETPU *Training Bulletin*, No. 1, March, 1983: 1).

As with other trade unions, EETPU opposed the closure of the ITBs and has seats on EITB and CITB, in the industries covered by this project. In the sectors in which the ITBs have been wound up, despite the proliferation of voluntary training bodies, the trade union seeks representation on most of them. In chemicals and the food and drink industry this is because although they represent a minority interest in terms of membership numbers, they have a major interest in training activities because the major training effort is in maintenance work. EETPU has representation on the CGLI, BTEC, and on professional institutes and the Engineering Council which are relevant to the interests of members in supervisory and managerial grades in their white-collar section, the Electrical and Engineering Staff Association (ESSA) and in the United Kingdom Association of Professional Executives (UKAPE), a section resulting from amalgamation in 1979.

With respect to the objectives of the New Training Initiative, EETPU supports YTS, training to standards and the opening up of opportunities for adults. Training to standards is viewed as a means of defending electrical training against dilution, and whilst the trade union has no objection in principle to adults learning skilled trades by undergoing full apprenticeship training, under present funding arrangements it opposes training in electrical skills aimed at adults through short courses.

The whole concept behind standards-based schemes is enhancing skills. We can't have a high failure rate because we would have problems with people coming out with a basic understanding of skills which is dangerous. We have blackballed short-term schemes and college schemes attempting to introduce broad-based training. Drop-in Skillcentres had six week schemes but we stopped the electrical scheme. You can't have broad-based training in electrical services (EETPU).

EETPU supports apprentice training through YTS in the electrical contracting industry and actively seeks representation on the Area Manpower Boards and at the time of fieldwork it had members sitting on 15 of the 54 AMBs.

In engineering, EETPU is involved in training policy formulation through the CSEU. Though they adhere to CSEU training decisions they are free to take a separate stance and put members' interests above policy which may not be favourable to EETPU. In chemicals, they work closely with the other craft unions which meet with the CIA on training. In construction, they are the only trade union in the electrical contracting sector which, they argue, allows them to be more radical than they can be where there are joint trade union negotiations.

## UCATT

UCATT is a trade union which has a relatively large number of officials due to the difficulties of establishing and maintaining trade union organization on sites in the construction industry. The instability of site work combined with the hostility of many employers to trade unionism results in the dependence of the membership on the services of officials. Eaton and Gill argue:

> Recruitment and maintenance of membership is particularly difficult in the building industry, largely because of the cyclical nature of employment, the continued prevalence of the practice of labour-only sub-contracting (the 'lump'), and the inevitable mobility of labour from site to site following work completion. The difficulty is compounded by the fact that the building industry attracts and moulds workers who seek high earnings, yet who are highly individualistic, independent, 'hard' and highly conscious of craft differences (1983: 157).

In the absence of strong bargaining power and trade union controls at site level, and in the face of the threat posed by the 'lump' to the control of apprentice training and wages, the representation of trade union interests through the participation of its officials in the structures of joint regulation at national and local level for apprenticeship training constitutes a means of controlling the construction labour market. Austrin argues:

> The lump was understood to be an attempt to lower the standards of training in the industry. In this sense it was a practice aimed at lowering wages. The craft form of control, then, was rooted in the

attempt to control and regulate apprenticeship training in order to maintain both craft standards and wages.

The success of the British building unions in achieving this form of control was however partial because they failed to develop any autonomous methods of regulating the labour market. In the casual conditions of employment of the construction labour market the tie of the worker to his union was his skill, but this tie was never unilaterally enforced through such practices as union control over hiring and firing (1980: 307).

Therefore UCATT has prioritized control over access to training as a means of combatting labour-only sub-contracting in a casual labour market over which it otherwise exercises relatively little control. As a result, policy on training is coherent; officials and lay members alike are well represented on bodies with a training remit to ensure that policy is implemented at local level.

The defence of apprenticeship is thus the priority of UCATT. The adaption of YTS to existing apprenticeship training has been part of this strategy. This is not because UCATT agrees with all that YTS implies. Because of the decline of apprenticeship training and demands being placed by the MSC on the building industry to provide placements, it was seen as the best option available.

We would rather have seen no YTS but we do see the need for a proper scheme of training. We support the concept of YTS in construction because we were presented with a *de facto* situation as far as the government and the MSC were concerned (UCATT).

Apprenticeship is defended against dilution primarily by restricting the assignment of MSC funding to CITB-approved schemes through participation in the process of approval of funding in the Area Manpower Boards. (In fact, representatives of the employers in the NJCBI, the Building Employers' Confederation follow the same policy where they have representation on the AMBs). This is reinforced through the apprentice registration scheme run through the National Joint Training Commission of the NJCBI, whereby six-months remission of the apprenticeship period is granted to apprentices trained under the Building Foundation Training Scheme (as the CITB's YTS scheme is known). The structure of the NJCBI is paralleled by the structure of the local and regional apprenticeship committees. At local level the NJCBI is concerned with hearing appeals from the employer and trade union side where the National Working Rule Agreement has not been met, whils the training committees are concerned with appeals and grievances of apprentices. These training committees are a recent development and have been set up in response to the changes in training brought about by YTS. When YTS was extended to a two-year scheme, the Area Manpower Boards became the vehicles through which UCATT's and subsequently the NJCBI's decision not to grant funding to schemes which fail to employ trainees and pay negotiated pay rates after the first year was implemented. The example of withdrawal of remission for the first year of apprenticeship in the case of the DLO reported in Chapter 2 provides another example of the way in which these sanctions can operate in this unstable labour market.

Within UCATT there is no national officer with specific responsibility for training. At national level UCATT has the majority of seats on the trade union side in the Training Commission of the NJCBI, of which an Executive Councillor holds the chair. There are no specialist working parties on training though the Executive usually discusses items on the agenda at the Training Commission. There is a five-man full-time Executive who are all national officers and if an item arises which requires a policy decision the Executive Councillors report to the Executive Council which will reach a decision on the matter. The policy positions taken at this level are usually endorsed by the Biennial National Delegate Conference. For example, policy on YTS has been endorsed by conference, but concern has nevertheless been expressed by conference delegates that the scheme is being used to manipulate the unemployment figures.

UCATT opposed the proposal to close CITB and argued that closure would not support the government's alleged policy objectives in the field of training. They made strong representations, including the lobbying of Parliament. Four senior UCATT officials have seats on the CITB Board, though one of them was nominated in his capacity as a member of the Civil Engineering Conciliation Board. However, to a large extent the Board of CITB authenticates decisions made within the committee structure of CITB, which have a high degree of autonomy over subsectoral decisions (see Rainbird and Grant, 1985a). UCATT has representatives on the Building and Specialist Building Committees, the Sub-committee on Craft Training amongst others and participates in the working parties concerned with developing the training schedules for the new Training Initiative. Apart from CITB, the trade union has representatives on CGLI and NEDO in the construction industry. It does not have a seat on CAITREC and the main changes in the chemical industry have related to trades other than their own. There are UCATT representatives on the boards of governors of technical colleges and the local advisory committees which make an input into the content of courses.

There is no liaison between the different trade unions in the construction industry on their input to CITB though the subject matter, such as the industrial relations dimension of training comes up at meetings of the trade union side of the NJCBI. They have informal contacts with the employers' associations, for example on developing a response to YTS and as an individual trade union they had informal meetings with the Building Employers' Confederation on this. In this industry, it was argued that there is a reasonable degree of accord with the employers on training objectives, which stops short of agreement on wage rates.

UCATT runs a regular programme of industrial relations training for shop stewards. These are organized nationally though there are also weekend regional schools for branch secretaries and shop stewards for construction trades generally and for specific industries. There is a Health and Safety Officer, and health and safety is incorporated into the education programme. There is no programme of training run by the trade union in craft skills.

## USDAW

USDAW like UCATT is a trade union which is relatively well-staffed by officials due to weakness of the workplace bargaining. This is because the majority of its membership is in retailing, a sector with a very high turnover of the workforce due to widespread use of casual, part-time and seasonal employment. It has been estimated that USDAW has 36 per cent annual turnover and has to recruit 100,000 new members per annum just to maintain its size. (Eaton and Gill, 1983: 210). This situation leads to the recognition by the trade union that there is a difference between what members can achieve in well-organised workplaces and trade union policy. Even where there are national guidelines, for example, that YTS should be introduced in consultation with the trade unions and that trainees should form no more than five per cent of the workforce, there is a problem with translation into action at local level. For example, it was stated that with one of the major retailing chains it was impossible to introduce a good programme however active shop stewards were because the company just uses trainees as cheap labour.

Internally, the Education Officer, with responsibility for industrial relations training, is also responsible for occupational training. He represents the trade union on a number of external bodies primarily related to the implementation of YTS. Other officials with responsibilities for negotiations deal with it in their capacities as national officers and may have seats on training bodies as part of their brief. However, there is a problem in formulating national policy in this area; trade union officers admit that there is no coherent policy and do not know the line taken by national officers on training bodies. Policy evolves on a piecemeal basis, with felt and agreed views on direction. The advent of YTS has brought the trade union to a situation in which it has to create greater policy coherence on youth training. In December 1985 a two day workshop was organized in order for the trade union to obtain a systematic analysis of what was happening in practice with the scheme and as a result to prepare a policy paper and a Executive Council statement for presentation to the Annual Delegate Meeting.

The bulk of USDAW membership is in retailing, the remainder being in chemicals, food manufacturing, distribution and warehousing. As a result, there is little centralized information about training issues affecting the membership in food processing and chemicals. This was explained in the following terms:

> USDAW has limited information on these industries and the impact of training because the bulk of the membership is in retailing and wholesaling. There are masses of bits and pieces of membership but national officers and local officers with responsibilities for these sections do their own thing. At the centre we know very little about the outposts of the union, which are run as autonomous sections. The national officer with responsibility for the industry liaises in general terms with the rest of the union. We don't go out into the field so there is little centrally collected information except on retailing and wholesaling. This is a problem for general unions. We have framework policies for our mainstream interests and when problems come up we refer them to our specialist departments (USDAW).

Despite this, USDAW does have seats on a number of national training bodies and opposed the closure of the ITBs. Their main focus of training input had been the Distributive ITB, until it was abolished and they made an input into developing training modules, depending on the interests of particular officials. There was not the same level of involvement in the work of the FDTITB. Currently the trade union is entitled to representation on 16 voluntary bodies in food manufacturing and CAITREC in chemicals, as well as other voluntary bodies outside these sectors. However, the proliferation of voluntary bodies means that USDAW has to be selective and sit only on some of them. Primarily national officers are concerned with representing interests at this level and one national officer has a seat both on CAITREC and on FMCIT. Training comes up as an issue on some of the EDCs of NEDO; participation in the Employment and Training Sub-committee of the Food and Drink EDC was mentioned as one of these. At divisional level some officers have seats on the Area Manpower Boards, and whilst it was reported that some of them were very involved in this work, at national level it was not known what happened on the ground. It is recognized that the trade union has a limited input in occupational training but, it was argued, that this reflected the general state of affairs in occupational training, the speed of implementation of government policy and its lack of coherence. The trade union regrets the loss of the ITBS, but recognises that its training interventions were not very effective;

> The union was not effective on training when the statutory organizations existed, but it endeavoured to intervene and some people were genuinely interested in the work. Now they have gone so there is no urgency about training since it is not on our list of negotiating priorities. These are determined by what members shout loudest about and training only comes out as a niggle. The quality of training is not an issue though the exploitation of the kids is. With the ITBs there were centralized national bodies concerned with specific trades and industries which collected information. Under this system USDAW had a reputation of making an input into the specifics of training. This input has gone now (USDAW).

Whilst participation in the ITBs provided the trade union with information and a monitoring role, this source of information no longer exists and USDAW does not have the resources, nor the prioritization of training policy to make effective intervention;

> National negotiators sit on training bodies but they are so busy with redundancies, closures and wages that they tend to sit on training bodies as a guardian or monitor, gaining a general perspective of what is happening. They are not geared up to making a positive contribution (USDAW).

and,

> In the absence of the ITBs there are many more training bodies and officers do not have the time to sit on them. Trade unions can't develop expertise when there is chaos elsewhere. For the negotiators, training is not their métier (USDAW).

The trade union organizes its own education programme for shop stewards, branch officials and full-time officials, geared to their representative role. Courses are also organised on health and safety but occupational training programmes are viewed as being outside the remit of the representational role of the trade unions.

## TGWU

The TGWU is the largest trade union in Britain: it is multi-industrial, organizing in many different sectors and general, open to workers in all types of occupations. Since the end of the 1960s decentralization of collective bargaining, which had been occurring on a piecemeal basis, was made more systematic and shop stewards and lay representatives were invested with greater power. The TGWU has a trade group structure through which industry-wide and national negotiations are conducted in different industries. It also has a regional structure composed of 11 divisions, whilst at local level district committees bring together the interests of different branches and trade groups (Eaton and Gill, 1983). As a result of TGWU structure, there are different levels within the trade union at which responses to training are formulated and negotiated. There has been a general, central response to YTS, formulated through the Biennial Delegate Conference, which is reflected in a series of Training Bulletins and a negotiators' guide prepared by the Research Department. Within the TGWU there are no national officers with responsibility for industrial training, but responsibilities and representational roles are taken up by national officers as part of their trade group responsibilities. Each trade group has a degree of autonomy in determining sectoral policies through its own National Committee, which deals with the interests of the membership in that sector. This committee considers reports and resolutions from regional trade groups and district committees (Eaton and Gill, 1983) but may also set up specialist sub-committees. For example, the Power and Engineering Trade Group refers proposals on engineering training to an *ad hoc* sub-committee, which makes recommendations to the committee.

The existence of members in a range of different industries and occupations means that many training issues (for example, multi-skilling in chemicals) arise in national negotiations conducted by trade group National Secretaries and Officers. This may also be the level at which representation of interests on external bodies such as ITBs may take place, though this is not exclusively the case. The trade union's commitment to decentralization means that local officials may take on these responsibilities. At the same time, the plant bargaining culture of the trade union means that training issues may be raised at plant level, though this is more likely to concern the terms and conditions of employment during training (for example, the negotiation of 'top ups' to the YTS allowance) than the content of training.

If the range of occupations, organizational decentralization and the trade group structure all tend to militate against a unitary response on training issues, then this has been reinforced by the fact that historically many TGWU members have received little industrial training. In the occupations and industries in which members have received training, for example, process operators in chemicals, semi-skilled workers in engineering, this has taken place through non-apprenticeship methods of training and so resistance to YTS as a method of training (as opposed to an attack on youth wages) has not been as great as it has been in craft areas. Furthermore, these industries are undergoing net job losses particularly in the occupations in which the TGWU organizes and so the training of new workers arises as fairly low priority as a workplace bargaining issue compared to redundancies, flexible working practices and casualization. In contrast, in construction, the trade union organizes in craft as well as non-craft occupations, but in this industry YTS has been adapted to apprenticeship training and the trade union position is one of support for the CITB managing agency and for schemes meeting CITB approval. At the level of plant bargaining, training may be bargained over informally rather than formally; that is to say, it arises in the form of informal job controls and knowledge of the job rather than an item which is on the agenda in wage negotiations (Spies, 1984). TGWU prepares its members to bargain over these skill-related issues insofar as it has produced publications, for example, on how stewards should respond to the introduction of quality circles and to job evaluation exercises (TGWU 1984 and 1983, respectively).

TGWU opposed the abolition of the ITBs and officials continue to have seats on the boards of EITB and CITB, in the industries covered by the project. Seats are held by National Secretaries on the boards of both ITBs, though in construction a Regional Officer and the Women's National Officer have seats as well and a further TGWU officer has a seat, nominated through the Civil Engineering and Construction Conciliation Board. In both instances, the trade union is represented in committee structures as well. In food processing the closure of the ITB was seen as inevitable, and although it was felt that FDTITB had done a lot of good work, ordinary members were scarcely affected by it. As a result, although TGWU opposed closure, the abolition of the ITB in this sector has not made a great difference to TGWU members. Though a National Officer has a seat on the Food Manufacturers' Council for Industrial Training, its activities are viewed as academic and training has been devolved to company level in the absence of the financial incentive of the ITBs levy-grant mechanism. In chemicals, the replacement of the ITB by the CIA's NSTO was denounced as a 'charade' (*Financial Times*, 12 January 1983), though TGWU has subsequently taken up a seat on the Chemical and Allied Industries' Training Review Council. TGWU is represented on the Economic Development Committees of

NEDO, some of which have a training and employment interest, as well as on City and Guilds, BTEC and boards of governors of colleges at local level. TGWU has members, usually Regional Officers, with seats on Area Manpower Boards.

Nationally the TGWU has an officer with responsibility for industrial relations training and this is replicated at regional level. The devolution of power to shop stewards has resulted in particular emphasis being placed on the education of lay representatives and the Research Department has a wide range of publications aimed at members involved in local negotiations. Health and safety training is provided but industrial training is seen as the responsibility of the employer.


## GMBATU


GMBATU is the third largest trade union in the UK and like the TGWU is both multi-industrial and general. It has members in all four industries covered by the project, though interviews were not conducted on its interests in the construction industry. Historically, it has had a reputation for hostility towards rank-and-file movements and officers are relatively powerful. Furthermore, Regional Secretaries have greatest seniority within the trade union structure after the General Secretary and this has resulted in the ten regions of the trade union operating with considerable autonomy from the centre (Gill and Eaton, 1983). This structure, combined with the wide range of industries and occupations covered by the membership results in little information being available on training centrally beyond a negotiator's guide to YTS and recruitment literature for trainees. There are, of course, sub-sectoral variations, and the policy issues relating to training are more clear cut in engineering and chemicals then they are in food processing.

At national level there is no one officer with responsibilities for training though one National Industrial Officer was one of the TUC-nominated commissioners on the Manpower Services Commission, and has a research resource to back this up. At Head Office, the research department has a training sub-group which monitors the situation and from time to time produces guidance. Committees on training are occasionally convened but are not constitutional. The annual conference is the normal policy-making body, but occasionally specialist conferences have been called, for example on YTS, and there is an annual youth conference at which YTS appears on the agenda. National Industrial Conferences discuss industry-specific interests. At regional level, officers are assigned responsibilities for industrial sectors and this may include training amongst other collective bargaining issues.

In chemicals the main issue relating to training has been that of multi-skilling and this has come up in the context of national pay negotiations and the discussion of flexible working practices rather than as a straight-forward training concern. GMBATU policy was to oppose the introduction of multi-skilling though it was admitted at the national office that very little was known about what was happening on the ground. In engineering the relationship between YTS and apprenticeship training has been a major concern. On YTS the trade union has sought to enforce the additionality rule under the one-year scheme, whereby YTS funding was given for five trainees, if two were taken on in addition to the normal intake. GMBATU has not sought 'top up' agreements so much as deals on back pay and service when trainees have been taken into full employment. It was believed that problems relating to the scheme and its relationship to apprenticeship training would be exacerbated by its extension to two years.

GMBATU opposed the closure of the ITBs and was particularly critical of the closure of the Chemical and Allied Industries' ITB. The National Industrial Officer for the Chemical Industry stated:

> The so-called Training Review Council offers nothing except a cheeky attempt to get a few union names on its notepaper to give an air of acceptabillity for laundering grants from the Manpower Services Commission to individual firms. I said it was a sham in 1982 – it still is in 1984 (GMBATU, *Chemical Union News*, January, 1984: 3).

In 1985, the trade union continued to take the position of non-involvement in CAITREC, and at the time of interviewing (November 1985) it was reported that the trade union was not represented on any of the NSTOs in the food industry either. It is represented on the board of EITB, on the Economic Development Committees on NEDO, on City and Guilds and the National Joint Industrial Councils relevant to collective bargaining in each sub-sector. It is a constituent of the CSEU and training arises every year on its agenda. At local level officials have seats on the Area Manpower Boards and on boards of governors of colleges.

GMBATU runs it own training programmes in industrial relations for stewards and activists, both at its own college and in conjunction with the TUC. This includes the training of safety representatives. The provision of industrial training is not viewed as being within the remit of trade union concerns, though as a policy issue it is viewed as one of the more important ones after their standard work on terms and conditions of employment.

## Conclusion

A review of the priorities of training policy and the structures through which it is formulated and implemented indicates considerable variations amongst the nine trade unions studied. This reflects the characteristics of trade union structure, organization and membership, on the one hand, and institutional structures related to training and collective bargaining, on the other. However, the most important single factor determining training policy – and this seems an obvious point – is whether training exists as an item to be bargained over in workplaces in the first place. Trade unions with long-standing concerns with apprenticeship and the training of skilled labour have more highly-developed policies and structures for formulating and implementing it, internally and in relation to external institutions, than do those whose members have historically had little access to formal, job-related training.

Recently, the introduction of YTS has resulted in all trade unions developing a policy response to youth training, or rather, to government schemes aimed at young people, which pay an allowance rather than a wage, which involve no formal contract of employment with the employer, and include a period of off-the-job training. However, there has been no one single coherent policy response from the trade union movement as a whole to YTS (Eversley, 1986; Wrench, 1986). The evidence presented here and in Chapter 2 indicates the range of responses from different trade unions to the scheme. These vary from those trade unions which regard it primarily as a scheme for the young unemployed with little bearing on skill training, through the construction industry unions which, though critical of the non-training aspects of the scheme, have negotiated for it to fund apprenticeship training, to those that are concerned at the exploitation of young people on the scheme, but see some potential for developing training programmes where none formerly existed. In some cases new organizational structures are being developed often on an *ad hoc* basis, to formulate a policy response. This has often resulted in the issuing of negotiator's guides to YTS and recruitment literature aimed at trainees. The trade union movement as a whole has made policy inputs into schemes such as YTS originating at national level through the TUC's involvement in the Manpower Services Commission.

In the background to these developments have been the structures, usually linked to specific sectors, which are concerned with training and on which trade unions may or may not be represented. In chemicals and food processing, the abolition of the ITBs has resulted in a reduction in trade union inputs into sector-level training policy and, particularly in food processing, the fragmentation of decision-making and expertise.

# 6

# Organizational Implications of a Changing Skill Base

## Introduction

The British trade union movement is characterized by its organization along occupational lines rather than by industrial sector or by political affiliation. Though there are exceptions to this rule, for example in coal mining, the four industries currently under examination; chemicals, construction, engineering and food processing, are representationally diverse. In each industry a number of trade unions have representational rights and recruit amongst different occupational grades. Though they may be in the process of extending membership into new areas, for example into managerial and white-collar grades, most trade unions have a core occupational identity. The jobs and skills of the membership are decisive in shaping trade union identity and, in the same way, the identification of a trade union with particular clusters of occupations will define its appeal to new and potential members. These identities are by no means exclusive and there may be competition between trade unions to recruit in particular occupational categories. The representation of members' interests in matters relating to their professional and occupational formation is, therefore, significant to trade union organization insofar as it shapes the organization's occupational identity, and allows it to intervene in the socialization of new members in the workplace.

Economic restructuring in the recession, the transformations in employment produced by the introduction of information technology, government support for privatization and deregulation and anti-union legislation have combined to provide an environment which is hostile to trade union organization and to which trade unions have had to respond. Not only has there been a shift in the locus of employment from manufacturing to the service sector, from larger to smaller establishments, but there have been changes in occupational structure and in conditions of employment which affect the characteristics of membership bases and trade unions' ability to organize them. Though similar processes affect trade union movements in all industrialized countries, the dynamics of occupational change are of particular significance in Britain for relationships *between* trade unions since they bring to the fore questions of occupational identity, the definition of recruitment territories and hence areas of potential alliance and conflict between trade unions.

Trade unions represent their members' interests in the field of training policy not only because it forms part of the process of formation of new members, but because this process of reproduction of members allows the trade union as an organization to replace members lost through redundancy, job changes and retirement. This was most clearly articulated in the concerns expressed by trade union officials about the decline in apprenticeship training and in particular, the EETPU's decision to strike a deal with the Electrical Contractors' Association on YTS to ensure continuity in the supply of new recruits. It has also resulted in a number of trade unions changing their membership rules so that YTS trainees who are not employees can be recruited. In a period of occupational change, training and, in particular retraining, of the existing workforce takes on a new significance; that of reconstituting the structure of occupations. Therefore, in order to adapt to the changing content of jobs and hence to changes in the structure of employment, trade unions must also respond collectively to opportunities for retraining if they are to claim to represent new occupations as they evolve and emerge from pre-existing ones. It is also a means of ensuring that members retain their jobs in line with changes in technology and industrial organization and thus constitutes a means of retaining and strengthening membership bases.

Training in the broadest sense of the term (cf. the French concept of 'formation') concerns the process of preparing the worker for employment, which includes the acquisition of a complex set of attributes through the formal education system, socialization in the home, formal training and socialization in the workplace. The skills acquired are of a technical nature and of a social nature insofar as each occupation has its characteristic practices and requires an understanding, acceptance and ability to operate within the rules and norms governing the social division of labour. However, this process does not only occur through initial training and socialization but also through *continuing* training and socialization in the workplace. In the contemporary context of changes in jobs brought about by the introduction of new technology combined with the employers' offensive on working practices, training may be the means not just of passing on new technical skills to workers, but also in legitimizing and recognizing new working practices which may undermine existing notions of demarcations between jobs and trade union spheres of influence.

New technical and social skills may be introduced with or without formal training. As documented in Chapters 3 and 4, new technology and new working practices are often introduced in the absence of formal training, though this absence does not mean that new skills are not learned nor that the skill content of jobs is not affected by the changes. On the contrary, informal learning on the job through *experience* can be an effective way of transmitting new skills, but the significance of informal learning lies in the fact that although new skills are learned on an individual basis by one worker instructing another on the job, the training itself is not mediated by worker organization and the outcome cannot readily be negotiated in the wages structure. It is in the interests of trade union members and of trade unions as organizations that new skills should be acquired through formal rather than informal training and thus become subject to collective negotiation and recognition in the wages structure. However, there is another reason why trade unions should support formal training over informal learning and this concerns the 'capacity inherent to formal training to structure jobs' (Maurice *et al.*, 1986). For whilst socially negotiated and recognized training increases bargaining power and wages, the real technical skills acquired and their recognition beyond the immediate workplace means that jobs can be structured around known skill dimensions and expectations, whereas informal learning on-the-job is by definition specific and is based on the assumption of a limited range of non-transferable tasks. In other words, there is a tendency for formal training in transferable skills to result in more varied and interesting work for the individual worker and a greater role for trade union organization in negotiating qualifications, on the one hand, and their social recognition in the wages structure, on the other.

Despite the often limited training received by the membership of some of the trade unions interviewed in this project, industrial training in one form or another is increasingly on the agenda in negotiations at plant level (concerning wages and conditions of employment during the training period and the subsequent recognition of the training received on completion) and in national bodies which concern the negotiation of curricula and qualifications relating to training. Currently, many aspects of the training system are undergoing change and trade unions are involved in negotiating them. In the general education system, a new role for industry in the curriculum has emerged with the growth of the 'new vocationalism'. The Youth Training Scheme, regardless of concerns expressed about the quality of the training received and the objectives of social engineering in its hidden curriculum, has to a large extent universalized initial training as a policy issue for trade unions. Vocational qualifications have been under review and the subject of consultations (MSC, 1985). All the features of the training system are subject to negotiation, though some of the institutions on which trade unions have until recently been represented, such as the ITBs, have themselves been subject to change. Occupational change requires trade unions to develop a coherent response to training issues in order to retain membership, lay claim to new skills and maintain spheres of influence. At the same time, these organizational considerations require trade unions to develop a policy response towards the process of negotiation of new qualifications and skills to ensure that they as collectivities exert influence over the process of definition of new occupations.

The significance of training which leads to the acquisition of formal qualifications and recognition in the wages structure is not mitigated by the development of new *methods* for imparting training. This is especially true of open learning which is usually conducted in the worker's own time either at home or in the workplace. Besides being cost-effective for the employer, open learning is of significance to trade unionists for a number of reasons. Firstly, new skills are acquired on an *individual basis* in a *privatized* learning process. Secondly, because it is presented as a neutral phenomenon, 'training', and does not refer to existing formal methods of training, it may be used as a means of avoiding or circumventing industrial relations conflicts that might otherwise arise from transmitting skills, either new ones or old ones in new combinations, that might be subject to contention by trade unions claiming them. Thirdly, unless trade unions are involved in the negotiation of the curriculum, the resulting qualification and its recognition in the wages structure, workers will find that their new skills increase productivity with no benefit to themselves and in this way encounter the same problems as posed by informal learning.

Trade unions have a representational role for their members but, as with any representative body, this organization may acquire bureaucratic interests of its own. With respect to training, there can be tension between organizational interests, on the one hand, and the interests of individual members, on the other. The relationship between socially recognized skills and wages illustrates this point. Cockburn (1983) has argued that trade union organization is concerned primarily with the market value of skill, that is the level at which it is rewarded, rather than the actual content of the job concerned and its relationship to the technical skills and accumulated experience of the worker performing it. With technological change the real level of skill required to perform a job may change, but the strength of trade union organization may allow workers to retain wage differentials. In the case of the linotype operators she studied, trade union organization maintained skilled wage levels although the compositors themselves felt that their jobs had been de-skilled:

> The predominant feeling amongst ex-operators however was clearly one of resentment: at the loss of the stimulus of piece-work payment, at the scrapping of the lino. Since they continued to belong to the craftsmen's union and to be paid craftsman's rates, some of the men, reduced to what they saw as fumbling incompetence in a job that thousands of teenage girls could do better, felt fraudulent and ashamed (1983: 99).

However, trade unions are not only concerned with maintaining the bargaining power of their members in the workplace but have organizational interests of their own which concern the retention of their power and financial base through maintaining and preferably expanding numbers in membership. To pursue this strategy the real and supposed qualifications of the membership may assume a significance in attracting new members especially in occupational categories in which there is competition for membership. Skills are not, of course, the only criteria by which trade unions attempt to recruit and services offered, the political outlook of the trade union and other factors may be presented in recruitment literature. Therefore, their association with particular kinds of workers with claims to defined skills which are negotiable in the workplace may also lead them to maintain an image of the technical skills of their members which may be at variance with the membership's own perceptions on the effects of new technology and changes in working practices on the skill content of their jobs. Multi-skilling provides a particularly good example of this. Moreover, there appears to be considerable debate within the trade unions affected whether it leads to de-skilling or the upgrading of skills. Regardless of the subjective feelings of the workers concerned, the issue of significance is in the translation of new skills into wages structure and, from an organizational perspective, its affect on the trade union's ability to recruit members and operate spheres of influence.

In earlier chapters the processes of occupational change were documented in chemicals, construction, engineering and food processing as they are perceived by trade union officials with a sizeable membership in these sectors. The aim of this chapter is to examine trade union responses and, in particular, to indicate the implications for trade union organization of changes in the structure of employment and occupations. Strategies directed towards structural change, such as reorganization and merger activity will be considered alongside new policies and services which are aimed primarily at recruitment.

## Declining Membership

The single most important factor influencing trade union organization apart from legislation aimed at reducing effectiveness in pursuing disputes, has been the decline in membership which has occurred alongside the growth of mass unemployment. This decline is illustrated in the fall in TUC membership to 9.6 million in 1986 (*The Guardian*, 19 January 1987) from its peak of 12.2 million in 1980. In 1985 TUC membership fell below 10 million for the first time since 1972 (*Financial Times*, 27 June 1985). Not only have the numbers of unemployed increased, but the period of unemployment has lengthened. The recession of the 1980s has been characterized by the vulnerability of *all* workers, not just the unskilled, to unemployment. Unemployment has risen as a result of the restructuring and rationalization of companies, leading to redundancies, as well as bankruptcies. Technological redundancy has affected some occupations, though the extent to which new technology has contributed to overall unemployment is disputed (Gill, 1985).

Amongst the trade unions studied in this project, there has been considerable variation in the effect of the recession on numbers in membership, with the white-collar unions with actual and potential membership growth in high technology sectors least adversely affected. Fluxes within the TUC in the composition of membership alters the number of seats each trade union holds on the TUC General Council. For example, in 1985 the TGWU lost one of its five seats as membership fell below 1.5 million and membership losses resulted in APEX falling below the 100,000 cut-off point for automatic representation on the General Council. AUEW, with a membership of 1 million increased its representation from three seats to four (*Financial Times*, 27 June 1985) though by the end of the same year it had fallen back below 1 million (*The Guardian*, 19 January 1987). Similarly, GMBATU, only 25,000 members short of 1 million in 1979 (as the GMWU), had lost nearly a quarter of a million members by 1985 and expected to lose more despite amalgamations and mergers with smaller unions (*Financial Times*, 4 June 1985).

Regional factors have been important in determining patterns of losses in membership and declining numbers of members in branches, combined with these changes in regional distribution have prompted changes in full-time officer distribution which receive an impulse themselves from financial problems, the principal cause of which is declining income from subscriptions. Regions characterized by heavy manufacturing industry are the most severely affected by job losses though even in more prosperous areas there are pockets of high unemployment in declining inner city areas. These shifts in regional employment patterns affect not only absolute numbers of trade unionists but regional balances in membership composition. The AUEW illustrates this point. In the post-war period AUEW membership was concentrated in London, Lancashire, the West Midlands, South Wales and Glasgow/Paisley, but the decline in membership by 1979 was much greater in these areas than in areas which had previously been peripheral to the trade union. Between 1979 and 1981, AUEW membership fell by 17 per cent overall but in its former heartland areas, the decline was a massive 22 per cent (Bassett, 1986: 23). As a consequence of this continuing decline in membership, in January 1987 the (by then) AEU announced the cutting of one-third of the trade union's full-time officer posts and pay freezes for all staff (*The Guardian*, 2 January 1987). By the April 1987 National Committee meeting in Eastbourne, the trade union's financial crisis was manifested in an annual income for 1986 only 1 per cent higher than the 1980 figure of £17.4 million. Falling numbers of subscriptions were set against increases in wages of staff and officers of 53 per cent. The Executive proposed a number of organizational solutions to be presented to the following rules revision conference including a reduction in the number of branches by disbanding those with less than 100 members, a cut of one-third in the number of National Committee delegates, a switch from a monthly to a quarterly journal and an increase in contributions linked to national engineering pay agreement weekly rates (*The Guardian*, 7 April 1987). In a similar vein, GMBATU considered cutting the number of its constituent regions in 1985, reducing officer costs through voluntary redundancies and approved a rule change to devolve branch administration to lay branch seretaries (*Financial Times*, 4 June 1985). Other trade unions have had to consider and implement similar organizational changes.

The financial problems of the trade unions are intensified by the fact that increasing numbers of their current membership are not located in large unionized workplaces. With greater dispersal and casualization of the workforce the recruitment and retention of members is more difficult. In the Midlands, a GMBATU official commented that where employers were substituting part-time for full-time hours, income from subscriptions had decreased in some workplaces even though membership numbers had increased due to the lower contribution rates paid by part-timers. An USDAW official reported that in his region, with rapid turnover of membership, the trade union had to recruit 15,000 new members a year for contribution levels to stand still. Indeed, membership categories may mitigate against effective retention; USDAW, for example, was recruiting YTS trainees into its part-timer category, though their distinctive interests and potential retention of membership on a longer-term basis would suggest that this was not the most appropriate form of recruitment. The combination of these factors has produced three distinct organizational strategies; firstly, trade unions have developed measures aimed at retaining members and volumes of membership contributions through offering new packages of services, computerizing membership files, and making check-off arrangements with employers. Secondly, in recognition of the changing structure and distribution of the working population, attempts have been made to appeal to and organize sections of the labour force which were formerly marginal to trade union organization, particularly to women and members of minority groups, and more recently, to the self-employed. Finally, there is the option of expanding into new areas of employment by claiming new skills on the one hand and seeking membership in new establishments for example, in high technology sectors, and in new plants opened by US and Japanese multi-nationals.

### Appealing to Members

A number of trade unions now provide a range of services for their members in addition to the traditional benefits of trade union membership. A package introduced by UCATT in late 1986 included discounts on car equipment, hire and breakdown recovery services, holidays, health insurance and some Channel crossings. The financial services offered included advice on mortgages, home insurance, life assurance, pensions, investment and conveyancing, though in contrast to other trade unions such as the EETPU and AEU who provide these services in-house, UCATT has contracted the scheme out to a private company (*Financial Times*, 6 November 1986). Whereas UCATT General Secretary Albert Williams claimed that he hoped the scheme would increase membership by up to 25,000, the EETPU regards its range of services, which include access to its training courses in electronics, more soberly, as not so much a means of recruiting new members but as a means of retaining existing ones.

The introduction of computers into trade union offices has enormous potential for those trade unions wishing to keep membership files up-to-date. The EETPU and AUEW, both craft unions with a tradition of individual membership were amongst the first to computerize their membership records. Apart from their existing practices of pre-strike balloting and postal voting in elections, which contributed to their predisposition to accept government funds for balloting in compliance with trade union legislation, it has been argued that they were amongst the few trade unions which would actually have been able to organize the postal balloting required by legislation (*Financial Times*, 2 August 1985). In contrast, other trade unions, particularly those with large memberships in the public sector, do not have centralized records. In 1985, it was reported that a trade union-backed banking institution, Unity Trust, had negotiated a central computer facility allowing trade unions to keep a central register of members and thus comply with the 1984 Trade Union Act (*Financial Times*, 5 December 1985). This data access service to members is linked to a direct mailing company and gives trade unions discounted bulk mailing through the Post Office.

A number of trade unions have established policies on equal opportunities and encourage the participation of women and ethnic minorities in their organization. This is evidenced in the existence of women's committees and caucuses in a number of trade unions as well as publications or sections of publications directed at women. However, the mere existence of conference motions supporting equal opportunities and public statements to that effect do not necessarily indicate equal opportunities *practice*, nor do they ensure equality of representation in the power structure of the trade union.

The AUEW for example, was anticipating a thorough review and overhaul of its policy on racial discrimination following a long-running dispute with the Commission for Racial Equality, initiated in 1979 when a CRE report on racial discrimination at British Leyland found that AUEW members (as they then were) had put pressure on the management to discriminate against applicants from ethnic minority backgrounds (*Financial Times* 5 August 1986). In other instances, discrimination may be indirect and result from an absence of *positive action* to encourage participation in the trade union and, in the field of training policy, the encouragement of women and members of ethnic minorities to train in occupations in which they organize. Both TGWU and GMBATU have placed particular emphasis on recruiting women, based on their analysis of part-time female employment as being one of the few major growth areas of employment with employers' moves to increase labour flexibility.

GMBATU has been at the forefront of trade union moves to come to terms with the changing structure of employment, particularly since John Edmonds was elected General Secretary in 1985. He has argued strongly for trade unions to turn outwards and to be seen to represent the interests of the working class as a whole rather than narrow sectional interests. This analysis is based on the assumption that there are sections of the working class which, because of their precarious employment situation, their mobility, or unemployment itself, are extremely difficult for trade unions to organize. Furthermore, they have little bargaining power. This is especially true in sectors of the population and areas in which there is little or no tradition of labour movement involvement. It is nevertheless important for trade unions to defend these workers' interests and to fight for changes in the law which will give them economic and employment rights. It includes trade union involvement and support for popular culture (Edmonds, 1985; *New Statesman*, 27 June 1986).

Whereas part-time and casual workers may be difficult to organize, trade unions have no difficulty as recognizing them as exploited members of the working class in need of organization. In contrast, attitudes to the self-employed are more ambivalent, particularly in construction where the growth of self-employment and labour-only sub-contracting has been at the expense of direct employment. The EETPU/ECA agreement in the electrical contracting industry specifically prohibited the use of self-employed electricians and the withdrawal of JIB recognition from operatives and employers alike who do not subscribe to direct employment. A measure of the degree of control exercised over the labour market in this sub-sector by the joint industry arrangements was the setting up of the Self-employed Electricians' Union in 1986 because the self-employed were finding it impossible to get work (*Financial Times*, 8 September 1986). Subsequently, the Electrical Contractors' Association unilaterally set up ESCA Services in 1987 to provide temporary, self-employed labour to its members (IDS, 1987). In contrast, in building trades the National Joint Council for the Building Industry exercises much weaker control over conditions of employment and the Building Employers' Confederation is less willing and/or able to discipline its own members using labour-only sub-contracting. In September 1987, the Building Employers' Confederation announced it wished to alter the industry's National Working Rule Agreement to include self-employed workers as well as directly employed labour (IDS, 1987). Both UCATT and TGWU see labour-only sub-contracting as a major threat to trade union organization and UCATT has debated the question of membership for the self-employed on a number of occasions at its Biennial National Delegate Conference. TASS estimates that one fifth of its membership work for sub-contractors, but due to its monopoly of representation of drawing-room staff it is party to a national agreement with the sub-contractors aimed at avoiding the development of self-employment. GMBATU in an innovative move launched a pilot specialist unit in April 1987 which will recruit and give advice to the self-employed through its white-collar section MATSA. It will offer the self-employed legal, tax and accountancy advice, secretarial help and access to computing facilities. The trade union estimates that in its northern region there are more than 93,000 self-employed and an appeal to them is aimed at boosting membership and revamping the trade union's image in line with changes in the structure of employment (*The Guardian*, 30 April 1987).

## 'New Realism'

If some of the strategies outlined above to appeal to existing and potential members have represented an accommodation to changes in the industrial relations climate and structure of employment in the 1980s, then the 'new realism' in industrial relations represents a response which not only recognizes changes in the nature of trade union members, but seeks to substitute traditional union ideologies of class struggle for one of co-operation with employers. The reasoning behind the adoption of the 'new realism' as a trade union ideology and practice was succinctly stated by Frank Chapple at the 1983 TUC conference:

> The working class movement that is being fashioned by recession, new technology, 40 years of welfare state and ever-developing aspirations, is profoundly different from that in which most of us grew up. In a few years' time women will constitute nearly half of the workforce; industry will be more concentrated in the south-east; a larger number of our members will be home-owners, new skills will have replaced the ones we know. If British trade unionism is to avoid the mistakes which have weakened our colleagues in other countries, we have to adapt to these changes and provide the kind of movement that they imply. We will have to stop wishing that the world was like it once was, and face up to what it is (quoted by Bassett, 1986: 47).

What distinguishes EETPU strategy towards recruitment towards new members is that it is not just directed towards individual employees, but particularly in the new high technology industries, it is directed at *employers*. This has occurred through its recruitment mission to Japan to establish contact with Japanese companies considering investing in the UK and in the attendance of Eric Hammond at the Confederation of British Industry conference in 1984, at which he suggested the idea of the trade union applying for CBI membership (Bassett, 1986: 69). The EETPU presents itself as a moderate, responsible trade union which wants to work *with* rather than *against* employers. In addition to the range of services it offers to members, including its electronics training courses, which many employers including British Rail, GEC, the CEGB and British Aerospace have used, it has shown a willingness to accommodate to the changed climate in industrial relations. The agreement with the ECA to cut apprentice wage rates in order to maintain numbers in training is one example of this. Its pragmatism towards new technology and multi-skilling are others, but perhaps its greatest notoriety has been bred from its willingness to allow members to work in new technology jobs which are claimed by and have displaced members of other trade unions (as at the *News International* dispute at Wapping) and to sign single-union and 'strike-free' agreements, both of which fly in the face of central notions of the sources of trade union strength and solidarity.

Despite the notoriety acquired by the EETPU for its support of 'strike-free' and single-union agreements, it is not the only trade union so engaged. Moreover, *all* unions are confronted by an employer offensive on labour flexibility which is often conditional on the selective withdrawal of negotiating rights and the acceptance of new procedures for arbitration. The problem is to avoid a deterioration in inter-union relations where pressures from the introduction of new technology, flexible working practices (especially where this crosses existing demarcations between trades) and employer strategies to reduce or alter bargaining units. These conflicts were clearly stated in interviews:

> For the trade unions the biggest problems of the future will be over who has which job and the employers will always opt to please the majority . . . new technology is severely straining the sense of brotherhood in the movement . . . Multi-skilling has caused abrasions between the EETPU and the AUEW. The employers see the need to develop multi-skilling. The bulk of them see this as a need for sophisticated handymen. It has been a significant move for the trade unions to accept some degree of skill-sharing between previously isolated crafts. Some unions are terrified of the prospects of going too far, not just because of how it may affect their members' interests, but also how it will affect the future of the unions. These problems arise because we can't amalgamate as fast as the rate of change (AUEW).

There is evidence not only of shifts in the structure of employment and the strategies of trade unions towards the recruitment and retention of members, but a recognition of the need to respond as *organizations* to the changing structure of the workforce. Changes in working practices and working conditions, *alongside* the development of new skills, the demise of others and/or their recombination in new forms, create the preconditions for realignments in the trade union movement along lines of occupational identity and political orientation.

## Changing Occupational Boundaries

New technology and changes in management and employment practices have the effect of changing the boundaries between occupations and between different elements in organizational hierarchies. Jobs are constantly undergoing a process of formation and reformation both as categories within an organizational structure and as posts which individuals fill. A number of comments in interviews suggested changes in specific occupations which reflected changes internal to the occupation on the one hand and changes which were significant for the boundaries between them on the other. In addition, where companies undergo major restructurings of their operations, including the selling off of subsidiaries, sub-contracting of certain categories of work and redundancies or even failure to recruit to replace losses through 'natural wastage', all these factors will have repercussions throughout the organizational structure and will affect the relationship between occupations, patterns of mobility betwen them and the legitimation of hierarchy in the wages structure. ASTMS, for example, argued that patterns of recruitment had not changed but that the craft manager, who had reached managerial status through occupational mobility from the shopfloor was being replaced by the 'all-purpose' manager who had a university rather than a craft apprentice background. In some companies, the reorganization of production and maintenance functions on the shopfloor has resulted in greater emphasis on engineering skills in first-line management. Organizational changes of this kind may bring trade unions into conflict as some benefit to the detriment of others, or may bring previously uncontested occupational categories into the job territory occupied by another trade union.

Information technology, perhaps more than any other factor, seems likely to bring about greatest changes in the interface between jobs of different status and thus have greatest implications for wages and conditions of employment. The introduction of CNC machinery has enormous potential to de-skill craft jobs and thus makes control of the new technology an object of struggle between different occupational groups on the shopfloor and in design functions. In the same way control of CAD/CAM in construction is a source of conflict between professional groups in design, planning and site management (Campagnac and Caro, 1987). New technology has the potential to wipe out whole layers of white-collar jobs as shopfloor workers become involved in ordering spare parts and management gains greater control in handling information. At the same time it has the effect of proletarianizing white-collar workers by tying them to machinery, increasing control of their work and breaking their privileged relationship to management. The established basis of trade union organization based on representing craft, skilled, semi-skilled and white-collar grades is undermined by occupational change and posits merger and amalgamation as a strategy of conflict avoidance and for maintaining organizational viability in the context of declining membership rolls.

## Merger Activity

Trade unions can become involved in merger discussions for both defensive and offensive reasons (Undy *et al.*, 1981). As argued earlier, declining membership has been a major factor contributing towards decisions to merge and amalgamate, though the decision may also be made on the basis of a strategic assessment of the value of combining by trade unions which are not facing severe financial difficulties. An example of the former would be the formation of UCATT in 1971 from the transfer of engagements from the Amalgamated Society of Painters and Decorators and the Association of Building Technicians to the Amalgamated Union of Building Trade Workers. The recent merger between TASS and ASTMS aimed at forming a high technology trade union with members throughout manufacturing industry would be an example of the latter. The occupational spaces in which the trade unions organize may be one consideration in the decision to merge, though in a number of mergers, both past and currently under consideration, the political outlook of the trade unions concerned may be a factor. The structure for integration of one trade union into another, its ability to retain a separate identity and to employ existing officials may be decisive in affecting the successful conclusion of merger discussions.

APEX is one trade union in which it is explicitly recognized that merger is central to its future. Since 1979 a third of the membership has been lost as a consequence of the reduction of clerical employment, particularly in its base in the engineering industry. With information technology shopfloor workers are increasingly encroaching on traditional white-collar jobs, which could eventually lead to the elimination of a range of clerical work. The onus is, therefore, on the trade union to extend recruitment to other areas and to do this by extending the range of occupations in which it recruits by alliances with trade unions in contiguous occupational spaces. For strategic reasons, it is particularly appropriate to merge with trade unions with which the changing structure of occupations is already creating areas of friction. In the 1970s the logic of trade union organization would have suggested merger with another white-collar staff union resulting in a horizontal extension of membership across industries. In 1979 an approach from ASTMS was turned down and in 1981/82 an approach from the GMWU met a similar fate although it was more favoured. By the 1980s, however, APEX was approaching craft unions, such as the National Society of Metal Mechanics (which eventually merged with TASS) on the grounds that increasing similarities between craft, technical and clerical work were bringing them into membership disputes with manual rather than other white-collar unions (Eaton and Gill, 1983: 308).

The unsuccessful amalgamation between TASS and the construction, foundry and engineering sections of the AUEW is an example of a merger with considerable industrial and occupational logic which failed for differences in political orientation and disagreement on constitutional matters. In 1970 the Draughtsmen's and Allied Technicians' Association (DATA) joined the AUEW as the Technical, Administrative and Supervisory Section. The AUEW, which up until then had had no white-collar section, had formerly lost members as they moved from craft to technician and supervisory grades. TASS therefore benefitted in acquiring new members from the amalgamation as well as from being part of a larger organization. The national committee of the AUEW Engineering, Foundry and Construction sections decided to sever links with TASS in May 1985, stating that TASS had obstructed amalgamation through failure to agree to constitutional changes. However, from 1980 onwards TASS had been pursuing a strategy of expansion through merger with craft unions, starting with merger with the National Union of Gold, Silver and Allied Trades (NUGSAT) in 1981, followed by the National Union of Sheet Metal Workers, Coppersmiths, Heating and Domestic Engineers (NUSMWCHDE) in 1984, the Association of Patternmakers and Allied Craftsmen (APAC) and the National Society of Metal Mechanics (NSMM) in 1985. In December 1985 a special delegate meeting of the Tobacco Workers' Union (TWU) voted to merge with TASS, extending its membership beyond the engineering industry for the first time. It has been argued that the merger between NUSMWCHDE and TASS had little industrial logic, and that the shared left politics of the two leaderships represented an attempt to form a 'CGT-style' political union. (*Financial Times*, 29 May 1985). Whilst TWU was also a left-led trade union, the same could not be claimed of the leadership of the NSMM and the APAC. Nevertheless, the logic of occupational change and particularly, the effect of new technology on craft jobs, has been a major factor in creating favourable preconditions for these mergers:

> . . . the union's expansion also has the more basic motivation of a typical staff/technician union taking advantage of the direction of

new technology. For several years while Tass was still part of the AUEW the union was always being accused of poaching engineering section members as craftsmen increasingly donned white-coats and became technicians.

It is this belief that merger with Tass will place a small union on the right side in the new technology battles plus increase its members' chances of acquiring staff status that has been decisive (*Financial Times*, 29 May 1985).

The political and occupational appeal of TASS, combined with the high degree of autonomy allowed to smaller unions joining its craft sector has made TASS one of the fastest growing trade unions in the 1980s.

If the logic of occupational change has made white-collar unions such as TASS an attractive proposition to craft unions seeking amalgamation, then the changing structure of industry and its domination by multinational companies has clearly been a factor in the merger talks between ASTMS and TASS. Ratified by their respective conferences in 1987, the merger created a 700,000 strong Manufacturing, Science and Finance union with a major presence in manufacturing industry and particularly, in expanding new technology sectors. In addition, it was envisaged that this would have the effect of taking the two trade unions out of competition for membership in industries such as aerospace and electronics and would rationalize negotiating rights and procedures in many sectors common to both trade unions (*The Observer*, 19 April 1987).

Opponents of this merger were the political right within the two trade unions themselves (primarily Conservatives and Social Democrats within ASTMS who fear domination by the pro-Soviet leadership of TASS) as well as the right of the trade union movement, notably the EETPU, which also has claims to a high technology membership. Its white-collar section, the Electrical and Engineering Staff Association sees itself as presenting a 'democratic and responsible alternative to the Tass/ASTMS axis' and has been seeking a closer relationship with the right-led Engineers' and Managers' Association (*Financial Times*, 3 November 1987).

At the time of writing other mergers were on the horizon, which could be categorized as having both a political and an occupational logic. EETPU and the then AEU have been discussing the possibility of a merger (*The Guardian*, 8 May 1987). Although progress had yet to be made on the unification of their structures, the AEU having a district and the EETPU a centralized structure, the rationale for merger was clearly one of political affinity on the right of the trade union movement. However, multi-skilling and flexible working practices bring the occupations of members of the two trade unions increasingly close together and the AEU clearly wishes to capture, belatedly, some of the EETPU's kudos in claiming new technology skills and in presenting itself as a modern trade union of common sense and moderation particularly to younger members. APEX was also considering the possibility of combining with the ASTMS/TASS amalgamation, on the one hand (*The Guardian*, 11 March 1987) and with GMBATU, on the other, with a view to taking over its white-collar section MATSA. The APEX conference voted to start talks on merger with GMBATU in 1987 (*The Guardian*, 23 June 1987).

### Expansion into New Technology Industries and Occupations

The TUC has repeatedly called for the support and involvement of trade unions in the integration of high technology into British industry. Norman Willis, TUC General Secretary has further called on the government to remove its unofficial ban on trade union representatives serving on a number of national committees which examine technology and research (*The Guardian*, 21 April 1986). As indicated in Chapter 3, all trade unions are faced with the introduction of new technology into specific work processes and occupations and have adopted policies to deal with them. However, if they are to adapt to the changing structure of employment, they must not only develop policies towards the introduction of new technology as it affects their existing areas of recruitment, but must also seek to recruit members in new occupations which emerge from the application of new technology to different labour processes, in new plants using new technology and in the new technology industries themselves.

Of the trade unions interviewed in this project ASTMS, EETPU and TASS have interests in recruiting workers in high technology industries. However, to date, workers in these industries have been remarkably resistant to trade unionism. In part this is attributable to the individual-ized nature of high technology work processes, for example, working with a VDU screen, which results in limited contact with workmates (Bassett, 1986). Furthermore, because of the buoyancy of the labour market in some new technology skills, many workers are able to negotiate high wages without trade union intervention. This is particularly true of software personnel who are in considerable demand. The equivalent work they do in software houses used to be done by directly employed TASS members in companies, but it is now contracted out (*Financial Times*, 4 November 1985). Whilst the EETPU has used traditional methods to attract members in Silicon Glen in Scotland (leafleting factories, public meetings, recruitment drives in disputes) they are also offering employers complete packages with 'no-strike' deals. Other trade unions have offered single union agreements at plants using high technology, for example, the AEU's agreement with Nissan at Peterlee. TASS has used the tactic of mail shots of trade union recruitment literature to every household in areas such as Bracknell which have a large proportion of employment in high technology jobs (*Financial Times*, 25 October 1985).

However, a trade union's appeal to workers in high technology industries is not just based on its attempts to recruit them but the way in which it appeals to their economic and professional interests. This may be through offering courses in new technology skills, as the EETPU does through Cudham Hall training centre, or it may be through the arguments put on a broad range of issues. TASS for example, produces a glossy *Electronics Bulletin* aimed at high technology workers, which highlights issues such as low pay in the electronics industry, the advantages of collective bargaining for professional groups, the existence of high technology skill shortages and their relationship to the underfunding of higher education and research. Despite the restricted inroads made into recruitment in these areas there is a certain confidence, based on historical experience in other industries as they emerged and developed, that unionization will eventually spread. (*Financial Times*, 25 October 1985).

## Conclusion

In this chapter trade union responses to changes in employment and occupational structure have been examined with the aim of highlighting their implications for trade union organization. A number of factors have combined to make it harder for trade unions to recruit and retain membership with shifts in the nature of the employment contract and hours of work, alongside the loss of membership in traditional strongholds of unionization in manufacturing industry. There can be no doubt that trade unions are adapting organizationally and ideologically to the challenges presented by developments in employment structure in the latter part of the 1980s; sectors of the trade union movement are demonstrating a vitality in their capacity to innovate and to appeal to new members, whilst also seeking solutions through new alignments between themselves and other trade unions with similar political outlooks and/or with complementary membership characteristics.

The decline of some occupations and the constitution and growth of others requires trade unions to take initiatives in defining and redefining their occupational identities. This means taking stock of the current reforms affecting the institutions which oversee the formation of different professions and trades; making an assessment of the best methods of intervening as organizations and on behalf of members; and using bargaining power at different levels to negotiate the expression of the new structure of qualifications in the wage relationship.

The labour market has always been characterized by segmentation, and workers outside large, unionized workplaces have been relatively disadvantaged in terms of their access to skill training, wages and conditions of employment. Redundancies and unemployment, combined with the contemporary extension of casual forms of labour, particularly in the youth labour market, represent an assault not just on individual workers but on the trade union movement as a whole. Yet at the same time that employer strategies attempt to divide worker from worker, and trade union from trade union, they can produce its antithesis; co-operation, amalgamation, unity, solidarity. With vision the trade unions may be able to respond to this challenge. However, this requires an analysis of the changing structure of the labour force and its bargaining power, and the pursuit of a strategy which is more explicitly political and addressed to wider working-class interests than the sectional interests which have characterized the trade union movement in recent years.

# 7

# Conclusion

In the mid-1970s, the long period of post-war economic expansion and full employment came to an end in Britain. In order to maintain profitability in the face of increasing international competition, manufacturing companies restructured their operations, and have pursued a number of strategies including the shaking out of labour and investment in new technologies. The results of this process on employment have been extremely complex. My focus in this book has been on its effect on the demand for labour and, in particular, the changing structure of skills and occupations as manifested in the availability and demand for occupational training.

In order to examine training it has been necessary to develop an analysis which views it both as an acquisition of technical skills and as a process of socialization into the workplace and the routines of working life. In other words, training is a preparation for the wage relationship. This concerns the development of individual capabilities, on the one hand, and the learning of tasks associated with a specific job and its place in the hierarchy of work organization, on the other. However, it should be stressed, that individual talents and the demands of a particular job are not one and the same. Just as training can result in the development of individual capabilities, an extension of the range of skills, the possibility of mobility between jobs and increased job satisfaction, it can also result in the restrictions of job aspirations and mobility, and socialization into monotonous, undemanding work. Training in the abstract does not automatically increase skills, but is linked to employment and specific jobs which demand different levels of technical, intellectual and social competences. Though individuals acquire skills through training, this is a process which is socially determined and negotiated at different levels. Negotiation takes place over the *content* of training, over its *form* and over its *expression* in the wages structure.

In this book I have dealt specifically with the analysis of trade union perspectives and policies on training in four industries. I have examined policies towards initial training and adult retraining, placing them in the context of wider processes of occupational change. The structures through which trade unions formulate and implement training policy have been considered, as well as the significance of training to trade unions as organizations which recruit in territories defined by occupation. The research method employed, that of interviewing officials at different levels within trade union hierarchies provides a broad rather than a narrow view of the processes taking place, and focusses on formal policy-making rather than implementation and practice at plant level.

The point in time at which this study was conducted was one during which there was considerable debate about training policy; an increase in volumes of training and retraining was widely held to be necessary to improvements in competitiveness. The West German, French and Japanese training systems were all under consideration as models capable of increasing employers' investment in the skills of the labour force, yet the solutions found seemed to fall far short of these objectives. Apprenticeship training fell to an all-time low despite massive injections of state funding for youth training. The mechanisms for encouraging and monitoring training through the levy-grant mechanism of the Industrial Training Boards, already weakened by the legislation of 1973, were abolished altogether in many industries. The 'poor law effect' training schemes for the unemployed of the 1930s (Finn, 1986; Perry, 1976; Sheldrake and Vickerstaff, 1987) were reintroduced in new guises; the Special Temporary Employment Programme, the Training Opportunities and the Youth Opportunities Schemes of the 1970s and the Youth Training Scheme, the Community Programme, the Job Training and Employment Training Schemes of the 1980s. And whilst the long-standing demand of the labour movement of 'training for all' could potentially have been met by YTS, in the absence of adequate funding and an appropriate industrial and employment strategy, the promise was not fulfilled.

Adult retraining, whether aimed at increasing labour flexibility or at updating the skills of the labour force when new technology is introduced, is negotiated primarily at the level of the establishment rather than through training arrangements at sectoral level which require a formal policy input by trade union representatives. However, the evidence presented in Chapters 3 and 4 indicates that new technology and flexible working practices are often introduced in the absence of formal training programmes. The reason for this may be employers' unwillingness to invest in the training of the workforce and to reward the acquisition of new skills. In the interests of short-term cost-cutting, workers may be expected to learn new skills through experience. The logic of this strategy is one that leads towards job division and task specialization rather than one which increases the range of tasks performed and increases workers' adaptability. In this respect it *decreases* flexibility. It is a short-term rather than a long-term strategy towards labour force planning. It is not conducive to the adding on of additional skills at a later stage; either from the point of view of the practicalities of learning or from the perspective of potential conflicts which may arise when existing patterns of work are changed and job controls threatened. In contrast, formal training, though more expensive in the short term, combines theoretical, and practical knowledge which increases productivity more rapidly than through the slower process of learning by experience. If combined with security of employment and appropriate incentive systems to reward new skills, this strategy increases the long-term adaptability of the labour force.

The exception to local negotiation of training has been in instances where national negotiations have concerned multi-skilling. Though full-scale multi-skilling requires investment in training programmes, it is not the fact of training which is problematic for trade unions. Rather, conflict arises over employers' demands for changes in working practices which concern the way in which individuals work and how trade unions organising different categories of worker relate to each other. Multi-skilling may lead to a process of deskilling or upgrading of skills for the individual worker, but at a time of restricted employment opportunities, increases in productivity may lead to redundancies, and this certainly conditions trade union responses to multi-skilling.

Though initial training also arises as a policy issue at establishment level, it is more likely to be subject to policy development at higher levels of trade union structure. In the case of craft unions, apprenticeship has been a long-standing concern and union representatives have been involved in both the development of curricula and certification in different bodies, as well as in negotiating with employers over the wages and conditions of employment of apprentices. More recently, with the introduction of the Youth Training Scheme, all unions have had to develop a policy response to it. However, it should be stressed that there has been no coherent response to it as a training scheme, since the way it intersects with existing training arrangements varies enormously. Rather, the policy response has been conditioned by its effects on the wages and conditions of young workers and has tried to combine the defence of adult workers from the threat of job substitution, on the one hand, with the protection of young people from exploitation, on the other.

In general, trade union policy towards training can be characterized as defensive rather than offensive. For some unions it is a peripheral issue and for others more central because of the tradition of apprenticeship. The focus has been on defending existing patterns of training and skills from employer-initiated changes and in responding to government policy. The exception has been where trade union policy has explicitly linked training to industrial strategy (as in the case of AUEW/TASS) or where trade unions have taken initiatives in providing training themselves (as in the cases of EETPU, AUEW and the craft sector of AUEW/TASS).

The findings of the study suggest that training, employment conditions, wages and the ability to organize are all closely linked. Training can not be analysed in isolation from the employment relationship and must of necessity be examined in relation to industrial policy and the general political and economic environment in which trade unions organize. The study has focussed on training and the policies of trade unions towards it at one particular moment in history, a moment during which they were on the defensive across a range of organizing issues. A number of conclusions can be drawn: firstly, relatively little training activity has been taking place due to cutbacks caused by recession, the emasculation of the ITBs and the return to voluntary training arrangements. Despite the claims made for YTS, it is unlikely to provide the skilled labour force of the future. Rather, it is producing young workers with low-level skills and low wage expectations appropriate to the more casualized sectors of the labour market. That is to say, with exceptions where it has been adapted to existing apprenticeship schemes, it is not a substitute for industrial training. Secondly, employers will not invest in training if they view their workforces as dispensable. Exhortation to employers to train is meaningless if there is no long-term planning of labour force requirements and if workers' rights to security of employment are being eroded. Regardless of the structures that exist for training and bargaining over training, there is no guarantee that training will take place unless workers' rights to secure employment are protected and employment is available in the first place.

Finally, this study has examined training and trade union policies towards it at a specific conjuncture. It nevertheless throws light on issues relating to training which are of a more general nature. These concern the relationship between training and the wage, the relationship between training and job design, the significance of formal qualifications in negotiating strategy, and the significance of training to the identity of collectivities of workers both in the workplace and in broader groupings in the labour movement. It has also attempted to demonstrate the range of issues relating to training both within the workplace and in the wider labour market, particularly in relation to schemes for the unemployed, which require trade unions to formulate policy. If the experience of government schemes such as YTS and the Community Programme has not been particularly positive, it is clear that it has made a major contribution to trade union policy-making, insofar as training has been placed on the agenda for many trade unions which previously had little need to formulate perspectives on training. As the cohort of school leavers declines in the 1990s, increasing the bargaining power of young workers in the labour market, and as manufacturing industry emerges from the recession, it is important that this learning experience is put to good effect. Trade unions should not only seek improvements in wages and conditions of employment but also to retain and pursue gains that have been made in the training of young workers. This greater awareness of training issues also needs to be applied in workplace bargaining as a means of pursuing wage claims linked to retraining and to avoid de-skilling. There are, of course, very important questions which need to be posed which concern not what is, but what trade unionists might expect of the training system in Britain. These could be formulated in the following terms: What level of commitment to the training of the workforce will deliver the high technology skills that will be required in the next century? What system of rights and obligations will make it effective? What are the most appropriate arrangements at national, sectoral, local and plant level to ensure this? What should the structure and powers of these bodies be? Finally, if trade unions are to participate in them, what will be the basis on which they are represented and what resources will be made available to ensure that their participation is effective?

# References

Andersen, M., and J. Fairley. 1983. 'The Politics of Industrial Training in the United Kingdom'. *Journal of Public Policy*. Vol. 3, Pt. 2, 191–208.

APEX. 1980. 'Automation and the Office Worker'. *Report of Office Technology Working Party*. London: APEX.

APEX. 1983. 'New Technology Job Content and Grading', London: APEX.

Armstrong, P. 1982. 'If It's Only Women It Doesn't Matter So Much'. *Work, Women and the Labour Market*. Ed. J. West. London: Routledge & Kegan Paul.

Atkinson, J. 1985. 'Flexibility: Planning for an Uncertain Future'. *Manpower Policy and Practice. The IMS Review*. Vol. 1, Summer, 26–9.

AUEW. *Journal*.

AUEW/TASS. *News and Journal*.

Austrin, O. 'The "Lump" in the UK Construction Industry'. *Capital and Labour*. Ed. T. Nicholls. London: Fontana.

Bamber, G. 1988. 'Technological Change and Unions'. *New Technology and Industrial Relations*. Eds. R. Hyman and W. Streeck. Oxford: Basil Blackwell.

Barker, B. 1987. 'Pre-vocationalism and Schooling'. *Skills and Vocationalism: the Easy Answer*. Ed. M. Holt. Milton Keynes: Open University Press.

Bassett, P. 1986. *Strike Free: New Industrial Relations in Britain*. London and Basingstoke: Macmillan.

Bates, I., J. Clarke, P. Cohen, D. Finn, R. Moore and P. Willis. 1984. *Schooling for the Dole? The New Vocationalism*. Basingstoke and London: Macmillan.

Becker, G.S. 1975. *Human Capital: A Theoretical and Empirical Analysis with Special Reference to Education*. Chicago: National Bureau of Economic Research.

Benn, C., and J. Fairley. 1986. *Challenging the MSC. On Jobs, Education and Training*. London: Pluto.

Bowles, S., and H. Gintis. 1975. 'The Problem with Human Capital Theory – A Marxian Critique'. *American Economic Review*. Vol. 65, No. 2, 74–82.

Braverman, H. 1974. *Labor and Monopoly Capital: The Degradation of Work in the Twentieth Century*. New York and London: Monthly Review Press.

Brent LERU. 1987. *Training for a Million Jobs. Contrasts and Opportunities in Construction*. London: Brent LERU. June.

CAITS. 1986. *Flexibility: Who Needs It?* CAITS: Polytechnic of North London.

Campagnac, E., and C. Caro. 1987. 'CAD/CAM for New Strategies in Construction'. *Working Papers from the Seminar CAD/CAM in Construction.* Ed. E. Frydendal Pedersen. Technical University of Denmark, Department of Construction Managament, Lyngby, 2–4 March.

Campbell, A., and M. Warner. 1986. 'Innovation, Skills and Training: Microelectronics and Manpower in Britain and Germany'. Paper Prepared for Conference on 'Industrial Structure and Industrial Policy: the Rise of Flexible Specialisation and its Implications'.

Campinos–Dubernet, M. 1985a. *Emploi et gestion de la main-d'oeuvre dans le BTP: Mutations de l'après-guerre a la crise.* Centre d'Etudes et de Recherches sur les Qualifications (CEREQ), Dossier No. 34. Paris: CEREQ.

Campinos–Dubernet, M. 1985b. 'The Rationalisation of Labour in the Construction Industry: An Example of the Limits of Orthodox Taylorism'. Translated by Jean Gordon. Paper Presented at the Seminar 'Training in Construction and the Construction Labour Process', 19 April, Bartlett School of Architecture and Planning, University College, London.

Centre for a Working World. 1986. *MSC Area Manpower Boards – Their Rules and Roles – An Outline Description.* Bath: Centre for a Working World. July.

Centre for a Working World. 1987. *The Boards and Beyond. Breaking Away From the MSC.* Bath: Centre for a Working World.

Centre for a Working World. (Colin Randall). nd. *MSC Good For Business.* Bath: Centre for a Working World.

Centre for a Working World. (Colin Randall). nd. *Manpower – Serving Whose Interests?* Bath: Centre for a Working World.

CITB nd. 'CITB Levy and Grant Policy'. Construction Industry Training Board. Reproduced in Rainbird and Grant 1985a, 100.

Clarke, L. 1985. 'The Determinants of Training Provision in the Construction Industry: the Applicability of Notions of Deskilling, Transferable Non-transferable skills and General/Specific Skills'. *The Production of the Built Environment. Proceedings of the 7th Barlett International Summer School,* 144–63.

Cockburn, C. 1983. *Brothers: Male Dominance and Technological Change.* London: Pluto.

Cockburn, C. 1987. *Two-track Training. Sex Inequalities and the YTS.* Basingstoke: Macmillan Education.

*Construction Board News.*

*Construction Industry Training Board News.* 1986. Press Release. 3 June.

Coopers and Lybrand Associates. 1985. *A Challenge to Complacency. A Report to the Manpower Services Commission and the National Economic Development Office.* Sheffield: MSC.

Cross, M. 1985. *Towards the Flexible Craftsman.* London: Technical Change Centre.

Dale, R. (ed.) 1985. *Education, Training and Employment. Towards a New Vocationalism?* Oxford: Pergamon Press.

Dutton, P. 1982. 'The Development of Industrial Training Policy 1979–82'. *The*

*Politics of Industrial Training Policy*. Papers Presented to a Conference in the Centre of European Governmental Studies, University of Edinburgh. Eds. M. Anderson and J. Fairley. Edinburgh.

Dutton, P. 1984. 'YTS – Training for the Future'. *Public Administration*. Vol. 62, No. 4, 483–94.

Dutton, P. 1985. 'YTS – What are the Facts?' Discussion Paper No. 33. Institute for Employment Research Report. Coventry: University of Warwick.

Dutton, P. 1987. *The Impact of YTS on Engineering Apprenticeship*. Institute for Employment Research Report. Coventry: University of Warwick.

Eaton, J., and C. Gill. 1983. *The Trade Union Directory. A Guide to All TUC Unions*. London: Pluto.

Edmonds, J. 1986. *Democracy in Trade Unions*. Warwick Papers in Industrial Relations No. 2. Industrial Relations Research Unit. Coventry: University of Warwick. January.

EETPU. *Contact*.

EETPU. *Training Bulletin*.

EITB. 1987. *Economic Monitor*. Watford: Engineering Industry Training Board.

EITB. 1987. *Annual Report 1986–87*. Watford: EITB.

*Engineering Training Today*. 1988. Watford: EITB. January.

Erridge, A., and M. Connolly, 1986. 'Comparative Study of Industrial Training Boards'. Paper presented to the ESRC Workshop on 'Tripartism and Training' at the Polytechnic of Central London. 14 November.

ETUI. 1986. *Flexibility and Jobs: Myths and Realities*. Brussels: ETUI.

Evans, S., and R. Lewis. 1989. 'Destructuring and Deregulation in the Construction Industry'. *Manufacturing Change: Industrial Relations and Industrial Restructuring*. Eds. S. Tailby and C. Whitson. Oxford: Basil Blackwell.

Eversley, J. 1986. 'Trade Union Responses to the MSC'. *Challenging the MSC on Jobs, Education and Training*. Eds. C. Benn and J. Fairley. London: Pluto.

Finn, D. 1986. 'YTS: The Jewel in the MSC's Crown?' *Challenging the MSC: On Jobs, Education and Training*. Eds. C. Benn and J. Fairley. London: Pluto.

Finn, D. 1987. *Training Without Jobs. New Deals and Broken Promises* Basingstoke and London: Macmillan Education.

Friedman, A. 1977. *Industry and Labour, Class Struggle at Work and Monopoly Capitalism*. London: Macmillan.

GMBATU. 1984. *GMB Survey of New Technology in the Food and Drink Industry*. Esher: GMBATU.

GMBATU. 1984. *Chemical Union News*. January.

Gill, C. 1985. *Work, Unemployment and the New Technology*. Oxford: Basil Blackwell.

Goldstein, N. 1984. 'The New Training Initiative. A Great Leap Backwards'. *Capital and Class*. No. 23, Summer, 83–105.

Grant, W. 1983a. *The Organisation of Business Interests in the UK Chemical Industry*. International Institute of Management Discussion Paper. Berlin.

Grant, W. 1983b. *The Organisation of Business Interests in the UK Food Processing Industry*. International Institute of Management Discussion Paper. Berlin.

Grant, W. 1985. 'What is Neo-corporatism?' *The Political Economy of Corporatism*. Ed. W. Grant. Basingstoke and London: Macmillan.

Grant, W., with J. Sargent. 1987. *Business and Politics in Britain*. Basingstoke: Macmillan Education.

GLTB. 1984. *Training in Crisis*. London: GLTB.

Hall, K., and I. Miller. 1971. 'Industrial Attitudes to Skills Dilution'. *British Journal of Industrial Relations*. Vol. 9, No. 1, 1–20.

Hardman, R. 1981. *The British Chemical Industry*. London: Jordan & Sons.

Hartman, G., I. Nicholas, A. Sorge and M. Warner. 1983. 'Computerised Machine Tools, Manpower Consequences and Skill Utilisation: A Study of British and West German Manufacturing Firms'. *British Journal of Industrial Relations*. Vol. 21, No. 2., July, 221–31.

HMSO. *Housing and Construction Statistics*. London: HMSO.

Holroyd, K. 1985. 'Job Design–New Technology Union Guidelines'. *Topics*. September.

Holt, M. (ed.) 1987. *Skills and Vocationalism: the Easy Answer*. Milton Keynes: Open University Press.

Hyman, R. and T. Elger. 1981. 'Job Controls, the Employers' Offensive and Alternative Strategies'. *Capital and Class*. No. 15, 115–49.

IDS. 1986. *Flexibility at Work*. Study No. 360, April.

IDS. 1987. *Building Workers' Pay*. Study No. 396, October.

IDS. 1988. *Employing School Leavers*. Study No. 414, July.

IER. 1987. *Review of the Economy and Employment*. Institute for Employment Research. Coventry: University of Warwick.

Jackson, R. 1984. *The Formation of Craft Labor Markets*. London: Academic Press.

Johnson, R., and E. Singer. 1982. 'A National Strategy for Education and Training'. *Personnel Management*. June. 36–9.

Keep, E. 1986. *Designing the Stable Door: A Study of How the Youth Training Scheme was Planned*. Warwick Papers in Industrial Relations, No. 8. Coventry: University of Warwick.

Keep, E. 1987. *Britain's Attempt to Create a National Vocational Educational and Training System: A Review of Progress*. Warwick Papers in Industrial Relations. No. 16. Coventry: University of Warwick.

Keep, E. 1988. 'What Do Employers Want From Education?–A Question More Easily Asked Than Answered'. Paper Presented to the Vocational Education and Training Forum. Coventry: University of Warwick, 20 May.

Labour Party/TUC Liaison Committee. 1985. *Jobs and Industry. A New Partnership. A New Britain*. London: TUC/Labour Party.

Labour Research Department. 1987. *Temporary Workers. A Negotiator's Guide*. London: Labour Research Department.

Labour Research Department. 1988. *Training. A Negotiator's Guide*. London: Labour Research Department.

Lee, D. 1979. 'Craft Unions and the Force of Tradition'. *British Journal of Industrial Relations*. Vol. 17, No. 1, 34–49.

Lee, D. 1981. 'Skill, Craft and Class: A Theoretical Critique and a Critical Case'. *Sociology*. Vol. 15, No. 1, 56–78.

Lee, D. 1982. 'Beyond Deskilling; Skill, Craft and Class'. *The Degradation of Work? Skill, Deskilling and the Labour Process*. Ed. S. Wood. London: Hutchinson.

Lee, D., D. Marsden, M. Hardey and P. Hickman. 1986. 'Youth Training, Life Chances and Orientation to Work'. Paper presented to the British Sociological Association Conference. March.

Lee, G., and J. Wrench. 1983. *Skill Seekers: Black Youth, Apprenticeship and Disadvantage*. Leicester: National Youth Bureau Studies.

Leek, R. 1985. 'Flexible Manning in Practice; Control Data'. *Manpower Policy and Practice. The IMS Review*. Vol. 1, Summer, 30–1.

Leighton, P. 1986. 'Marginal Workers'. *Labour Law in Britain*. Ed. R. Lewis. Oxford: Basil Blackwell.

MSC. 1981. *A New Training Initiative: An Agenda for Action*. Sheffield: MSC. December.

MSC. 1984. *A New Training Initiative. Modernisation of Occupational Training. A Positive Statement*. Sheffield: MSC. July.

MSC. 1985. *Review of Vocational Qualifications In England and Wales. Interim Report*. Sheffield: MSC. September.

Manufacturing, Science, Finance. 1988. 'Training for the Future: Can Britain Compete?' May. London: MSF.

Marsh, D., and W. Grant. 1977. 'Tripartism: Reality or Myth?' *Government and Opposition*. Vol. 12, No. 2, 194–211.

Marsh, S. 1986. 'Women and the MSC'. *Challenging the MSC on Jobs, Education and Training*. Eds. C. Benn and J. Fairley. London: Pluto.

Mason, C., and R. Russell. 1987. *The Role of the Social Partners in Vocational Education and Training (including Further Education and Training.) The United Kingdom Final Project Report*. CEDEFOP Study No. 1236. Berlin.

Maurice, M. 1984. 'The Interdependence Between Training Systems and Work Organisation: The Case of the Use of NC Machine Tools in France and Germany'. *Work Organisation, Incentive Systems and Effort Bargaining in Different Social and National Contexts*. Eds. R. Deppe and D. Hoss. Frankfurt a.M.: Institut für Social Forschung. Mimeo.

Maurice, M., F. Sellier and J.J. Sylvestre. 1986. *The Social Foundations of Industrial Power. A Comparison of France and Germany*. Translation of *Politiques d'Education et Organisation Industrielle en France et an Allemagne*. Translator, Arthur Goldhammer. Cambridge, Mass. and London: MIT Press.

Mincer, J. 1962. 'On-the-Job Training: Costs, Returns and Some Implications'. *Journal of Political Economy*. 70, No. 5, 50–79.

Moon, J., and J. Richardson. 1984. 'Policy-making with a Difference? The Technical and Vocational Education Initiative'. *Public Administration*. Vol. 62, Spring, 23–33.

NEDO. 1986. *Working with New Technology*. Construction Equipment,

Mechanical Handling and Mining Machinery Economic Development Committees. London: NEDO.

NEDO/MSC. 1984. *Competence and Competition. Training and Education in the Federal Republic of Germany, the United States and Japan*. London: NEDO.

*National Labour Movement Inquiry into Youth Unemployment and Training*. 1987. Report of the Birmingham Trade Union Resource Centre.

*New Statesman*.

Osburg, L. 1984. 'Star-spangled Economies'. *Marxism Today*. September.

Overbeek, H. 1986. 'The Westland Affair: Collision over the Future of British Capitalism'. *Capital and Class*. No. 29, Summer, 12–26.

Perry, P.J.C. 1976. *The Evolution of British Manpower Policy. From the Statute of Artificers 1593 to the Industrial Training Act 1964*. London: Eyre and Spottiswoode.

Piore, M., and C. Sabel. 1984. *The New Industrial Divide: Possibilities for Survival*. New York: Basic Books.

Phillips, A. and B. Taylor. 1980. 'Sex and Skill: Notes Towards a Feminist Economics'. *Feminist Review*. No. 6, 79–88.

Pollert, A. 1986. 'The MSC and Ethnic Minorities'. *Challenging the MSC on Jobs, Education and Training*. Eds. C. Benn and J. Fairley. London: Pluto.

Pollert, A. 1987. *The 'Flexible Firm': A Model in Search of Reality (or a Policy in Search of a Practice)?* Warwick Papers in Industrial Relations. No. 19. Industrial Relations Research Unit. Coventry: University of Warwick. December.

Poole, M., W. Brown, J. Rubery, K. Sisson, R. Tarling and F. Wilkinson. 1984. *Industrial Relations in the Future. Trends and Possibilities in Britain Over the Next Decade*. London: Routledge & Kegan Paul.

Prais, S.J., and K. Wagner. 1983. 'Some Practical Aspects of Human Capital Investment: Training Standards in Five Occupations in Britain and Germany'. *National Institute Economic Review*. August, 46–65.

Price, R. 1980. *Masters, Unions and Men: Work Control in Building and the Rise of Labour, 1830–1914*. Cambridge: Cambridge University Press.

Purcell, J., and K. Sisson. 1983. 'Strategies and Practice in the Management of Industrial Relations'. *Industrial Relations in Britain*. Ed. G.S. Bain. Oxford: Basil Blackwell.

Raffe, D. 1987. 'The Context of the Youth Training Scheme: An Analysis of its Strategy and Development'. *British Journal of Education and Work*. Vol. 1, No. 1, 1–31.

Rainbird, H., and W. Grant. 1985a. 'Employers' Associations and Training Policy. A Study of Industrial Training Arrangements in Four Industries; Food Processing, Chemicals, Machine Tools and Construction'. Institute for Employment Research Report. Coventry: Institute for Employment Research, University of Warwick.

Rainbird, H., and W. Grant. 1985b. 'Non-statutory Training Organisations and the Privatisation of Public Policy'. *Public Administration*. Vol. 63, No. 1, 91–5.

Rainbird, H. 1986. 'Union Involvement in Tripartite Training Structures'. Paper presented to the ESRC Workshop 'Tripartism and Training' Polytechnic of Central London, 14 November.

Rainbird, H. 1987. 'Government Training Policy and Apprenticeship in the British Construction Industry'. *The Production of the Built Environment. Proceedings of the 9th Bartlett International Summer School*, 88–93.

Rainbird, H., and L. Clarke. 1988. 'Self-Employment and Training in the British Construction Industry: A Contradiction'. Paper presented to the Conference 'Europe et Chantiers: France–Grande Bretagne–Italie–République Fédérale d'Allemagne'. Paris, 28–30 September.

Rees, A.M. 1973. 'Trade Union Officials and Government Training Centres'. *British Journal of Industrial Relations*. Vol. 11, No. 2, 229–41.

REITS. 1987. *YTS Not White TS*. Racial Equality in Training Schemes. Coventry Workshop.

Rubery, J., R. Tarling and F. Wilkinson. 1984. 'Industrial Relations Issues in the 1980s: an Economic Analysis'. *Industrial Relations in the Future. Trends and Possibilities in Britain Over the Next Decade*. Ed. M. Poole *et al*. London: Routledge & Kegan Paul.

Ryan, P. 1984. 'The New Training Initiative After Two Years'. *Lloyds Bank Review*. No. 152, April, 31–45.

Ryan, P. 1986. 'Trade Unions and the Pay of Young Workers'. *From School to the Dole Queue?* Ed. P.N. Junankar. London: Macmillan.

Scarbrough, H. 1984. 'Maintenance Workers and New Technology: the Case of Longbridge'. *Industrial Relations Journal*. Autumn, 9–16.

Scase, R., and R. Goffee. 1982. *The Entrepreneurial Middle Class*. London: Croom Helm.

Schnack, K., and R. King. 1986. 'Corporatism and the Youth Training Scheme'. Paper Presented to the Annual Conference of the Political Studies Association. Nottingham. 9 April.

Sheldrake, J. and S. Vickerstaff. 1987. *The History of Industrial Training in Britain*. Aldershot: Avebury.

Society of Civil and Public Servants. 1986. *Work for the Future. A New Strategy for Training and Employment*. Northern College: Society of Civil and Public Servants.

Spies, B.G. 1984. 'Vocational Training, Apprenticeship and the Trades Unions . . . the Case of West Germany'. *Training in Crisis*. Greater London Training Board. London: GLTB.

Spies, B.G. 1985. 'Does Myth Blur the Facts of West German Training?' *Transition*. September, 22–4.

Streeck, W. 1989. 'Skills and the Limits of Neo-Liberalism: The Enterprise of the Future as a Place of Learning'. *Work, Employment and Society*. vol. 3, No. 1, March.

Streeck, W., and P. Schmitter. (eds.) 1985. *Private Interest Government: Beyond Market and State*. London: Sage.

Streeck, W. and J. Hilbert, K-H. van Kevelaer, F. Maier, H. Weber. 1987. *The Role of the Social Partners in Vocational Training and Further Training in the Federal Republic of Germany*. Berlin: Wissenschaftzentrum.

Stringer, J.K. and J. Richardson. 1982. 'Policy Stability and Policy Change: Industrial Training 1964–1982'. *Public Administration Bulletin*. No. 39, 22–39.

TASS. 1982. *TASS on Training*. London: AUEW/TASS.

TASS. 1985. *VDUs Health and Safety Guidelines*. London: AUEW/TASS.

TASS. nd. *Westland in Crisis. The TASS Solution*. London: AUEW/TASS.

TASS. *Electronics Bulletin*.

Taylor, B., and P. Lewis. 1973. 'Informal Learning, Training and Industrial Relations'. *European Training*. Vol. 2, No. 2, 160–80.

TGWU. *Herald*.

TGWU. 1979. *Microelectronics: New Technology, Old Problems, New Opportunities*. London: TGWU.

TGWU. 1983. *Management Consultants–Friends or Enemies?* London: TGWU.

TGWU. 1984. *Employee Involvement and Quality Circles–A TGWU Guide*. London: TGWU.

Trade Union Resource Centre, TURC. 1984. *The Great Training Robbery*. Birmingham: TURC.

TURC. 1985. *Unequal Opportunities–Racial Discrimination and the Youth Training Scheme*. Birmingham: TURC.

TURC. 1986. *The Great Training Robbery Continues . . . A Follow-up Investigation of the Role of Private Training Agencies in Birmingham and Solihull*. Birmingham: TURC.

Training Research Group. 1981. *Training on Trial. Government Policy and the Building Industry*. Birmingham: Training Research Group. October.

*Transition*. 1987. November.

Turner, H.A. 1962. *Trade Union Growth, Structure and Policy*. London: Allen & Unwin.

Undy, R. *et al*. 1981. *Change in Trade Unions. The Development of UK Unions Since the 1960s*. London: Hutchinson.

USDAW nd. *New Technology Action Pack. Advice on How to Meet the Challenge of New Technology*. Manchester: USDAW.

USDAW. *Dawn*.

Wilkinson, B. 1983. *The Shopfloor Politics of New Technology*. Aldershot: Gower Publishing Company.

Wilkinson, F. (ed.). 1981. *The Dynamics of Labour Market Segmentation*. London: Academic Press.

Wood, S. (ed.). 1982. *The Degradation of Work? Skill, Deskilling and the Labour Process*. London: Hutchinson.

Woodall, J. 1986. 'The Dilemma of Youth Unemployment: Trade Union Responses in the Federal Republic of Germany, in UK and France'. *West European Politics*. Vol. 9, No. 3. July, 429–47.

Wrench, J. 1986. *YTS, Racial Equality and the Trade Unions*. Policy Paper in Ethnic Relations. No. 6. Coventry: Centre for Research in Ethnic Relations, University of Warwick.

Ziderman, A., and A. Walder. 1975. 'Trade Unions and the Acceptability of GTC Trainees: Some Survey Results'. *British Journal of Industrial Relations*. Vol. 13, No. 1, 78–85.

# Index

The index uses the abbreviations of union titles as found on pages xi – xii

*Index compiled by Meg Davies*
*(Society of Indexers)*